THE EUROPEAN UNION IN THE 1990s

THE EUROPEAN UNION IN THE 1990s

Paul Taylor

OXFORD UNIVERSITY PRESS

Oxford University Press, Great Clarendon Street, Oxford OX2 6DP

Oxford New York

Athens Auckland Bangkok Bogota Buenos Aires Calcutta
Cape Town Chennai Dar es Salaam Delhi Florence Hong Kong Istanbul
Karachi Kuala Lumpur Madrid Melbourne Mexico City Mumbai
Nairobi Paris São Paolo Singapore Taipei Tokyo Toronto Warsaw
and associated companies in
Berlin Ibadan

Oxford is a registered trade mark of Oxford University Press

Published in the United States by
Oxford University Press Inc., New York

British Library Cataloguing in Publication Data
Data available

Library of Congress Cataloging in Publication Data
Taylor, Paul Graham.
The European Union in the 1990s / Paul Taylor.
Includes bibliographical references and index.
1. European Union. 2. European Union Community countries-
-Politics and government. I. Title.
JN30.T39 1996 341.24'2—dc20 96-20419
ISBN 0-19-878185-7
ISBN 0-19-878186-5 (pbk.)

3 5 7 9 10 8 6 4 2

Printed in Great Britain
on acid-free paper by
Bookcraft (Bath) Ltd
Midsomer Norton, Somerset

Contents

INTRODUCTION

....

THIS book is a portrait of the European Union in the mid-1990s, an attempt to capture its essential character, written by someone who has lived close to it as researcher and teacher for around twenty five years. As a portrait it inevitably reflects a certain attitude, a feeling about what it has all been about, and an anxiety that it should not be misunderstood. Accordingly although this is a book for students, it is not a textbook: the details of the history and mechanisms of the Union are available from a wide range of sources noted in the text. Rather it tries to get the essential outlines, and shapes them into a coherent whole, which it is hoped, will be recognized and acknowledged.

What is the European Union?

For some it is simply a set of intergovernmental institutions, useful for specific purposes, but without any wider implications. For others it is a device in a strategy which has lost its purpose: that of cornering the USSR or containing Germany; for others it is a delusion of European unity which now has to be thrown off in order to preserve the natural and enduring primacy of the nation states; others think it is the transcending of evil in the lives of nations, a unity which reflects the greater good for individuals. Finally there is the view that it is none of these, that it is something unique in relations between states which have retained their sovereignty and equality.

Which view is correct? The short answer is that the jury is still out, but in the body of the book an answer is suggested. In the 1990s public anxiety about what the European Union(EU) was about, and what it implied for the traditional forms of organization—especially the nation state—became more intense. Those who were against it, such as the Eurosceptics in Britain, found demons in Brussels, and catastrophe for the nations. Too often the counter-claim, that federal Europe was better for its citizens, was welcomed by its opponents as a way of increasing people's fears. In this book these conceptions of the future of Europe are both rejected. The kind of Europe which the present writer sees in the mid-1990s, and which is likely to be consolidated in the future, does not threaten the nation state, and yet brings with it the advantages of integration for its citizens. The European Union is seen as a unique arrangement between states, which benefits the majority of individuals without threatening national sovereignty.

This is not a position that depends upon the alteration of the Union's institutional arrangements to stop Brussels. Neither does it require that the nation states put a stop to new proposals for cooperation which involve the joint exercising of sovereignty. It does not demand any invention, or new determination to resist pressures from the Union, but merely the clearer recognition of what Europe now is. This is a matter of perception and not of fact, and is inevitably contrary to the sceptical position as well as the idealistic one.

Indeed the facts about what the European Union *is* have increasingly indicated that it is neither a federation in the making nor a society of states in the betraying. One of the many ironies about the development of the organization, and there were a large number, was that as this became clearer so those with the false perception began to shout more loudly. In the mid-1990s, in the press and in news programmes on radio and television, it was hard to avoid cries that the fabric of the state was afire. These alarms threatened to trigger the sprinkler systems, with costs that would have been large and uncalled for. The facts demonstrated there was no fire, and there was no need for this continuing commotion.

The five chapters which follow cover the major aspects of the subject, and they are rationally connected. Chapter 2 may be seen as the core chapter: it says what the European Union *is* in the 1990s. In Chapters 1, 3, and 4 issues are identified which reflect the features discussed and illustrated in Chapter 2. Chapter 1 is intended to reveal patterns in institutional development which explain the main features of the Union's arrangements in the 1990s, discussed in Chapter 2. The EU came to have a particular shape and character by the 1990s, and the pattern of its institutional development was a part of the explanation for this. Chapter 3 discusses the appropriate relationship between the EU and the outside world, especially the states now seeking admission; the character of that relationship is discussed as an aspect of what the EU had become by the 1990s, and the direction in which it should develop. What relationship suited it and which would destroy it? Chapter 4 discusses what the citizens of the EU think about it, and finds that patterns in public attitudes in the 1990s match its character. And Chapter 5 proposes a range of overall conclusions.

The greatest concern about the EU in the 1990s was found amongst observers who started from two different perspectives on the same event: the Second World War. Both views tended to resolve into the argument that the traditional form of the state should be kept. The first view, argued vehemently by those who were, or thought they were, on the winning side, held that the hero state had to be preserved at all costs because it had saved Europe and the world. The European Union was a threat to key national values, the right to be different, even the roots of democracy. Those who thought this way were often obsessed with history and constantly recognized in the present, shadows of dangers from the past. Europe was the Austro-Hungarian Empire, or the modern equivalent of the Tartars dressed as Brussels bureaucrats, or, as Mrs Thatcher suggested in her speech at Bruges in 1988, an attempt to centralize and impose conformity in the West precisely when those aims had been abandoned in the East, the ex-Soviet Union.

There was also often a sense that the traditional inner order of the states of which they were members was sacrosanct and to challenge it was anathema. Perhaps the up-front arguments were sometimes the manifestations of the hidden fears of individuals who felt personally threatened, as social status and career positions were involved, turning big fish in small pools into minnows in a minor sea.

The second view was that the European states had to be absorbed into a new united state, which transcended the older entities. The old states had betrayed the peoples of Europe, in that they had failed to provide security in two world wars, or adequate welfare. But those who believed this did not specify any fundamental alteration in the concept of the state, but merely the same thing on a bigger scale in the form of a Federal Europe: there was to be a single bigger state, rather than a number of smaller ones. Their hope was that the larger entity, though similar to the ones it replaced as a form of organization, would somehow behave differently. Often concealed in their arguments was a particular image of the USA, which was thought to have provided better for its citizens. But when it came to the external relations of this new leviathan, its role in international society, the image was less clear. By default, the image which seemed to be favoured was an introspective, withdrawn, isolationist mega-state, over that of an involved, active international one. Such larger states would be kinder, based on the enthusiasm of the people, but less involved with each other. Very few considered whether the new Europe could be a superpower in the making, given as much to con-flict as its predecessors.

Neither of these positions represented a real challenge to the international society which had produced the wars of the past. The view of the saviour state, the prejudice of the Eurosceptics in Britain, stressed the heroic national tradition, but tragically edged towards encouragement of a world in which it was more likely that heroism would again be necessary. It was rooted in pride about the perfor-mance of the states that had resisted fascism in the two world wars, yet could contribute to the recurrence of circumstances in which they would have to fight again. The heroic was a self-fulfilling prophecy in that it was too easily perverted into an anti-Europeanism, a little 'island' or 'provincial' mentality, a policy of divide and rule on the continent, associated with a hankering after the kind of loose balance of power arrangement that arose in the late nineteenth century. Already, by early 1996, there were elements in the British government which eagerly welcomed any appearance of discord between France and Germany! There were reasons for this which were peculiarly British, but there were parallel reactions in a number of other states, and an increasing fear that they would become stronger and spill over into extreme nationalism. There was support for looser and larger frameworks. But in such frameworks the conflictual tendencies in the international system would be more likely to become manifest.

This position implied a world in which the existing states kicked back the traces of the increasing range of social, economic, and other interdependencies which had been developing in the modern world: the latter would be hedged anew by the frontiers of states, and each would be less involved economically, socially, and politically with the others. In other words, if the Eurosceptics had their way, the value of national autonomy, in a crude form, would be stressed above the pursuit of efficiency, effectiveness, and economy. This is illustrated by their attitude towards the notion of subsidiarity contained in the Maastricht Treaty. It was seen, mistakenly, as allowing the repatriation to the states of competence exercised by the Union, not because they would be exercised better, but because they would be exercised by them.

But a federal state, if that were to be set up in Europe, would also tend to be more exclusive in its social economic and political relations than the individual states in the interdependent world of the 1990s. Its sub-units would be pushed towards greater involvement with each other by constitutional doctrine and pressured to discriminate against non-members with which relationships could be more rewarding. The implications of hard forms of intergovernmentalism and of federalism were similar in that both risked lessening the degree of global integration. Both would mean less involvement in economic, social, and other forms of cooperation with other states, which would be capable of acting as constraints upon their behaviour.

In the 1990s the goal of a federal Europe was not, however, a realistic one, although the hard intergovernmentalists acted as if this were the case. The real, practical problem for the Union's member governments, with which they had to deal every day, was that of learning to live with profound changes in the conditions of national autonomy, which resulted from increasing links with each other. There was a search for new forms of sovereignty, appropriate to the modern world, with which all states, inside or outside the EU, had to deal. But this increasing interdependence had more revolutionary implications for the nature of the state in international society than federalism.

This book argues that the arrangements which reflected and promoted interdependence between the member states, which were concerned primarily with economic activities, but increasingly involved social and a wide range of political and security dimensions, had themselves become discrete forms of activity. They were structures which extended across the Union, and had the effect of changing the conditions of sovereignty and of posing new problems for national governments about how they managed their affairs. They also increasingly created pressures for internal change in the member states.

This is different from the view that the European Union should be seen merely as a mechanism which rescued the nation state. (See the discussion of this in Chapter 2.) This may have been true for a short period in the history of the Union, say in the late 1940s and 1950s. But by the 1990s the situation had greatly changed. This was the decade in which the states were being confronted with pressures to change by the Union, and they were not simply using the Union to defend their traditional forms. The politics of the Union interacted substantially with those of the states, but had also acquired a degree of self-containment, with values being sought which were not necessarily identical with those preferred in any of the states, by groups which were not primarily national organizations. Now there was a struggle between those who wished to accept the challenge of this new reality, and to adapt to a new world, and those who would resist. It is argued in this book that to fail to adapt would carry a heavy price.

The European Union was in fact a very powerful illustration of the limits of the argument that the behaviour of states was determined solely by the international political system. In Europe the structures of cooperation had begun to impinge upon the behavioural disposition of the state members, and had increased pressures upon them to change and become different from non-members. The way in which they were arranged internally, increasingly affected by the EU, was of the utmost importance in influencing the pattern of their mutual relations. This challenge to the traditional version of the concept of international society is also one of the themes of this book.

The argument between Eurosceptics and Europhiles, whoever they were in the different member countries, was not just about federal or intergovernmental approaches to the European Union, but also about how far to respond to, or resist, pressures to change within the state. Hankering after the heroic state, and for looser arrangements, was a reflection of a determination to protect the traditional form of the state, and to resist the pressures to change deriving from the structures of the European Union. This hope was based upon a delusion, an attempt to hold back the tide of increasing interdependence, which in the mid-1990s was swirling especially strongly among regional groupings of states. It was not confined to Europe, though probably most advanced there. Anti-federalism was the hook on which these inclinations were placed.

Such adaptations are seen in this book as leading not to a federation, however, but to a new and unique form of international system. This is a special grouping of states, and this is the most important point to be made in this book. It is the point that needs to be made over and over again, in the face of the dangerous arguments of the Eurosceptics and the misplaced hopes of the federalists, who feed each other's anger. In the extent of its common arrangements, and the changes in the conditions of the sovereignty of its members, it would be radically different from previous groups of states. It is truly a departure from the world preferred by traditionalists or federalists, but is more consciously addressed to fundamentally altering the society of existing states, than to creating a new transcendent state. To put it bluntly: this book is *anti*-federalist, but *for* forms of adaptation of the state which are beyond the ken of Eurosceptics. The character of the group of states thus adapted is as much a product of pressure deriving from the nature of the sub-units, the states, as of systemic forces.

Traditionalists might argue that the backlash by Eurosceptics is a manifestation of the inevitable tendency for the state to reassert itself in a traditional form. They imply that there are dark forces defending the state which cannot be denied. The same argument was proposed with regard to Charles de Gaulle's resistance to the Community in the mid-1960s (see Chapter 1), and to the reaction against the dynamics pushing towards integration in the mid-1970s. The hard realist view in these cases was the same: the primacy of the state will out. But this was always a viewpoint rather than an argument. After the two oppositions mentioned, the tide of integration moved on: there was a point at which someone thought the state was facing great danger, but always somewhere down the line it was realized that what had been opposed was now accepted, and the state was as alive as ever.

In the 1990s the battle has been joined between the modernizers, who are among the ranks of the pro-Europeans, and the traditionalists, who defend the traditional form of the state. The fact that this is a struggle, with sides being taken, and points won and lost, is an indication that nothing is inevitable. This book is a part of the struggle for successful adaptation by the states to the EU. Their survival is assumed: they do not require to be rescued, but they do require to adapt. The answer to the question at the start of this introduction will in large part depend upon the outcome of this struggle.

1

THE DEVELOPMENT OF THE EUROPEAN UNION: A CONCISE HISTORY

IN the development of the European Community there were a number of key moments, defining various phases in its historical evolution. This chapter is concerned with the main features of these defining moments. They may be listed as follows:

the setting up of the institutions and the logic of the founding agreements;

the crisis in 1965 and the resulting institutional changes;

the proposals of the Hague Conference in 1969 and their outcome in the early 1970s;

the new intergovernmentalism and the Paris Summit of December 1974;

the new phase of integration starting in 1984: the progress towards the Maastricht Treaty;

the Maastricht Treaty and its context.

These key events defined the shape of the evolution of the European Union and also the main contours of its character in the late 1990s. They allow the achievement to be judged: what existed in the mid-1990s could only be understood by reference to what was added at each of these junctures. A non-historical understanding of the European Union of the 1990s, say in terms of a contemporary account of the role and powers of the institutions, would be misleading, in that it would miss the way in which new arrangements at each stage were the product of a timely reconciliation of different ambitions for integration. This chapter does, however, include a brief evaluation of the contribution of the key institutions to the integration process, a theme which is developed throughout the book.

Opponents of the Union often referred to national histories in defending their realms, and implied that, whereas national histories had deep cultural resonance, the history of the European Union was merely a set of technical adjustments in the machinery of cooperation. Such national histories were usually described in terms of key events which explained and legitimized key aspects of the nation's current being. In this chapter the attempt is made to produce this kind of history for the European Union. Wherever possible, developments in the history of the Community are related to what appears to be true about the Community in the mid-1990s. This conveys the weight of the inheritance, and is suggestive of the underlying adjustment to the norms of Community behaviour as the system evolved.

This is not a detailed account of its evolution—there are a large number of excellent examples of this. It is a selection of critical founding moments, which explain and legitimize the current form, and which, as is shown in Chapter 4, also have a cultural resonance. A brief résumé of the defining moments will indicate the overall shape of the history of the evolution of the European Community.

There were three main phases in the development of the European Community, which in 1991 was rechristened the European Union. In the first phase, from the signing of the Rome treaty until 1965, the process was relatively straightforward, in that it seemed to enthusiasts that integration was about transferring powers to the centre, and it seemed to the supporters of the nation states that this should be resisted. Both sides thought that the states' relationship with the Community was a zero-sum game: what went to the centre was equal to what was lost from the parts; and there was difficulty about any notion of mutual benefit. Given the personality of the first President of the European Community—Walter Hallstein—the arguments of the main integration theorists—the Neofunctionalists—and the climate of Euro-enthusiasm,[1] the prevailing view among students of integration was that Europe was likely to move towards more centralization.

After the *first* phase of enthusiasm, there was little or no forward

[1] For an excellent account of the early development of the European Community from a Neofunctionalist perspective see Leon Lindberg, *The Political Dynamics of European Economic Integration* (Stanford, Calif.: Stanford University Press, 1963).

motion, from 1965 until 1969. But the Conference of the Heads of State and Government of the Community at the Hague in December 1969 led to a *second* phase of integrative development, which reached its climax at the Paris Summit meeting of Heads of State and Government in December 1972.[2] This Summit produced a communiqué which supported the idea of European Union by 1980, and proposed a great push towards a European *Great Society*, illustrated by the efforts made to push the European social programme forward at that time, which no member government opposed. In December 1974 another meeting of the Heads of State and Government at Paris instigated a set of changes in the workings of the Community's institutions which established their major shape until the early 1990s.[3] But the integration process did not accelerate into its *third* phase until the mid-1980s, and it then continued through until the Maastricht Treaty of 1991, which marked the beginning of another phase of retrenchment in the mid-1990s. This successive acceleration and slackening of pace was a characteristic of the historical evolution of the European Union.

Alongside this process was that of developing the institutions. In the first period the institutions' shape was relatively simple. It was dominated by the Commission of senior officials, appointed for a four-year period by the governments, but required to act independently of them in the general interest; and the Council of Ministers, made up of representatives of national governments. These two institutions remained at the heart of the Community's arrangements. But several new institutions were later added to the core. In early 1966 the first adjustment was made when agreements concluded in Luxembourg led to the enhancement of the role of the Committee of Permanent Representatives of the member states in Brussels, and placed a major impediment in the way of majority voting. The Luxembourg Accords, as they were called, in effect postponed the introduction of majority voting in the Council of Ministers. Majority voting became an unusual procedure until the mid-1980s, despite the terms of the Treaty of Rome, which held that in the third four-year period of the transitional phase—1966–70—majority voting should be used more often.

Then, the December 1974 Summit introduced a further set of

[2] See Roy Pryce, *The Politics of the European Community* (London: Butterworths, 1972).

[3] See Paul Taylor, *The Limits of European Integration* (London and New York: Croom Helm and Columbia University Press, 1983).

adjustments, chief amongst which was the strengthening of the role of the General Council of Ministers, made up of the Foreign Ministers of the member states, in managing the business of the Community. This had the effect of strengthening the role of the state which held the Presidency in the Community's decision-making; that state provided for its six-month period of office all the chairpersons of the institutions responsible to the Council of Ministers, and was now to play the leading role in formulating the agenda of the Community and managing its business. The institution of the Presidency was to become the archetypal institutional feature of a new model of Europe, discussed in Chapter 2. Another significant change in December 1974 was the setting up of the European Council, which turned the meetings of the Heads of State and Government into a permanent Community institution.

In the mid-1980s a new set of institutional adjustments began: as will be seen, the Single European Act enhanced the powers of the European Parliament, and confirmed that a system of qualified majority voting should operate in the Council of Ministers in ten named policy areas. The Maastricht Treaty was the culmination of these changes, with its introduction of the notion of the European Union, which embodied a number of new features concerning foreign policy and civil arrangements going beyond the original European Community.[4]

The Logic of the Founding Agreements

The evolution of the European Union owes a great deal to the character of the Treaty of Rome. This permitted a pragmatic adjustment to circumstances and the legitimization of various alternative models of community development. It was not tied to a particular prescription: its purpose was not made wholly explicit and it enunciated principles rather than details. It was like the American Constitution in that its level of generality was precisely pitched to allow it to be a focus of the hopes and expectations of a wide variety of different groups, and for these to be adjusted and to find a new reconciliation with each other at various points in the Union's history. Had it been detailed and precise, it would probably have been broken long since,

[4] See Desmond Dinan, *Ever Closer Union? An Introduction to the European Community* (Basingstoke: Macmillan, 1994).

as any formal commitment to federalism would have lost the states, and any firm enunciation of intergovernmentalism would have lost those who wished to transcend the existing political forms. Beyond that it conveyed a vague optimism about a better future which anti-federalists could not explicitly renounce. Even Charles de Gaulle and Mrs Thatcher went along with that. Agreed, it did postulate in the preamble an 'ever closer union of peoples', but this large purpose was not one which any leading politician in the member states could explicitly reject, because to do so would have seemed tantamount to recommending a return to the disorder and incipient violence of the 1930s.

The Treaty showed the impact of the disappointment of earlier hopes for rapid federation with the rejection of the European Defence Community (EDC) in the French National Assembly in August 1954.[5] The statesmen were reluctant to start again down that path, and in the debates about the proposed Treaty in the French Assembly, and in the *Bundestag*, it was made clear that ambitious supranationalism was out. In his speech to the *Bundestag* in support of the adoption of the Rome Treaty, Ludwig Erhard, the German Economics Minister, seemed to his audience to be in the process of recommending its rejection; his support was explicit only in his con-cluding remarks. Indeed in the actual wording of the Treaty there was no explicit promise of federalism. The word *supranationalism*, which was in Article 9 of the founding treaty of the ECSC, the Treaty of Paris, before its amendment in the Merger Treaty of 1965, did not recur. There was no mention of foreign policy, or of monetary inte-gration; and legal aspects of the Treaty, such as the requirement that amendment could only be carried out on the basis of the consent of all members, underlined the point that this was a Treaty between sovereign states, and not a constitution. It was, indeed, concluded *for an unlimited period*, according to Article 240, but this was not the kind of resounding assertion of perpetuity which is to be found in consti-tutions.

The Treaty was also a *framework* treaty. It was detailed in those areas which referred to the establishment of the common market, such as the stages by which tariffs on trade between members were to be abolished, and the linked establishment of the common exter-nal tariff. As John Pinder pointed out, this was the area of *negative*

---

[5] See Daniel Lerner and Raymond Aron (eds.), *France Defeats EDC* (London: Thames and Hudson, 1957).

integration.[6] But the ways of creating the economic community, of harmonizing the policies and instruments of intervention in national economies, were not spelled out. They were largely statements of the intentions of the signatories, and declarations of principle. This was the case with the Common Agricultural Policy, the common commercial policy, social policy, tax policy, transport policy, fisheries, and of course, non-tariff barriers to trade under Article 100. The details in these areas were to be agreed in the future as governments realized that consensus could not be found at the time of negotiation. It was as well that they did not try, or they would quickly have discovered the things which divided them.

The Treaty was indeed also capable of being interpreted as a hard commercial deal, a set of rather specific bargains between the signatory states, at the core of which was the central bargain between the French and the Germans. The French were unsure about the common market in manufactured goods, as in the mid-1950s they lacked the confidence that their industry would compete effectively with that of a Germany which was already well into its economic miracle. Indeed the major safeguard clauses in the Treaty were the result of French pressure. But they *did* want the common market in agriculture, because of the surplus in food which they produced. In the mid-1950s around 20 per cent of the French were still directly dependent on agriculture. The Germans, for their part, wanted the common market in manufactured goods, and were prepared to risk French dominance of the agricultural market. The deal, therefore, was that the French would get the common market in agriculture, and the Germans would get the common market in manufactured goods. In the event French industry adapted very effectively to the common market, and held its own in competition with that of Germany.

But there was another kind of understanding between France and Germany which was a subtext of the Treaty of Rome. This was not set down in a form of words, but was nevertheless a part of the Treaty's meaning. The French also wanted to take further the constraints placed on West Germany by the common framework of the European Coal and Steel Community (ECSC) in the Treaty of Paris of 1951. The ECSC was an important stepping stone towards the European Economic Community and the Treaty of Rome. It combined attempts to solve specific problems with highly innovative

[6] Pinder, John, 'Positive Integration and Negative Integration: Some problems of Economic Union in the EEC', *The World Today*, 24, London: RIIA, (Mar. 1968), 88–110.

institutional arrangements which provided a model for those of the European Community. A measure of its brilliance as a creation of French diplomacy was that it abandoned traditional approaches to the problem of obtaining French security in relation to Germany— alliances, Maginot lines, and the like—in favour of supranational institutions placed in charge of key economic sectors, which at that time included the coal and steel industries. The main institution was the High Authority, an executive committee independent of national governments, headed until 1955 by the founding father of European integration, Jean Monnet. Its powers were without precedent, having more direct executive and quasi-legal authority than the Commission, albeit in a carefully defined area. It was required to regulate in a common framework the sections of the separate economies which had been particularly important in sustaining Hitler's regime. For the French the supranational principle was absolutely essential: it was the best way of restraining capabilities which could lead to war, and the new West German government of Konrad Adenauer accepted this. Intergovernmental approaches simply would not do.[7]

A grand purpose of the Treaty of Rome, as with the Paris Treaty before it, was to bind West Germany to Western Europe, and to meet continuing French concerns about their security in relations with Germany. The German government saw the framework of the European Community as the place where they could define themselves as a state, find a new sense of identity to replace that which had been so tarnished by the Third Reich, and adapt to their new constitutional and legal mechanisms—to rediscover Germany as a nation and as a state. In return for this grant the French were to be given a more secure environment. From the beginning, therefore, the European Community was as much about state creation as about integration.

It was about four things each of which was of vital importance. First, it was to provide specific benefits of a utilitarian kind. Second, it was to provide a framework for the recovery of statehood, a need which was always present but which was particularly clear with regard to Germany, and the new members such as Greece, Spain, and Portugal. Third, it was to provide for the security of the member states in their relations with each other. And, fourth, it was to

[7] See John Gillingham, *Coal, Steel and the Rebirth of Europe, 1945–55: The Germans and French from Ruhr Conflict to Economic Community* (Cambridge: Cambridge University Press, 1991).

offer the prospect of fundamental changes in the governance of Europe, though these were not spelled out. For some that meant transcending the nation states, for others it meant serving them better. Sight of this range of purposes was often lost in the debate about federalism in the 1990s.

The institutional arrangements of the Community themselves reflected these various purposes. They were designed in such a way that the gaps in the framework treaty could gradually be filled on the basis of proposals from the Commission, which was asked to promote the European interest, and to reconcile that with the common interests of the member states. Its members were forbidden from receiving instructions from governments, though they were to be appointed by the general agreement of the states. The Council of Ministers in turn was to legislate on the basis of the Commission's proposals. That was where the general interest was to be related to the separate interests of the member states.

The Council's decisions would add to the law of the Community, in particular through regulations, which were directly binding on the persons to whom they were addressed, without the need for any further enactment by governments; and directives, which required governments to achieve the goals stipulated within a specific period.[8] Thus the working method of the Community, from the outset, required the general interest and the interests of the states to be reconciled; and it was the governments which determined the content of the law of the Community, either through agreeing to the Treaty or to subsequent enactments. As is shown in other parts of this essay, the supranational legal arrangements had intergovernmental roots. This crucial ambiguity was to be a great source of strength for the Community over the years.

Yet this point, which was so important in the history of the European Union, is often ignored. The origins in the ideas of the founding fathers, Jean Monnet, David Mitrany, and the presiding statesmen in the early years—Adenaur, Di Gasperi, Shuman and Paul Henri Spaak—always contained a duality of purpose, namely increasing unity in continuing diversity. If federalism meant an overweening drive to centralization, none of these founding fathers were federalist, but they did share a common ambition to introduce profound changes into the relations between the European states.

[8] See P. S. M. F. Mathijsen, *A Guide to European Community Law*, 5th edn. (London: Sweet and Maxwell, 1990).

This explains the appearance early on of two ways of proceeding in the Community: first, the *community method*, with its insistence on timely concessions and an awareness of the common advantage, and a certain way of doing things, and, second, a fraught intergovernmental diplomacy, involving endlessly protracted and often bitter negotiations in the formation of package deals. After observing the latter it was common in the early years for British students of the Community to complain about the hypocrisy of the continentals in talking about cooperation whilst grabbing what they could.[9] It was only after accession that a British statesman, Sir Christopher Soames, was led to understand and praise the community method.[10] The evolution of the European Union involved the gradual ascendancy of a form of qualified intergovernmentalism, at the expense of an insistent federalism, which it was probably necessary to pursue more energetically in the early years in view of the tendency towards the fragmentation of the European state system. But the duality of community and state, unity and diversity were constant themes. The community method and the techniques of intergovernmentalism existed side by side from early on, and there was nothing hypocritical in resorting to the other if the one would not do. The fights were in the family.

Stronger common frameworks were necessary to contain the instincts of individuals who were inclined to fight: such frameworks could be allowed to retreat as the individuals themselves developed surer instincts for cooperation. But any states which did not understand where the margin lay between concern with self and support for the community were dangerous partners in this enterprise. Neighbours who thought the nightly squabbles were between enemies could be mistaken. The problem with the dangerous partners was not that they were concerned with their own interests and the survival of their own states—that wish was common to all states. It was rather that they had not understood the history of the Community, and credited members with a malice which they had begun to forget. The danger with the British in the mid-1990s was precisely that: having refused to believe that the enemies of the Second World War could be anything but hypocritical when they said they agreed, they tried to amplify their disagreements, as the opportunity arose, into something more sinister.

[9] See William Pickles, *How Much has Changed? Britain and Europe* (Oxford: Basil Blackwell, 1967).

[10] European Parliament, *Debates* (July, 1973), 91.

The Crisis of the Late 1960s

The crisis in 1965 was the dominating event of the mid to late 1960s. This was the occasion when Charles de Gaulle withdrew French participation from the main committees of the European Community, partly because of a dispute over the financing of agriculture, and partly because of a more fundamental disagreement about the future of the Community. De Gaulle quarrelled with the others about the ways of financing the intervention mechanisms which were now being introduced, and from which France was to be a major beneficiary. He reacted strongly against what he took to be an attempt by the Commission to extend its supranational power by linking the financing of the Common Agricultural System to a scheme for introducing a Community budget which it would command, and giving greater powers to the European Parliament. When Germany showed signs of supporting this package, de Gaulle withdrew from the discussions, and from French participation in key committees in the Community.[11]

But there was another level of the dispute. The General realized that the quarrel about agriculture also provided an opportunity to press his vision of a more intergovernmental Community, a *Europe des Etats*. In the first phase, in what looked like a simple stand-off between Community and state, it looked as if the Community was winning: all powers were in the process of going to the Community, and de Gaulle, like Mrs Thatcher twenty years later, was determined to stop this.

There was a sense in which de Gaulle won the argument. But there was also a sense in which he failed. On the one hand he headed off the further development of the first image of European cooperation that involved a fairly straightforward shift of power and authority to Brussels. President de Gaulle was a French patriot and was determined to restore French self-confidence and power. But there was also a sense in which he lost. The Community proved to have acquired strength enough to withstand his attack, in terms of the effectiveness of the institutions, the status of its leadership, and the level of more general support. It had begun to emerge as a political system with resources of its own.

Other developments at the time helped to establish the regime.

[11] John Newhouse, *Collision in Brussels: The Common Market Crisis of 30th June 1965* (New York: Norton, 1967).

For instance two decisions by the European Court of Justice reinforced very effectively the Community legal system. The Costa versus Enels case established the legal arrangements of the Community as a self-contained system with its own Court at the head: national systems were now denied the right to intervene in the application of the law of the Community or to decide what it meant in particular circumstances. And the van Gend en Loos case established the principle of direct effect, meaning that individuals within the states had acquired the right to sue, and could be sued, under Community law; they had acquired the right even to sue their own government.[12]

One of the fascinating aspects of these developments was that they proved so uncontentious among governments, despite the fact that they represented major reinforcements of the fabric of the Community. The governments accepted the partial detachment of an important area of the law—that which followed from the Rome Treaty—from their national jurisdiction without complaint. Of course it was recognized that there were sound reasons for this: to maintain the coherence of the system over the territory of the Community as a whole. But good reasons are frequently not enough for governments to accept alterations in the conditions of their sovereignty.

In France itself the resilience of the Community system was demonstrated in the pressure brought to bear upon the General to keep France in the Community. French farmers in particular were anxious at the prospect of losing the common market in food. And French industry had begun to feel that it could after all compete with that of Germany. In the French Presidential election of December 1965 de Gaulle had to face a humiliating second round of elections in a run-off against the pro-European candidate François Mitterand. It was clear that anti-Europeanism was a vote loser, though the General's experience may have reinforced his determination to preserve unanimity in the Council of Ministers, and to take greater care to resist any attempt by the Commission to enter into direct relationships with the French people, thus undercutting the position of the government. In retrospect it may be seen that de Gaulle's attack on the Community, though it helped to change its direction of development, confirmed its growing strength. Indeed the French Presidential election of December 1965 was the last election within the original six member states in which the question of membership of the European Community was an issue.

---

[12] See Mathijsen, *A Guide to European Community Law.*

But the crisis certainly led to greater stress on the intergovernmental aspects of the Community. The Luxembourg Accords reinforced the trend towards turning the Community into a kind of
complex standing diplomatic conference. The number of issues
being dealt with at the Community level was increasing, which itself
led to the need for more meetings between national officials, and the
gradual introduction among national officials of standard operating
procedures which centred around Brussels. But unanimity naturally
required that all governments should be persuaded to accept any
proposal made, and this in turn meant that more diplomatic effort,
and more personnel, had to be involved in reaching agreement. In
particular that meant that the Committee of Permanent Representatives of the member states in Brussels became more important. This
Committee, meeting on a weekly basis, became a primary framework of negotiation between governments and of contact between
them and the Commission: it was to identify areas where agreement
was possible without further discussion, and areas which would
need further negotiation by the governments, and possibly reconsideration of the proposal by the Commission. This body, with its
associated supporting committees, became central in the
Community's decision-making. And increasingly the work of
national governments involved liaison with other governments
through national representatives in Brussels, and direct participation
by officials from national centres in community business.

The crisis marked a change in the centre of gravity of the
Community's institutions: more weight was attached to intergovernmental committees, as the agenda expanded, and because of the
need for unanimity. But the challenge by de Gaulle revealed the
strength of the Community's arrangements rather than their weakness. As the challenge was made so the regime was being consolidated in the member states. Expanding the scope of common
concern, together with the requirements of reaching consensus,
helped to reinforce the process of educating national officials in the
ways of the Community. More of them had to deal with Brussels
than would have been the case if majority voting had been introduced on time. In attempting to contain the Community's institutions, and challenge its values, de Gaulle succeeded in consolidating
its norms and principles.

Another development was the fragmentation of the state in the
sense that increasingly links with the Community more frequently
went directly from national administrative departments to Brussels

or matching departments in other member states, rather than through foreign offices. Charles de Gaulle's critique of the Community was linked with his alliance with the Quay d'Orsay, which was also concerned with its own loss of authority in the Community context. A framework was being established in which national civil servants could develop much stronger transnational links which became communities of common expertise, across national frontiers in the Community. These links grew much faster than the countervailing coordination mechanisms within the state, which traditionally had centred around foreign offices, but which now found new forms. Despite the continuing efforts by governments to regain control of this process of *engrenage*, by setting up such mechanisms as Cabinet Committees and other devices, from now on the development of transgovernmental alliances in favour of European policies could not be prevented. Any political élite that was opposed to integration now had to deal with those alliances. Not that these were the only examples: professional organizations, interest groups, and those in business and commerce all began to cultivate links with their opposite numbers in partner states, and to set up offices in Brussels.[13]

Civil servants who were involved in the business of Europe on a day-to-day basis, and there were increasing numbers of them, inevitably acquired a perspective and a set of preferences which inclined to European solutions. But *engrenage* also carried with it other dangers. It certainly exacerbated a problem of modern society in democracies: the difficulty of maintaining the accountability of those who played the key role in taking economic and social decisions—the bureaucrats—to an elected assembly. In other words government became more remote. It is not suggested that this problem was caused by the Community but the appearance of a greater measure of *engrenage* in the late 1960s certainly made it worse. There were more officials, taking more decisions in cooperation with each other across national frontiers, who were more remote from publics or assemblies.

The mid to late 1960s was, therefore, a period of challenge to the European Community but also a period in which the regime was consolidated. Legal arrangements were strengthened, and working practices enhanced. In essence the period was when the Community emerged more clearly as a distinctive political actor. A crucial thresh-

---

[13] See S. Mazey and J. Richardson, *Lobbying in the European Community* (Oxford: Oxford University Press, 1993).

old was reached in the numbers of individual politicians and officials who had developed such links with the Community as to be attached to it as well as to the member states.

It was not just that there was an increasing number of civil servants in Brussels, but that national officials were routinely brought to defend Community positions to governments as well as the other way round. The Committee of Permanent Representatives was an excellent example of this.[14] At the stage of policy making, when Commission proposals were being formulated, its members often acted as a sympathetic adviser about what they could persuade their own governments to accept. It was only after the Commission proposals had been formally dispatched to the Council of Ministers, and on to the Committee, that their role as national representatives was reasserted.

In sum large steps were taken in strengthening the legal system of the Community, entrenching procedures through the process of *engrenage*, the fragmenting of national interests as different parts of national administrations dealt directly with each other and the Commission, and the enhancement of multiple loyalties, even among national officials. This was the time when de Gaulle threatened to undo the Community—whether he would have done so in fact is a different issue—but, although he nudged its development in a new direction, his effort demonstrated its growing strength rather than its weakness.

From the Hague Conference to the Summit of December 1974

A new cycle of integration, followed by consolidation, began with the Hague Conference of December 1969. The Summit of December 1974 was in many ways a conclusion of this phase and added a further layer of institutions to the Community. The Council of Ministers could be seen as an agent of governments at the service of supranationalism, doomed to sign itself away, in that its role was to agree upon legislation which would gradually fill out the gaps in the Rome Treaty, and in so doing transfer responsibility to the Commission. But strengthening the Presidency, and creating the

---

[14] See Fiona Hayes-Renshaw, 'The Role of the Committee of Permanent Representatives in the Decision-Making of the European Community', Ph.D. Thesis (London: London School of Economics, 1990).

European Council, at Paris in December 1974, had the effect of incorporating intergovernmentalism as one of the formal principles of the Community. From now on the key to understanding the Community was finding ways in which intergovernmentalism and supranationalism could be related together, not that of deciding whether either should or could triumph. The Summit changed the character of decision-making in a way which had enduring consequences, in that it made explicit the latent duality of the earlier periods. Chapter 2 takes these arguments further.

In the early 1970s an apparent drive towards integration, which had a measure of success, inadvertently gave birth to a set of countervailing pressures. The intergovernmental imperative was revealed even as integration was being sought. The most obvious trigger of the new phase was the series of initiatives taken at the Hague in December 1969. This led to a set of proposals which were still behind many of the issues on the agenda twenty-five years later. It was agreed that there should be a move towards monetary integration; that the Six should consider among themselves the question of enlargement of the Community, in particular to include Britain; that the budgetary arrangements of the Community should be finalized; and that there should be a move towards establishing a machinery for harmonizing the foreign policies of member states.

Each of these proposals was in part the consequence of a logic which was specific to itself. Monetary integration was agreed because of the turbulence in the international monetary system caused by the weakness of the dollar, and the excessive quantity of dollars in the Eurocurrency market. This currency, now capable of being moved at very short notice, was pushing the currencies of the member states of the Community further apart, thus damaging the common market. The stronger currencies, especially the German mark, were under continuing pressure to revalue in order to avoid inflation, and weaker currencies in the Community were driven down in value as they too were sold. The proposals for the Economic and Monetary Union (EMU), which emerged from the Werner Report in the autumn of 1991, therefore appealed as a way of establishing a zone of monetary stability in the Community which would safeguard what had been obtained in the common market. But monetary integration also appealed to those who wanted to push the integration process forward.[15] States involved would also

[15] See Walter Hallstein, *Europe in the Making* (London: George Allen and Unwin, 1972).

be required to coordinate their economic policies: adopting inflationary policies would create irresistible pressure to devalue currency.

Some thought that adopting monetary integration would in itself
compel coordination of economic policies, which was the French
view; others thought that it was necessary to deliberately carry out
such coordination, which was the German view. But the overall conclusion was that monetary integration in the Community was necessary for good practical reasons, to stabilize currencies in the face of
pressures towards instability from outside, and, for some, for more
idealistic political reasons: so that it would push the integration
process along. EMU was explicitly linked with the goal of integration from its beginning, and was linked to the ambitious goal of
European Union by 1980, which was in the communiqués issued at the
end of several meetings of Heads of State and Government at that
time.[16] The last occasion in the 1970s when such an ambition was
declared by the Heads of State and Government was in the commu-
nique of the meeting of December 1974. Its emergence as a leitmotif of the meetings of European statesmen for a time in the early
1970s indicated their great expectations about Europe. This was the
period of the Euro-optimists: Heath and Brandt led the way, with
Pompidou and Giscard reluctantly following on.

Each of the other proposals also had its own logic. Deciding to
consider admitting the British was the culmination of a long period
of internal wrangling between those who favoured admission, such
as the Germans, the Dutch, and Belgians, and those who opposed it,
chiefly the French. But the main opponent, Charles de Gaulle, was
now in retirement, and Britain seemed to be as capable of causing
trouble between members outside the Community as within it.
Germany was now prepared to push more actively for British membership, and was in a position to reward the French for accepting
enlargement. The French had long pushed for stronger arrangements for harmonizing foreign policy among the members—the
Fouchet discussions of the early 1960s were one example of this—
and were prepared to give ground on enlargement in return for creating such a mechanism now.

Completing the transitional phase of the Common Market, and
now going beyond that to deepen the Community, naturally raised
the question of harmonizing foreign policy. The members had more

[16] See Loukas Tsoukalis, *The Politics and Economics of European Monetary
Integration* (London: George Allen and Unwin, 1977).

economic interests in common, which required the harmonization of other aspects of foreign policy. Foreign offices in the member states were attracted by the idea of such an arrangement, as it would help to move them back to centre stage in the institutions of the Community. Hence the decision to open negotiations with the applicant states and the first steps towards creating the machinery for European Political Cooperation (EPC), took place in the same year: in June and October 1970, respectively.

With regard to the budgetary arrangements, the Treaty of Rome had required that they be completed at the end of the transitional phase. But states do not necessarily readily accept what they have agreed to in a treaty. Why was the French government now prepared to accept the right of the Community to finance, and the introduction of an automatic financing mechanism, when de Gaulle had so vigorously opposed a very similar arrangement only five years earlier? The Commission's proposal to finance the Common Agricultural Policy out of money raised in this way had been the trigger of the crisis in July 1965. The answer was that by 1970 the French government was more at ease with the kind of Europe which seemed to have emerged. The consequence of the 1965 crisis was that an apparent drive to increase the power of Brussels had been halted, intergovernmentalism seemed more secure, and in this situation, budgetary powers could be granted to the Community without risk. This way of thinking recurred in the history of the Community: governments were often prepared to make concessions to supranationalism precisely when they had been reassured that it posed no threat to their sovereignty.

Indeed the 1965 crisis also played a part in at least two other conversions in the attitudes of political leaders towards integration. The Benelux countries had been very hesitant about accepting the Fouchet proposals for foreign policy harmonization in the early 1960s, which appeared surprising in view of their strong support for integration. Given that inclination, why had they opposed the introduction of mechanisms for harmonizing foreign policies? At first sight such a step looked like a great leap forward, as such questions were traditionally close to the heart of sovereignty. The proposal appeared to provide General de Gaulle with an opportunity for heading off the move towards majority voting in the third transitional phase of the Treaty of Rome, and it created an opportunity for him to hive off Community matters to a more strictly intergovernmental framework. Given the way in which the Community was viewed in the early 1970s this no longer seemed a realistic objection. The British Labour Prime Minister, Harold Wilson, also said that he had realized that Europe posed no threat to national sovereignty because of the 1965 crisis, and that therefore an application to join for specific utilitarian reasons was acceptable. The application was made in May 1967.

These links illustrate the internal coherence of the history of the European Union, with attitudes and developments at one time having implications for different attitudes and developments many years later. This coherence may be reduced to two propositions: the higher the degree of intergovernmentalism the greater the degree of integration which may be tolerated; the higher the degree of integration the stronger the assertion of intergovernmentalism. These two propositions are often true of particular bargains but also of developments over a period of time.

West German government attitudes went through a cycle in the late 1960s and early 1970s which illustrate the second of the propositions. Under Willi Brandt there was enthusiasm for further integration. Brandt was a supporter of deepening, enlarging, and widening of the Community, and it was he who dominated the December 1969 conference at the Hague. This was partly because of his personality and partly because of the changes in the diplomatic position of West Germany and France over the preceding three years. France had declined from the high point of 1967, when de Gaulle had been able to increase French gold stocks to their 1913 level and put pressure on the Americans to devalue the dollar, and in December 1967 he had vetoed the British application to join the Community for the second time. But in early 1968 the French had gone through a period of very serious internal turmoil: there had been student and worker riots, concessions to their wage demands, and fundamental alterations in the administration of universities and industrial management. And the French had been compelled in August 1969 to do what de Gaulle had described as 'the worst anathema', namely devalue the French franc. By the time of de Gaulle's resignation France had been to some degree enfeebled.

At the same time the more active Ostpolitik pursued by Brandt had freed him from excessive dependence on the allies. The policy of his predecessors, which followed the Hallstein doctrine of not dealing with any states which recognized East Germany, except the Soviet Union, had led to caution even in the West. Eastern European policy was the context in which the Germans had developed and exercised increasing diplomatic muscle, which was more potent because of their economic strength. The settlements with Eastern European states, culminating with that with the Soviet Union in 1971, allowed Brandt to pursue a more energetic Western policy, and part of this was the abandonment of the Hallstein doctrine.[17] He was able to push for more integration in the face of French caution, without the continuing fear that German initiatives would suddenly be trumped by a threat from one or other of the Western partners to enter into diplomatic relations with an East European state. A more active Eastern policy was therefore closely connected with the appearance of a more active Western policy.

But the problem was that this stance was always subject to an inner contradiction. Pressure for more integration by Brandt followed from West Germany's greater self-confidence as a state, and indeed the abandonment of the view that West Germany was a temporary form. The settlements had the effect of confirming what appeared to be the permanence of West Germany. But in the early 1970s integration could be seen as having precisely the opposite implications in challenging the survival of the German state, and constraining its new-found energy: it followed from German strength but also threatened to drain it. It was but a matter of time before this contradiction was recognized. West German leaders, such as Brandt's successor Helmut Schmidt, began to express doubts about taking integration too far. There were complaints that Germany could not continue to be the paymaster of Europe. The context in which this became clear for the first time was the discussions about the Regional policy in 1973–74, when Germany refused to contribute significant sums to the new Regional Fund, to the disappointment of the British. West German statesmen were looking for a new balance between the prerequisites of integration and the survival of the state: the dynamic balance between federalism and intergovernmentalism had to be restored. This meant transcending the first model of the Community in a new synthesis of state and union.

The integrative momentum of the early 1970s was slowing down by 1973–4 for a number of reasons. The EMU proposal, which had been at its core, faltered because the states were unable to maintain their unity in the face of increasing monetary disorder in the international system. It had been created because of the realization that

---

[17] See Roger Morgan, *West European Politics since 1945: The Shaping of the European Community* (London: B.T. Batsford, 1972).

integration would help members to insulate themselves to some extent from turbulence in the international monetary system. But as the pressures from outside increased they could not accept the scale of internal monetary integration necessary to preserve the system; in the judgement of the time, it required such a degree of integration as to compromise their sovereignty. It would have been possible to extend that external monetary defence by strengthening the common institutions, by increasing resources available from the centre to defend narrowing exchange rate margins, and by accepting the limitation of national autonomy on various areas of internal economic policy. But this jump to a higher level of integration could not be accepted in the mid-1970s. As in the mid-1990s the question of whether a single currency would remove sovereignty from states was unanswerable, but in the mid-1970s the views of those who believed this prevailed.

The EMU proposal failed because of weakness in the sense of common identity and mutual confidence rather than as a direct consequence of any specific practical problems. The governments preferred to be more exposed to the disturbances in the international monetary system, as they saw the alternative as a loss of national sovereignty. The effect was that the exchange rate margins could not be further narrowed or held, the Monetary Authority remained a shell, and by 1977–8, only a small number of states remained linked to the German mark in the exchange rate system.[18] The slowing of the pace of integration was, of course, much encouraged by the disappearance of its major sources of diplomatic support, namely Brandt, who resigned in 1973, and of Edward Heath who was succeeded by Labour under Harold Wilson in February 1974. The British Labour Party at that time was deeply suspicious of the European Community.

Two main levels of developments in the early 1970s have now been discussed, that of the issues and initiatives, and that of statesmen and states. A third may now be identified, accepting that all three are closely related to each other. There were also developments that were concerned primarily with the institutional arrangements of the European Community. The initiatives of the 1969 summit also led to the further growth of Community institutions. This was due primarily to the proposals for EMU and for the harmonization of foreign policy, but also because of the continued

[18] See Geoffrey Denton, 'European Monetary Cooperation: The Bremen Proposal', *The World Today*, 34/11, London: RIIA, (Nov. 1978).

expansion of the scope of integration which had been identified in the late 1960s. Two particular growth areas were evident. First, the number of committees under the Council of Ministers showed rapid increase; these were committees that would be chaired by officials from the same state as that providing the chairman of the Council of Ministers. Second were an increasing number of committees which were concerned with areas that were outside the sphere of the Community institutions, because they were not areas covered by the Treaty of Rome. These included a wide range of meetings, such as meetings of central bankers to discuss monetary integration and a large number of other issues related to monetary integration. These issues were not in the Treaty, which only appealed for stable relations between currencies according to the principles of the IMF. Another area outside the Treaty was that of the harmonization of foreign policy. These involved the governments of the member states of the Community but not the Community itself.

The multiplication of committees, both in and outside the Community—strictly defined—led to the worsening of a long-standing problem of the Community: how was the business of the Community and of the member states to be coordinated? It was in the spirit of the times in the first years of the 1970s that the Commission was the main claimant of this role. The Treaty gave responsibility for managing the Community to the Commission. Could the new areas not be incorporated into the Treaty of Rome through amendment, so that the Commission's domain would be increased? This course of action was strongly supported by Commission Presidents, and pushed very vigorously by President Ortoli.[19]

With the waning of the pro-integration enthusiasm, and the failures of the main integrative ventures, especially the EMU, the answer to this appeal was not surprising. Responsibility for the European Community Summit in Paris in December 1974 was in the hands of the French, in particular those of President Valéry Giscard d'Estaing. He had his own combination of prejudices regarding Europe. On the one hand he was perceived as being a pro-European. On the other he was from the right of the French political spectrum, and, though not of the same party, an heir to de Gaulle's way of thinking. In the event, the conclusions of the Summit, agreed by partners including Helmut Schmidt and Harold Wilson, were that

[19] See President Ortoli's 'Introduction' to the *Sixth General Report on the Activities of the Communities* (Brussels and Luxembourg, 1973), 4.

responsibility for coordinating the business of the Community should be given to the General Council, the Council of Ministers meeting in the form of the Foreign Ministers. The Commission was to be consulted as a partner in this process, but its claim to be restored to its position of manager of the system was rejected.

The General Council was also given responsibility for the machinery for harmonizing the foreign policies of the member states, and the Chairman of the Council of Ministers was asked to act on behalf of Community members in relations with other states, subject to the members' agreement. The effect of this, of course, was to enhance the powers of the Chairman of the General Council, which was known as the Presidency: that state and its officials now had primary responsibility for seeing that the General Council exercised its functions effectively, and for managing the foreign policy of the members through its foreign ministry. The Foreign Ministries had been returned to centre stage in the Community's institutions with a vengeance!

This was one of the more important developments in the history of the Community's institutions, as it meant that for a period of six months each state in turn, following the rotation principle of the chairmanship of the Council of Ministers as stipulated in the Treaty of Rome, became the leading Community member both within the Community and outside it. Each of the states, large or small, became a leading diplomatic force in the world, able to push it own agenda, and project its own image, once every four and a half years in a Community of nine, and once every eighteen and a half years in the Community of fifteen states of the late 1990s. But it was soon learned, as was predictable, that no state could crudely pursue its national interests, and that every state had to project the interests of the Community and combine those as well as it could with its own interests. Here was a place where common interests and the separate interests of states were juxtaposed. This was the institution where the duality of the Community's character was revealed particularly clearly, and where the participating officials mysteriously quickly learned that this was the case. No state, most of all the small and medium-sized states, was prepared to abandon this arrangement by the time of writing: it helped them to emerge more clearly as separate sovereign states, whilst at the same time working for common policies where sovereignty would be pooled. This unique institution was the culmination of a long process of the adjustment of institutions and perceptions of interest, and of the learning of working habits.

But in the December 1974 Summit another institution was created, the European Council. This was the descendant of the earlier summit meetings of Heads of State and Government, and was convened in this form for the first time in March 1975. It was to meet three times a year, in Brussels and in each of the capitals of the states holding the Presidency. In the Single European Act of 1985 the number of meetings was reduced to two. The General Council and the Foreign Ministry of the state holding the Presidency would be mainly responsible for preparations for the meetings of the Council.

Why was it established at this stage? At one level the answer to this is banal: it had been wished for by the previous French President, Pompidou. But the underlying reasons were more complex. On the one hand it also symbolized the recapturing of the business of the Community by the governments, the reassertion of the intergovernmental model. The big decisions were to be taken by the Heads of State and Government and usually agreement on the basis of unanimity would be sought. New initiatives would also be taken by its members. It was also necessary, however, not merely because of governments' wish to defend their corner, but also as a facilitator of further integration. The development of the work of the Community had got to the point at which the separate Councils of Ministers often ran into barriers which could not be overcome without creating deals between the different policy sectors. Such cross-sector package deals could not be made within the specialized councils. They had to be made at a higher political level by the members of the European Council. The latter was, therefore, as much to ease forward motion, as to impose a timely brake. The Council was to link sectors in package deals to unravel the impasse of the specialists, to tackle major political obstacles, and to generate new grand initiatives.[20]

Like the Single European Act and the Maastricht Treaty the December 1974 Summit took three steps forward and two steps back—the regular mode of Community development. It is consistent with the themes of this chapter that further integrative decisions were taken, as well as decisions which reinforced the positions of Governments and Foreign Offices. Institutional adjustments seemed at first sight to entrench intergovernmentalism, but they also eased the path of integration. The German dilemma of the early 1970s, that there was an irreconcilable opposition between the

[20] For a discussion of these issues see Paul Taylor, *The Limits of European Integration*, ch. 3.

thesis and antithesis of the first Europe—the antagonism of integration and nationalism—had tentatively approached a new synthesis: the realization that state and community could reinforce each other, and need not be opposed at all. At the same meeting that established the European Council and reinforced the Presidency it was also agreed that there would at long last be direct elections to the European Parliament by 1978 (the resistance of the British, as ever hell-bent on democracy, meant that they were not held until 1979). A common form of European passport was also agreed, as was a proposal for a European Regional Fund. It was also agreed to set up the European University Institute in Paris.

The Role of the Institutions in the Integration Process

At this stage it is appropriate to consider briefly the role of the main institutions of the Community in the integration process. Enough has been said about the historical evolution of the institutional arrangements for the main features of this process to be apparent. A more direct focus on the institutions will further illuminate these features, before returning to the later stages of the process.

The Court of Justice[21]

The Court of Justice played a very important role in the promotion of the integration process. It was highly successful in protecting its reputation as an impartial legal actor whilst in fact acting in a highly political capacity as a motor of integration. It achieved this in a number of ways.

• It adopted a teleological role for itself, though it was able to retreat from this when the integration process appeared to be going well, or it looked as if it could attract significant criticism as it had become too exposed. This involved interpreting the founding agreements, especially the Treaty of Rome, in the light of what the signatories said they wanted to achieve, namely, an economic community, rather than on a more restrictive basis, such as a literal interpretation

---

[21] See Anne-Marie Burley and Walter Mattli, 'The Law and Politics of the European Court of Justice: Law as a Mask', *International Organization* (Oct. 1993).

of the terms use. The Court's strongest role with regard to integration came when it handed down what were called preliminary rulings under Article 177 of the Treaty. These rulings were essentially interpretations of the Community's constitution produced after a request for clarification by a court in a member state.

- It succeeded in building up a significant group of people who had an interest in protecting and strengthening the European legal system These included the community of European legal specialists in the academic world and judges and lawyers involved in the system. The former had developed an expertise which was at a premium in the evolving system. They could advise on its implications. The judiciary also acquired an interest in working within the system, and showed an increasing inclination to apply to the Court for interpretations of the law of the Communities. They liked the way in which the European system facilitated their empowerment with regard to national legal authorities.

- The Court had encouraged an arrangement within which this was possible because it had enunciated the main features of the new system. Three principles were at the heart of the Community's legal system, namely direct applicability, direct effect and the principle that European law had primacy over national law. Direct applicability was the principle that regulations approved by the Council of Ministers would be applicable within member states without further enactment by national authorities. This was contained in Article 189 of the Treaty of Rome. Direct effect created rights and obligations for individuals under Community law, and the principle of primacy held that courts within states would apply Community law in preference to national law if there was a contradiction between the two. (See Chapter 2.) The second and third of these principles were determined by the Court itself, and the member states had not been entirely happy about them, but did not bring themselves to overturn them. The judgements of the Court could only be overturned by using the amendment process of the Treaty of Rome, but three of the then six member states of the Community expressed doubts about the direct effect principle when it was handed down in 1964. The principles were thought necessary by the Court to achieve the goals sought in the founding Treaty, namely the setting up of a single economic community among the member states. Many authorities, including governments and specialists, supported this view.

- The Court extended the implications of these principles. Of particular importance was the extension of the principle of direct effect, which originally established that individuals could sue their government for infringements of the Treaty of Rome. It was expanded by the Court, however, to mean that individuals could sue each other under the law of the Community, and eventually to mean that rules contained in the Treaty, as well as directives, could create rights and obligations for individuals, even if a government had failed to introduce implementing legislation. The distinction between regulations, which were directly applicable to individuals within member states, and directives, which required governments to approve facilitating legislation, was eroded. The only condition was that the rule or directive should be clear and not conditional upon some other act: it should be capable of being applied without ambiguity with regard to circumstances or timing. Direct effect was therefore very skilfully used by the Court to increase the number of those who stood to benefit under the Community's legal system. It was also skilfully used in that a failure to comply with a directive was not inevitably turned into a contest between the Court and the member states. Individuals within states were given greater power to push their governments to act upon directives, as the consequences of directives for individuals could often not be evaded by governments' delay.

• The Court also played an important part with regard to specific acts of legislation. It consistently tried to clarify principles of the Treaty, with regard, for instance, to the promotion of the common market, so that restrictions upon its development could be eliminated. The right of governments to discriminate against goods produced in other member countries was limited in a number of ways by the actions of the Court, but an historic decision was the *Cassis de Dijon* case of 1979, which was the occasion on which the Court asserted the principle which was to become key in the freeing of trade in the single market programme agreed in the Single European Act. The Court ruled in this instance that any good that was legally produced and tradable in one country should be tradable throughout the Community. Any exceptions to this rule, for instance for reasons of public policy, or of safety, would themselves be subject to Community supervision. Another area where the Court played an important role was that of promoting freedom of movement for workers. Any account of the development of the principle of the freedom of EU citizens to reside in any member country would have to take account of the decisions of the Court.

• Why was the Court able to maintain its reputation for being solely concerned with legal questions? There was a sense in which its decisions were logical and necessary. The governments were persuaded that if they wanted to achieve what they had indicated in the Treaty of Rome then it was necessary to act according to the rules and principles handed down by the Court. Other considerations helped. For instance, the members of the Court—one judge from each state, and one additional member appointed by the judges themselves—were sworn to secrecy and their rulings, though taken by majority vote, could not be identified with individual judges. The judges were therefore protected from political influence. The point has also been made that they cultivated alliance with national judiciaries, and with the scholarly community, and that rulings could only be overturned by amendment of the Treaty. This always seemed too difficult, and the dissenters, including the British Eurosceptics, though they might complain, never had enough support or energy to pursue any judgements once handed down. The Court therefore became an unexpected but very important agent of integration.

The Commission

What was the Commission's Contribution to the Integration Process?

In other parts of this book the point is made that the Commission had a dual character. It both articulated the common interest, the interest of the collectivity, as required by the Treaty of Rome, and in various ways reflected the separate interests of the member states. The reality was more complex than the doctrine, and this was helpful from the point of view of integration. States were anxious to maintain their quota of nationals in the Commission, both in the body of the secretariat and in the Commission more narrowly defined. And they strove to get their people into key positions; Sir Roy Denman was put into a position concerned with trade policy, and Lord Cockfield was mandated to push for the Single Market Programme by the British government, which regarded these as key interests.

With regard to policy formulation the Commission was therefore able to push for integration in a much more subtle sense than is usually admitted. It was able to develop policies which reflected three perspectives on Europe, which in combination could create a powerful impetus towards integration. First, it had within it resources and attitudes which encouraged the formulation of the ideal solution to particular problems: the best way for Europe as a collectivity in the best of circumstances. Second, because of its extensive consultation, in the course of making policy with interest groups and government representatives, it developed a view of the solution that was likely to be acceptable to the majority of actors—the policy which reflected the lowest common denominator among the relevant interests. Thirdly it was able to identify the nuances of policy proposals which were likely to be acceptable to the most powerful coalition of interests. Such coalitions extended among members of governments and nationals within the Commission. The Commission was therefore most likely to be effective in promoting integration when these three interests coincided: when a supranational solution coincided with the interest of a powerful national–supranational coalition, and the interests of the majority of involved actors, non-governmental and governmental.

The Commission's power was also therefore likely to be subject to periods of upswing and periods of downturn. There was clearly a limit beyond which the Commission could not free itself from dependence upon these background factors, but it might be better or worse placed to exploit opportunities when they arose in its environment. It was more effective when a dynamic President of the Commission, from one of the more important states which favoured integration was in office. In this sense the Commission's perceived role, like that of the Court, was subject to a certain sleight of hand. It had a reputation of supranationality—this was the doctrine and it was important that this should widely appear to be well founded—but in practice it was most effective when its leading figures were from a powerful state, or group of such states, which favoured integration. The power of the Commission was a product of, not an alternative to, dominant state actors which were committed to integration. In the Union in recent years these had usually been France and Germany, but occasionally other states such as the Italians took up a lead role. This was a position which the British had never occupied, because the government had not been able to build and maintain effective alliance with the members of the Commission.

Aspects of the context of Commission action which enabled it to act more effectively were, therefore, the commitment of key national actors to integration, the capacity of an energetic Commission to add to the momentum of integration by making innovative proposals for action in a favourable environment, a favourable view in the relevant attentive public of experts, commentators, and other opinion formers, and the capacity in the Commission to capitalize on the implications of previous acts of integration. In other words the Commission could in the right circumstances capitalize upon a forwards momentum, but it probably could not itself generate *ab initio* that momentum. Jacques Delors could therefore take the lead in proposing monetary integration in his Report to the Madrid summit in 1989, but it was not he who initiated the new upswing in integration which started in 1984.

When the circumstances were right the Commission was able to use a number of other resources, some of which reflected its unique character as an international institution. There was no other international institution which had its particular mix of political and administrative skills. It was headed by a cabinet the members of which had designated mandates, approved by governments, and which acted as a college (the Secretariat of the UN was headed by a single officer, the Secretary-General, and there was in that organization no equivalent of the EU cabinet); it was working to a set of goals that had a degree of definition in the Treaty of Rome; it had quasi-judicial power in certain areas, such as the abuse of the market, and in areas inherited from the Coal and Steel Community; and it was working within, was subject to, and applied, a system of rules embodied in the legal system of the Community/Union. Other international institutions did not possess a measure of all these virtues: they were not controlled by a cabinet in the same way, were not pursuing such a well-defined programme, and were not subject to, nor did they uphold a legal system of the kind found in the EU. The Commission was also helped, of course, by its key position in the diplomacy of the EU, its ability to build coalitions among actors, which was enhanced by its direct participation in the discussions of the Council of Ministers, and its detailed awareness, in advance of Council meetings, of the difficulties facing the various governments with regard to particular policies. It could be proactive in building bargains between the members of the Council of Ministers.

In addition, of course, it was given influence by two rather basic resources: knowledge and money. It had played a part in developing a highly sophisticated system for collecting, and analysing information about the relevant aspects of the member states, and this also extended to collecting information through its various embassies in a large number of states and organizations outside the Union. It also dispensed not insignificant sums of money. The Court of Justice had its growing community of grateful clients, and this was also true of the Commission. There were an increasing number of persons and institutions in the EU which had received financial support through Community mechanisms, or which had been blessed in some other way by the Commission. Perhaps the most striking illustration of this was the development of direct links between the Commission and regions within states, especially in the southern European states. Such Commission-sponsored ventures were often worked upon by nationals of the receiving states in the Commission.

The Commission therefore had a range of resources of its own, which helped it to exert influence, and to promote integration. But it remained the case that the Commission was a dependent rather than an independent actor. Its effectiveness in deploying these resources depended crucially upon a chance coincidence of favourable factors in its environment, especially the support of lead governments, the dynamics of policy evolution, and the appearance at the right time of individuals with skill and energy in the Commission itself. But the latter may sometimes be a product of the former. Delors was close to Mitterand, and Hallstein close to Adenauer. Denman and Cockfield both had the support of the British government for a programme which they strongly supported, but the alliance could not be sustained.

The Council and the European Parliament

At this stage these institutions are discussed very briefly. The Council of Ministers, made up of the ministers of member governments, was a crucial player in the integration process, as it was the main lawmaker in the Union. Further integration depended upon the diplomacy between the members, and the Council was a key forum for such diplomacy, at the head of a hierarchy of committees headed by the Committee of Permanent Representatives, and since December 1974 overseen by a committee of Heads of States and Government, the European Council. These arrangements are discussed at various points in this book, and the main dynamics of the diplomacy between states is a central theme which need not be anticipated here.

A question of central importance in this context, however, is what did the Council of Ministers and its linked institutions contribute, as institutions and as sets of procedures, to integration? The issues raised, which were very important in the discussion about the Commission and the Court, are rather more limited. They concern primarily the voting arrangements of the Council, especially the implications of majority voting after its use had been increased by the Single European Act and the Maastricht Treaty. This issue is discussed at length in Chapters 2, and 4.

The European Parliament was relatively unimportant as a source of independent pressure towards integration. This is not to deny that it played an important part in the governance of the Union, and needed to be further developed in this role to remedy the problem of the democratic deficit—the perception that too many decisions were being taken in the Brussels institutions which were too distant from public accountability. But it only acquired a limited capability to initiate legislation in the Maastricht Treaty in that it was given the right to ask the Commission to make proposals on a particular matter. It first acquired more specific powers with regard to legislation in the Single European Act in 1985, and these were further enhanced in the Maastricht Treaty. But these powers were essentially negative. They represented the power to stop something from happening in a set of defined areas, which could be overruled by the Council in the case of the powers granted by the Single European Act, but not with regard to those given under Maastricht. It might be said, therefore, that the European Parliament proposed a large number of things but had only been able to initiate, in the sense of changing legislation, since the Single European Act. After that date it had more influence, which, however, was still modest when evaluated as a power to add as opposed to prevent. It was also conditional upon the commitment of the governments to the single market programme: they were prepared to accept compromise with the Parliament's wishes in order to get something done. The powers of the European Parliament are also evaluated further in later chapters.

In the 1980s and 1990s the one large-scale proposal from the European Parliament which had major consequences was the European Union Treaty, which was designed by a group in the Parliament headed by one of the grand old men of European integration, Altiero Spinelli, and approved in February 1984. But this was an exceptional input. It had consequences because it was taken up by the French, in part because President Mitterand liked the proposals for stronger European institutions, and in part because his support was part of a strategy for putting pressure on the British to behave better in the Community. This is discussed in more detail in the next section.

The Single European Act and beyond to Maastricht

In the mid-1980s, the pace of integration between the member states of the European Communities once more accelerated. This followed a period of consolidation in the early 1980s.[22] In this section, the reasons for this development are examined.

The main events included: the settlement in 1984 of the British complaint about what were judged to be excessive budgetary contributions, a problem which had led to quarrels between Mrs Thatcher and, in particular, President Mitterrand;[23] the initiation of a campaign to strengthen the European institutions, especially the European Parliament, which led it to adopt a Draft Treaty on European Union on 14 February 1984;[24] the agreement of the Single European Act at Luxembourg in December 1985, which included a plan to create a *Europe without Frontiers* by 1992;[25] and adopting budgetary measures on 11–12 February 1988 to increase the scale of the Community's resources, restrain spending on the Common Agricultural Policy, double the size of the Funds, and exercise financial discipline.[26]

There came a point in the mid-1980s at which President Mitterrand realized that expressions of support for a higher level of

[22] William Wallace, Helen Wallace, and Carole Webb (eds.), *Policy-Making in the European Community* 2nd edn. (London: Wiley, 1983).

[23] Geoffrey Denton, 'Restructuring the EC Budget: Implications of the Fontainebleau Agreement', *Journal of Common Market Studies*, 23/2 (Dec. 1984) 117–40. Stephen George, *The British Government and the European Community since 1984*, University Association for Contemporary European Studies, Occasional Papers 4, (London: Kings College, 1987), esp. 2–18.

[24] Otto Schmuck, 'The European Parliament's Draft Treaty establishing the European Union (1979–84)', in Roy Pryce (ed.), *The Dynamics of European Union* (London and New York: Croom Helm, 1987), 188–216. Commission of the European Communities, 'Draft Treaty establishing the European Union', *Bulletin of the European Communities*, 17/2 (1984), 7–28.

[25] Juliet Lodge, 'The Single European Act: Towards a new Euro-Dynamism?' *Journal of Common Market Studies*, 24/3 (Mar. 1986), 203–23. European Parliament, *A New phase in European Union* (Luxembourg: General Secretariat, 1985).

[26] European Council, *Texts of Agreement reached at European Council*, 11–12 Feb. 1988, including documents SN517/88 and SN461/88, p. 7.

integration, such as had been proposed by the European Union Treaty, were a very good strategy for putting pressure upon the British to accept a compromise in the settlement of their budgetary grievance. Helmut Kohl's government in West Germany, partly in response to the French, and partly on its own initiative, acted in ways which gave credence to this strategy. Its effectiveness rested upon the vulnerability of the British government, particularly a Conservative one, to the apparent threat to move a core of original members to a higher level of integration, if necessary to the exclusion of the British. A Conservative government had ignored comparable threats to its cost in the late 1950s, when the EEC had been formed without Britain.[27]

The British wanted no truck with any of the several variations of future development in the Communities which were then being discussed—except one.[28] They disliked the idea of a two-tier Europe very much indeed. One reason for this position was that it would reduce their ability to exercise influence in the EPC framework which they very strongly supported. At that time, however, they also disliked the idea of Europe à la carte or the idea of graduated integration as general principles of future European organization: the existing example of this, the EMS arrangement, and the proposal to reactivate West European Union, were to be regarded as exceptions to the rule. That everyone should go forward at the same gentle pace, one ideally suited to British capacities and inclinations, was ideal.

One problem for the British was that by early 1985 the various items on the agenda of integration, the completion of the Common Market, the strengthening of the machinery for political cooperation, and the rather ambitious proposals for institutional reform, had been refined and increasingly firmly linked together in a single package. The British had tried to prevent this. In the discussions of the Ad Hoc Committee for Institutional Affairs, which became known as the Dooge Committee, after its Irish chairman, the pattern was set. It established a 'convergence of priorities' in the particular sense that the need for a 'homogeneous internal economic area', the 'promo-

---

[27] Miriam Camps, *Britain and the European Community* (Princeton: Princeton University Press, 1964).

[28] Helen Wallace, *Europe: The Challenge of Diversity* (London: Routledge and Kegan Paul for the Royal Institute of International Affairs, 1985), 29–49; Bernd Langeheine and Ulrich Weinstock, 'Graduated Integration: A modest Path towards Progress', *Journal of Common Market Studies*, 23/3 (Mar. 1985).

tion of common values of civilisation', and the 'search for an external identity' was spelled out, and made conditional upon the
achievement of 'efficient and democratic institutions', meaning 'a
strengthened Commission', the extension of the powers of the
European Parliament and the reform of the Court of Justice.[29] A
method for obtaining these goals was recommended in the Report:
it was held that a 'conference of the representatives of the governments of the member states should be convened in the near future
to negotiate a draft European Union Treaty based on the *acquis communautaire*, the present document, and the Stuttgart Solemn
Declaration on European Union, and guided by the spirit and
method of the draft treaty voted by the European Parliament'.
President Mitterrand indicated his approval for this general line by
appointing a known Euro-enthusiast, Maurice Faure, as the French
member of the committee.[30] In other words, it proposed an explicit
and detailed programme for action leading to a new treaty.

The best that the British representative, Mr Rifkind, could do in
the face of this enthusiasm was to enter a number of reservations
which were noted in footnotes. Together with his Greek and Danish
colleagues he held that the proposals should be the 'subject of consultations between the governments before the June European
Council', and opposed the idea of the conference of government representatives. The latter probably looked to the British suspiciously
like the constituent assembly of a federal union.[31] Elsewhere in the
Report, Rifkind alone entered reservations on proposals to
strengthen the European Parliament—at most it should 'make more
use of its right to put forward proposals for community action', and
there should be 'improvement and extension of the conciliation procedure';[32] he opposed the proposal that the incoming President of
the Commission should nominate his own team of Commissioners
for the approval of the governments.[33] Governments should continue as at present to nominate and approve unanimously what Mrs
Thatcher now frequently referred to as 'our Commissioner(s)'. And
together with the Greek and Danish representatives he insisted that
the January 1966 Luxembourg Accord should continue to operate.[34]
No reservations on the policy objectives were entered.

This pattern of doubts on the proposals for institutional reform,
and support for the policies, remained the British position up until

[29] Ad Hoc Committee for Institutional Affairs, *Report to the European Council*
(Brussels, 29–30 March 1985), SN/1187/85.
[30] Ibid. 33.　　[31] Ibid.　　[32] Ibid. 30.　　[33] Ibid. 28.　　[34] Ibid. 26.

the meeting of the European Council at Milan in June 1985. It had, however, by then been somewhat refined in that the need for a state to justify in detail its wish to invoke the Luxembourg Accord was asserted by the Thatcher government, and the appeal was addressed to the others that majority voting should be used more frequently in the Council of Ministers' decision-making.[35] As William Wallace pointed out, the British reluctance to accept that institutional arrangements mattered was a problem: British exhortations to better behaviour in the use of the veto had little appeal.[36]

By the time of the June Summit, the attachment to the package of an explicit time constraint, namely, the achievement of a Europe without frontiers by a specified date, 1992, had further increased the difficulties for the British of steering a way between either accepting the package as a whole or risking the appearance of stronger pressures towards a two-tier Europe. The first mention of the 1992 deadline found by the present writer was in the President of the Commission's statement to the European Parliament, 14 January 1985, in which, speaking of the next meeting of the European Council, he said: 'now that some Heads of State and Government have decided to set an example . . . it may not be over-optimistic to announce a decision to eliminate all frontiers within Europe by 1992 and to implement it.'[37] This ambition was approved by the European Council at its meeting at Brussels on 29–30 March 1985. There would be less scope for the British to escape from the horns of their dilemma by procrastination.

On 1 July 1985 it was reported in Britain that the Milan Summit of 28–29 June had been 'extremely bad-tempered' and that Mrs Thatcher's 'anger and frustration' even 'undisguised fury' had shown through.[38] Unfortunately, however, from the British point of view, when viewed in the longer perspective, the dice can be seen to have been loaded against a favourable outcome. The French strategy, the refinement of the proposals for Europe without frontiers in the White Paper on Completing the Internal Market of May 1985, which was presented to the heads of government at Milan,[39] and the

---

[35] *The Times*, 27 June 1985.   [36] William Wallace, *The Times*, 2 July 1985.

[37] Commission of the European Communities, *Bulletin of the European Communities*, Supplement 1/85, 'The Thrust of Commission Policy' (Strasburg, 14 and 15 Jan. 1985), 6.

[38] *The Times*, 1 July 1985.

[39] Commission of the European Communities, *Completing the Internal Market: White Paper from the Commission to the European Council* (Luxembourg: Office of Official Publications, June 1985).

pressure of deadlines, meant that it was odds on that the British would now have to accept the intergovernmental conference. On its agenda would be the amendment of the Communities' decision-making procedures.

Only the Greeks and the Danes joined with the British in voting against the Mitterrand proposal for a conference. Again, Helmut Kohl attracted Mrs Thatcher's particular wrath by supporting the French. Mitterrand said that the outcome had 'sorted out those in favour of a strong united Europe from those who were hanging back'. *The Times* said disingenuously that his comments had 'rekindled speculation about a two-tier Europe'.[40] At a meeting of the Council of Foreign Ministers, 22–23 July 1985, Britain went along with the others in agreeing to the convening of an intergovernmental conference by the Luxembourg Presidency, in office in the second half of 1985, which was explicitly asked to consider the 'revision of the Rome Treaty' and the drafting of a treaty on political cooperation and European security.[41]

The British had at least gained the important concession that there would not be a new treaty. It was reported, however, that early on in the discussions of the intergovernmental committee, some governments, especially the Italians, the Belgians, and the Dutch, sought to put pressure upon the British by speaking explicitly of the possibility that some of the Ten could go ahead of the others.[42] It was, therefore, perhaps not surprising that in early October the British Foreign Secretary, Sir Geoffrey Howe, gave the 'first indications that Britain would accept treaty amendments on a pragmatic basis'.[43]

The underlying dynamics of the negotiations leading up to the conclusion of the Single European Act are now clearly visible. On the one hand were a group of states, which included in particular the French, the Italians, the Dutch, Belgians, Luxembourgers and the West Germans, which inclined to support a more ambitious set of changes for the European institutions, though probably Butler was correct when he pointed out that no member actually wanted to give the European Parliament the sole right both to initiate and

[40] Ibid.
[41] Commission of the European Communities, *The Inter-governmental Conference: Background and Issues* (London, 1985), 2.
[42] Richard Corbett, 'The Intergovernmental Conference and the Single European Act', in Pryce, Roy (ed.), *The Dynamics of European Union*, 242.
[43] Ibid.

approve legislation.[44] The French government by this time did not need to lead this faction at all stages, and indeed it was the Italians who in practice in 1985–6 usually carried the Euro-banner. The West Germans sometimes dragged their feet but generally and eventually inclined to this group much to the irritation of the British. At a meeting in London, 27 November 1985, Kohl and Thatcher agreed that economic and monetary union should not be included as a goal in the Single European Act. Later, however, Kohl changed his mind when the French and Italians liberalized their exchange control provisions and these goals were eventually included in the Agreement's Preamble.[45]

The British headed a group of doubters which included the Greeks and the Danes. The outcome of the negotiations between this group and the others could not, however, be completely explained by reference to the specific interests and exchanges on particular policies. The longer term dynamics which have been outlined meant that the British group was necessarily and invariably on the defensive in the negotiations, particularly with regard to the institutional questions. They were placed in the position of having to make specific concessions in order to avoid incurring non-specific and longer term costs and of having to fight a rearguard battle to prevent fundamental alterations in the structure of the Communities of which they did not approve. Thanks to the Mitterrand strategy, success in this depended paradoxically upon making concessions on precisely those questions, whilst at the same time struggling to make them as small as possible. The character of the Single European Act was largely explicable in terms of the outcome of this struggle and this feature was captured in Mrs Thatcher's remark to the House of Commons on 5 December 1985, on her return from Luxembourg: 'Part of our task the whole time has been to diminish their expectations and draw them down from the clouds to practical matters' (*The Times*, 6 December 1985).

The Character of the Single European Act

There is a sense in which the Single European Act of December 1985 was a considerable achievement for the British negotiators. A central

---

[44] Sir Michael Butler, *Europe: More than a Continent* (London: William Heinemann, 1986), 156.

[45] Corbett, 'The Intergovernmental Conference', 247.

feature of that achievement was that a way was found to make what appeared to be major concessions to those who wanted stronger European institutions, whilst at the same time introducing such qualifications as to significantly mitigate their implications. The British negotiators could comfort themselves, for the time being at least, with the judgement that what they had wanted all along had been achieved: a system which depended for its success upon the convergent interests, and political goodwill of governments rather than upon some constitutional relocation of the metaphysical bases of power.

Much depended upon the nature of the new powers of the European Parliament and upon the implications of the extension of majority voting in the Council of Ministers, and the policy areas to which these changes were to apply. The proposal to introduce co-decision-making for the European Parliament in its relations with the Council—in effect to give each of the partners a veto—was successfully resisted. Instead, a *cooperative procedure* was introduced which allowed a second reading to the European Parliament, as a result of which it could now either reject a Council proposal or amend it. If it did the former, the Council could only overcome its rejection by a unanimous vote; if the latter, the Commission was required either to incorporate Parliament's amendment into a new proposal for the Council, or, if it disagreed, send Parliament's amendment to the Council together with its own proposal. In this case, the Council could only accept the Parliament's amendment on the basis of unanimity.[46]

Richard Corbett concluded that the amendment procedure was 'in essence a second consultation of the European Parliament in more difficult conditions (needing an absolute majority to propose amendments and unable to use delaying tactics) than current practice in its single reading'.[47] On the other hand, the ability to 'reject' legislation from the Council could strengthen the European Parliament's hand in that the requirement of unanimity in the Council to overcome the rejection would strengthen the position of governments which sympathized with the Parliament's views. But if the Council had not acted within three months, which could be extended by one month by 'common accord between the Council

---

[46] Commission of the European Communities, *Bulletin of the European Communities*, Supplement 2/86, Single European Act (Luxembourg: Office for Official Publications, 1986), Title II, Sect. 1, esp. articles 6 and 7.

[47] Corbett, 'The Intergovernmental Conference', 262.

and the European Parliament' (Article 7, Single European Act, paragraphs F and G), the proposal could be 'deemed not to have been adopted'. This in effect severely curtailed the power of the European Parliament. In other words, in the ten areas to which this new procedure was to apply, the member governments could as a last resort avoid taking action which they did not like by vetoing attempts in the Council to overcome Parliament's wishes.

The most important area to which the cooperative procedure applied was the legislation covered in the new Article 100a, under which the Council was to take decisions by majority vote, on its first reading, to implement the establishment and functioning of the internal market—Europe without frontiers. If the members had the will to work for the latter, it was to be assumed that as a matter of good sense, and to avoid unnecessary delays, they would not use what amounted to a veto by inaction. But the arrangement, nevertheless, meant that states *in extremis* could stop the European Parliament from getting what it wanted.

In view of the British government's appeals to the others to rely more upon majority voting in the Council of Ministers, it might seem odd that the former British Prime Minister should have made it clear on her return from Luxembourg that 'the Luxembourg compromise [allowing a national veto] was unaffected'. This point is discussed more fully in the next chapter. She also said, however, that there had been 'no transfer of powers from [the British] Parliament to the Assembly'. She even avoided the use of the term 'European Parliament', which had been formally accepted in the Single European Act. And only a little earlier she had asserted that she did not believe 'in the concept of a United States of Europe' (*The Times*, 6 December 1985).

Other aspects of the Single European Act illustrate the theme of Britain's wish to minimize concessions to the European centre, whilst avoiding accentuating centripetal tendencies in other members, and obtaining desired specific ends. Many of these relate to a broad disagreement between those who were inclined to include in the Act explicitly what was thought necessary to complete the internal market, and those who wished to move forward in a more pragmatic fashion by only accepting the general principle now, and making further adjustments later in the light of experience. Amongst the latter group, naturally, the British occupied pole position, whilst the former included the Commission, Italy, France, and the Benelux countries, with the support usually of the West

Germans. The point has already been made that the British eventually accepted reluctantly the reiteration of the goal of the 'progressive realisation of economic and monetary union' (Preamble, Single European Act). But the list of exclusions from the range of specific goals linked with the completion of the internal market and the obtaining of monetary union, also reflected British interests. In Article 6, 'policy on credit and savings, medicines and drugs' was carefully excluded from the cooperative procedure. Similarly, in Article 18, according to paragraph 2 of the agreed new Article 100a of the Rome Treaty on the approximation by the Community of Laws, regulations, and administrative actions in member states to achieve 'the establishment and functioning of the Common Market'—a process which was also to involve the cooperative procedure—'fiscal provisions, and those relating to the free movement of persons' and the 'rights and interests of employed persons', were to be excluded.

From the British point of view the new arrangements on cooperation in economic and monetary policy had advantages. A new section on these matters was introduced into the Rome Treaty, which meant that the Commission now had responsibilities in the operation of the European Monetary System. This could be regarded as a further consolidation of the arrangements of the Community, as EMS mechanisms had previously not been a part of these formally. On the other hand, paragraph 2 of the new Article 102a explicitly required that 'in so far as further development in the field of economic and monetary policy necessitates institutional changes the provisions of Article 236 shall be applicable.' Proposals for new institutional arrangements for the EMS would, therefore, from then on be subject to the amendment procedures of the Rome Treaty, and could therefore be vetoed by dissenting states, even those, such as the British, which had not yet joined the EMS. The British had now acquired the means of preventing the others from creating a two-tier Europe with regards to money, a significant development in view of Mrs Thatcher's opposition to the British membership in the EMS, and her hostility to a Franco-German initiative in 1988 in favour of moving towards a kind of European central bank[48] (the latter proposal was indeed criticized by the Bundesbank in West Germany). At the Maastricht conference the British decided to opt out rather than veto the new monetary arrangements.

[48] John Palmer, 'Hard Pounding for the EMS', the *Guardian*, 18 May 1988.

On the environment they agreed that the 'polluter should pay' and that the Community was now to have a role in protecting the 'quality of the environment', 'the protection of human health', and 'the prudent and rational utilisation of natural resources' (Article 25 SEA; New Treaty of Rome Article 130r). But, having made that gesture, the reservation was entered (new Article 130s) that any Community action should be decided on the basis of unanimity in the Council of Ministers. Such behaviour may be judged as being no more than commercial caution; but it also helped British obstructionism on environmental questions generally, a particular instance of this being British obstruction to developing Community policies on control of the emissions which produced acid rain and other pollutants, widely accepted as gravely damaging forests in Germany and in Scandinavia.

Britain had also agreed to a Community effort to strengthen the 'scientific and technological basis of European industry', but insisted that the Multi-Annual Framework Programme in which it was to be embodied, should be subject to unanimity in the Council. In this they were supported, in particular, by the West Germans. Only a few months later the British revealed their underlying attitude to this great European enterprise: they refused to countenance anything other than a minimum budget, and at the same time limited their participation in the European space programme. The general British posture seemed to be to encourage technological innovation and the use of venture capital but not at the European level and not out of the public purse. Indeed, they seemed prepared to enter into commitments at the European level which they had no intention of honouring in order to ensure that they could be more easily frustrated. One illustration of this was the British behaviour with regard to the financing of the Horizon 2,000 project of the European Space Agency, which was described by Lord Shackleton a respected Labour member of the House of Lords as constituting 'appalling bad manners and arrogance' (the *Independent*, 5 October 1988, p. 2) The British had procrastinated about the level of finance for the Agency, and was currently refusing to endorse a 5 per cent increase in the budget to support Horizon 2,000, which represented a core science programme. The British were alone in opposing the increase but held a veto as the decision, according to the Single European Act, was subject to unanimity in the Council of Ministers.

There is, therefore, no doubt that in the circumstances of 1984 and 1985 the Single European Act can be judged as a considerable British achievement. In its details it reflected British interests in a remarkably nuanced and comprehensive way. On the other hand, the British, and, of course, the varying coalitions of states with which they were involved, had been placed in a situation in which they had indeed been required to make concessions. They had not wanted the Dooge Committee, the Intergovernmental Committee, formal amendment of the Rome Treaty, changes in the role of the European Parliament or Commission, or, indeed, any truck with the process which led up to the Luxembourg meeting. They wanted the completion of the internal market but even in this there was an element of ambiguity. The few areas where there was unambiguous enthusiasm were the liberalization of the capital market, and of the related arrangements for banking and insurance, and the EPC. In these areas, however, the method preferred by the British, in their usual way, was one of low-key negotiations between governments leading to specific commitments with no immediate implications for institutional change.

Despite its modest immediate effects, the Single European Act was a symbol of the constraints which had been placed in the mid-1980s upon those governments which preferred a minimalist approach to Europe. But would the concessions, despite the conscious intentions of these states, further strengthen those constraints? This question is considered in the detailed examination of the Maastricht Treaty in the next chapter.

Hugo Young wrote that 'Mrs Thatcher's concessions on the European Community budget were concessions to the idea of Europe. They were made in order to sustain the very notion of the Community' (the *Guardian*, 16 February 1988). There was, however, considerable doubt about whether she and her senior advisers intended this to happen. But the longer term tendencies in the development of the regional system, both before the Brussels 1988 meeting and when they are projected into the future, were such that such concessions might be seen to have become progressively more difficult to avoid. Despite British intentions, the British concessions on the visible agenda can be seen as Young implies as sustaining 'the very notion of the Community'. In the longer term, the political relationship of Britain with Europe may be seen to have been progressively consolidated. The political cooperation procedures were slowly acquiring new substance, and the British Foreign Office was increasingly committed to these. There had occurred a sea change in British thinking about where it stood in the world: that it was a European state was increasingly hard to dispute.

Within her Cabinet there was evidence of Mrs Thatcher's increasing isolation with regard to the level of her doubts about Europe. The Foreign Secretary and the Chancellor of the Exchequer both openly expressed their disagreement with her about the need to join the European Monetary System. The Home Secretary, though prepared to drag his feet on some matters, such as easing restrictions on the movement of people, as at a meeting of the Trevi Group in June 1988, was also inclined to support closer links with Europe. For a while in the late 1980s it looked as if the Conservative Party was resigned to Europe. In the Labour Party, too, change was evident. The new party document explicitly referred to the need to stay in Europe, though one reaction was the election of an anti-marketeer as leader of the Labour Party group in the European Parliament. The Communities' system looked like being consolidated within Britain.

But the Eurosceptic reaction, which was to pull the Conservative party apart in the 1990s, was about to gain momentum. Even the careful balance of concession and achievement won in the Single European Act, and, as will be seen, at Maastricht, could not assuage the fierce hostility to Europe of a small group of Conservative right-wingers. Mrs Thatcher made a speech about the future of Europe at the College of Europe in Bruges on 20 September 1988, which attracted considerable attention. It was sharply criticized as being 'unrelentingly negative' by those in the Commission, and states such as Italy and Holland, who favoured a more supranational Europe, and enthusiastically welcomed by opponents of a stronger Europe (*The Times*, 21 September 1988). It was, however, also an illustration of the emerging balance between the autonomy of the states and the integration of the European Community, remarkable in the views of someone who was the most forthright and indeed nationalistic of European leaders.

The speech contained clear indications of the perception that the extension of the scope of integration was necessary in order to promote the well-being of the various separate nation states: the latter had a symbiotic relationship with the former. Therefore 'willing and active co-operation between independent sovereign states is the best way to build a successful European Community', and 'Europe will be stronger precisely because it has France as France, Spain as Spain, Britain as Britain, each with its own customs, traditions and identity. It would be folly to fit them into some sort of Identikit European personality.' The states were to be served by the achievement at the

European level of a wide range of policies which 'encourage enter-prise'—'if Europe is to flourish and create the jobs of the future, enterprise is the key.' The *acquis communautaire* and the various ini-tiatives in the European Community of the mid-1980s were, there-fore, necessary and important, but not in Mrs Thatcher's view because of their contribution to strengthening regional arrange-ments, but because of their reinforcement of the distinctive life of the separate states.

Accordingly the European Community was definitely not to be a framework within which new regional administrative and govern-mental arrangements were to be nurtured. Indeed Mrs Thatcher's image of Europe seemed to be of a kind of macro enterprise zone, free of regulations which could increase the cost of labour and impede the movement of capital, and equally of the kind of central-ized supervision which could be the product of 'arcane institutional debates'. In this fashion Mrs Thatcher justified her opposition to a European Central Bank (this was not 'the key issue'—this was rather to 'implement the Community's commitment to free movement of capital'). Similarly those who wished to see stronger institutions in Brussels were derided: 'it is ironic that just when those countries such as the Soviet Union, which have tried to run everything from the centre, are learning that success depends on dispersing power and decisions away from the centre, some in the Community seem to want to move in the opposite direction.' 'We have not successfully rolled back the frontiers of the state in Britain only to see them reim-posed at a European level with a European superstate exercising a new dominance from Brussels.'

Yet even Mrs Thatcher's view at that time implied that regional arrangements had to be strengthened and the balance between inte-gration and autonomy restruck. If the goal of a Europe without fron-tiers was to be achieved a major extension of the scope of integration would necessarily follow. Business organizations in the various mem-ber states were to be permitted and encouraged to operate in the Common Market as a whole as if it were their own domestic market: hence the major effort to remove the range of restrictions and barriers which had previously discouraged this. To cope with the new compe-tition and use the new opportunities companies would need to 'Europeanize' themselves. In short what was being contemplated even by the most ardent intergovernmentalists was something that went far beyond the traditional practice of international cooperation between states: it amounted to the creation of a single economic space.

What were the implications of these developments for the level of integration, especially for the powers of the central institutions? Mrs Thatcher denied that there were any such implications. The President of the Commission, Jacques Delors was of a different opinion. He said that over the next few years the European Community would be responsible for some 80 per cent of all legislation in the Twelve, during which time an embryo European government might emerge (the *Guardian*, 21 September 1988). In the next section and in Chapter 2 the changing distribution of powers between the states and the Community in the 1990s will be considered.

The Maastricht Treaty and its Context

In the next chapter the Maastricht Treaty is considered in detail. In this chapter it is discussed as part of the history of the European Union, and is compared with the previous periods.

The reasons for the convening of the intergovernmental conference at Maastricht on 9, 10, and 11 December 1991 were strongly reminiscent of those which explained the meeting at Luxembourg which agreed the Single European Act. Indeed the meetings which preceded Maastricht echoed those which had preceded the earlier agreement. There was a meeting in June 1989 in Madrid at which a new intergovernmental conference, to begin in 1990, was proposed by the Spanish hosts. This was resisted by the British. The Report of that summit called for the setting up of an intergovernmental committee to prepare for the conference and for the Finance Ministers to prepare the way for EMU. This was the summit which received the Delors Report on Monetary Union, which had been requested at the EC meeting in Hanover on 27–28 June 1988. The Madrid meeting was the equivalent of the Milan conference in 1985: on both occasions the British were faced with a majority in favour of an intergovernmental conference in the face of their opposition, and both conferences proposed major new initiatives. In 1985 it was the proposal for a single market; at Madrid it was the proposal for monetary union. The Social Charter was also discussed, but lightly, and the British again expressed their dissent.

Echoing the speech of May 1984 to the European Parliament, President Mitterand again addressed the European Parliament on 25

October 1989.[49] As on the earlier occasion he called for a new treaty, a constitutional conference—to be held no later than the autumn of 1990—and strongly supported the EMU proposal 'as the lynchpin of European political integration', the centre of 'a real Union—that is European Political Union'. This was reminiscent of the hopes attached to the original EMU proposal in the early 1970s: European Union by 1980.

It was at the Strasburg conference of 8–9 December 1989 that the decision was taken to call an intergovernmental conference to open if possible in December 1990. On this occasion the British were out-voted by eleven votes to one. It was striking, however, that at the same conference, which took place shortly after the fall of the Berlin wall, the idea of German unification was also strongly supported. It was reported that 'Thatcher was ignored and subdued'. Neverthe-less she said 'there is no other European forum where we would rather be'. Mitterand gallantly replied: 'we are pleased to have you among us'.[50] Still the guest rather than the family member! The con-ference also supported the adoption of the Social Charter and the extension of further powers to the European Parliament. Thus once again the process was pushed forward by the dynamics of the rela-tionship between the core and the peripheral states. Mitterand took the lead in generating pressure against the British, Danes, and Greeks, who nevertheless could not avoid being dragged along by the succession of conferences. Even though outvoted they were not prepared to accept that the others could go on to form a stronger European core. The threat of signing a new treaty was also repeated by the more ambitious states.

There were of course other explanations of Maastricht. There was a momentum towards institutional reform that had been generated in the Single European Act. Individuals like Commission President Delors were pushing to solve the democratic deficit by increasing the powers of the European Parliament. At that point he was expressing strongly pro-federalist sympathies. The unification of Germany also pushed the process forwards. The old French security agenda was still alive: unification of Germany made it even more important to have a stronger Europe, and it was no accident that at Strasburg both stronger integration and German unification were welcomed. The Germans under Helmut Kohl sympathized with this

---

[49] The *Guardian*, 26 Oct. 1989.   [50] The *Observer*, 10 Dec. 1989.

position, but added a further dimension: if there was to be monetary union, political union was also necessary.

This was an extension into the political realm of the German 'economist' argument of the 1970s, that monetary integration demanded the harmonization of economic policies. Monetary union was now also seen by the Germans as requiring that states should not pursue divergent political interests, and foreign policies, which could be as damaging as economic divergences to currency harmonization. And, of course, the process of economic integration generated by the Single European Act also suggested a need for further steps. The single market could be extended and protected by further measures, in particular the achieving of monetary integration. The Delors Report, and the Cechini Report, amongst others, argued that the costs of variable currencies were excessive and unnecessary in a European Union.

In its precise terms the Maastricht Treaty once again was a mixture of forward movement and retreat. Forward movement was represented by the consolidation of the Union, which was to be served by a single institutional framework. There was indeed to be a European Union, and not a Federation, as had been proposed in an earlier Dutch plan. The image was of a temple with three pillars, the roof being the common institutional framework, and the three pillars being the economic community, the foreign and defence arrangements, now incorporated in a Common Foreign and Security Policy (CFSP), and a citizen's Europe, which involved the extension of the rights of European nationals to vote in each other's elections, more police cooperation, more common consular representation, and a move towards a common visa policy, to be agreed by 1996. There was also the expansion of the scope of the Union to include aspects of Education and Health policies, as well as cultural questions, economic convergence, and the setting up of a cohesion fund to pay for the building of new intra-European transport networks. New powers were proposed for the Union's institutions, in particular the introduction of a new Article 189b under which the European Parliament would be given the right of veto. The cooperative procedure of the Single European Act was now incorporated as Article 189c.

There were new institutions and new powers for existing ones. States could now be fined for not fulfilling an obligation under the Treaty, on the judgement of the European Court of Justice (ECJ). The Commission was required to keep national parliaments informed of their proposals, so that they could express an opinion. And a new Committee of the Regions, and a European Ombudsman, were created. A new Article 137a allowed the European Parliament a modified power of initiative: it 'may request the Commission to submit a proposal' on an issue about which it was concerned.

But the most important new item on the agenda was probably monetary union, which was to be achieved in three stages, subject to states' meeting a set of five convergence criteria. The United Kingdom obtained an opt-out from the third phase of this process; even if it met the criteria, it was still up to the British Parliament to opt in. In some ways the convergence criteria were the functional equivalent from the German perspective of the requirement to coordinate economic policies as a condition of monetary union, on which they had insisted in the early 1970s. States accepted an obligation to work for economic convergence. 'Economic policies are a matter of common concern.' Accordingly the Council was now given the power to address recommendations if states adopted disruptive behaviour. Adjustments to promote convergence could be required. The UK was explicitly excluded from 104/9 under which fines could be imposed on states which misbehaved, despite Council recommendations, for instance by allowing excessive government deficits. But the UK did accept an *obligation* to avoid such excessive deficits.

These were the major steps forward. But what were the steps back? Unfortunately for the ratification process most attention was focused on the former, indeed, deliberately so by Eurosceptics. The most important retreat was, of course, the adoption of the principle of subsidiarity, and more will be said about this in the next chapter. But there were a number of others which attracted very little attention. For instance, wherever scope was extended there were explicit limitations on the Community's competence. With regard to the environment, for instance, although 189c could be used to take decisions to implement environmental policy, unanimity was required in the Council of Ministers on any measures which involved provisions of a fiscal nature, on measures affecting town and country planning, and on measures significantly affecting choice between different energy sources. On education the Community could now be concerned with cooperation on such matters, but any harmonization of laws and regulations in the context of member states was excluded. This was typical of the approach on a wide range of matters: a limited extension of the role of the Community, but a firm indication of the limits of that role. As with subsidiarity the lines of defence of the sovereignty of the state were now being drawn more firmly than before.

Even the extension of the powers of the European Parliament was not unambiguous. The broad principle appeared to be that the greater power was given to the Parliament on the less important issues. But in those areas where it was introduced, there was a cynical as well as a more optimistic interpretation. One plausible argument was that 189b allowed states which had been outvoted in the Council of Ministers a second bite at the cherry. They could mount a second defence by organizing, through party links in the European Parliament, a majority in favour of a veto. Much depended on the strength of the parties in the European Parliament. When it was also recalled that the Committee of the Regions could be made up of government appointees, the likely calculations of anti-federalists about the implications of 189b were not hard to guess: they viewed it as making little difference.

Conclusions

What conclusions may be drawn from this account of the evolution of the European Union? The first is that the character of the relations between states and Community changed between the early period and the later one. In the early period the expectation was a very basic one, that the Community and the states were in opposition, and that integration was about the former replacing the latter. From 1974, however, a different model could be detected, which was that state and Community could have a positive relationship with each other. There was a tendency for the relationship to return to balance at higher levels of interdependence.

This tendency was reflected in the realization on the part of the supporting politicians that more integration did not necessarily lead to the abandonment of what they understood by sovereignty. It was also reflected in the tendency for concessions to be made to supranational arrangements when it was felt that the sovereignty of states had been assured. This same dynamic was visible in the tendency for further measures of integration to be linked with ways of reasserting the frontiers between state and community. This was clear as recently as the Maastricht Treaty. The pattern was also reflected in the tendency for integration to move in waves, with moves to a higher level of integration followed by periods of consolidation.

All this was not surprising. States frequently joined the Community in order to rediscover themselves as states, indeed in order to consolidate their national arrangements. There was a sufficient identity with the common values to allow this to be recognized as a possibility. But there was never a relaxation of concern with national identity, a point which is discussed in Chapter 4. The history of the Community reflected the idea of Europe as a unity in diversity. But the European Community level also acquired its own integrity and a degree of self-containment. It was not just a matter of providing a mechanism to help the state.

Unifying elements in the Community were as real as those making for diversity, and they became attached to a set of working arrangements which involved a large number of officials and citizens. They came to embody a set of shared values, principles, and norms. The next chapter takes this discussion further, but further conclusions are presented in Chapter 5.

2

THEORIZING ABOUT THE
EUROPEAN UNION IN THE 1990s

O NE of the consequences of the long and often acrimonious
debate that accompanied the ratification of the Maastricht
Treaty was the identification, for the first time in the history of
European integration, of an end to the process. Hitherto the idea
that this was a matter of establishing an 'ever-closer union' of the
peoples of Europe appeared to be just that, both to supporters and
opponents of union: it was difficult to see any end, or how far it
would get towards a tight federal union. But what seemed evident
was that it could move in that direction. Some thought this had to be
stopped; others welcomed it.

In the debate about the Single European Act there had been a similar problem, but those in favour of continuing with the *journey to an
unknown destination* won the argument.[1] There were in the Act several indications of that outcome: there were to be economic and
monetary union, economic and social cohesion, a union of peoples,
and further steps towards a common foreign policy. More important
in some ways, however, was the absence of any explicit challenge to
the traditional view of the process. Despite Mrs Thatcher's efforts,
the subtext of the Act, revealed in the style of its language and
expressions, was that of the Euro-enthusiasts. In the Maastricht
Treaty this was still the case, as was to be expected from the kinds of

Parts of this chapter are updated and modified versions of material from the
author's *International Organization in the Modern World*, (London: Pinter, 1993; and
his 'The European Union in the 1990s', in Ngaire Woods (ed.), *International
Relations since 1945*, (Oxford: Oxford University Press, 1996).

[1] Taken from the Reith Lectures, delivered by Andrew Shonfield in 1971, pub. as
Europe: Journey to an Unknown Destination (Harmondsworth: Penguin Books, 1972).

proposals which were considered in the diplomacy leading up to the decisive meeting of the European Council in December 1991.

But in the Maastricht Treaty a different tune was also to be heard. There was the statement of subsidiarity. And there was also the successful opposition of the British, and other countries, like Denmark, to the inclusion of the Federalist ambition in the Treaty. It might be argued that it is hard to see much practical difference between that and the idea of a European Union, as it was accepted, but the differences were real. The latter implied an association of sovereign states; the former suggested a move to European sovereignty.

The fierce determination to resist the former, in so many member states as ratification proceeded, was such that the President of the Commission, Jacques Delors, played down for a while the goal of a Federal Europe. The problems of giving the doctrine of subsidiarity any clear legal content were overwhelming, but that was not the point. Subsidiarity was always more important politically than legally. The Germans liked the idea, but it was also a concession to Britain; it allowed John Major a stronger hand in persuading the doubters in the House of Commons to go along with the Treaty. But it was essentially an injunction on behaviour, an assertion that some doctrine other than unification would now prevail, rather than a hard rule.

It was helpful in the more cautious states to let it be supposed that it also meant a repatriating of some functions of the Community, but that was never a practical possibility. In effect—though this was not the intention of the Eurosceptics in Britain—it stripped the integration process of ideological content, and replaced it with a utilitarian concept: that things should only be done at the European level if they were better done there. Anything which was the exclusive competence of the Community would stay with the Community, and if strict legal criteria were applied it was hard to see how this could justify repatriating anything. But it implied a way of working for the future in the Commission and in the Council: that nothing would be transferred to the Community on the basis of the doctrine that doing things at that level was of necessity a good thing.

Subsidiarity and Integration

In 1992 and 1993 an extended discussion of three related concepts concerning subsidiarity took place in the European Community.

These were the central principle of subsidiarity, and the related notions of proportionality and transparency. These could be translated into three kinds of concern, which were, respectively, with the level at which decisions about particular policies were to be made, the powers which were to be assumed by the agency entrusted with carrying out the policy, and the degree to which the policy-making process was to be open to the inspection of the public.

A series of declarations concerning these issues were produced by the Community's leaders in 1992, at meetings of the European Council in Lisbon in June 1992, at a special meeting in Birmingham in mid-October, and at the meeting in Edinburgh in December 1992. In addition there were a number of pronouncements by other authorities, such as Jacques Delors, President of the Commission, as, for instance, in a speech to the European Parliament in June 1992. The Commission also produced two major texts on the subject to which reference will be made later.

The level of the discussion was sharply differentiated between a set of rather theoretical arguments, which did, however, help to clarify the constitutional character of the system and its direction of evolution, a set of claims and counter-claims by politicians and journalists, intended primarily to boost their preferred cause in the domestic electoral context, and a set of heated ideologically based arguments from lobbies about the nation, the state, and Europe.

Typical of the latter was the fierce campaign mounted by the sentimental nationalists of the Bruges group—the Eurosceptics—in Britain, the campaign of the right-wing opponents of the ratification of the Maastricht Treaty in France, exemplified in a number of articles in *Le Figaro* before the referendum in France in September 1992, and the corresponding anti-European groups in Denmark. The arguments of the politicians obviously had to take these views into account, as well as those of the authorities. The views of the politicians and journalists were obviously bound up with the perceptions of the wider electorates, and these may be encaptured in what might be called the mood of the times. This seemed to be ebbing with regard to integration in the mid-1990s, and more will be said of this later. But discussion of subsidiarity was the most obvious symptom of this development, and this is discussed in more detail first.

Concern with subsidiarity was not new: it was discussed earlier in the Draft Treaty on European Union which had been approved in the European Parliament in February 1984.[2] But it moved up the agenda in the period before the agreement of the Maastricht Treaty in December 1991 primarily because of the concerns of the British government about what it saw as an excessive transfer of powers to the Brussels institutions, especially the Commission. The idea also became of importance in Germany; it arose out of the concern of the Länder (the main sub-units of the German federal system) for their powers, which they argued were being lost to the Federal Government in response to membership of the European Community, in breach of the division of powers stated in the German constitution. The British policy reflected an intensifying antipathy especially on the right, towards what seemed to be an increasing trend towards federalism, a position which for a while was reflected in some of the proposals of Jacques Delors. There were reports of Commission moves to significantly extend its own powers as a way of managing the Community if its membership was greatly increased. Delors did, however, quickly realize the unpopularity of such a strategy, and moved to strongly support the idea of subsidiarity.

In narrower political terms it was very important to John Major, the then recently elected British Prime Minister, in his first intergovernmental conference in the Community, that he should be seen to have obtained significant political concessions from his partners. He had to achieve tokens of success at Maastricht, regardless of their merits, in order to outflank the Thatcherites in his party, and subsidiarity was one of them. He could claim, as did his Foreign Secretary, Douglas Hurd, that the inclusion of the concept in the treaty, was a triumph for the British, for a moderate intergovernmentalism in Europe, and a defeat for the Federalists. The others were happy to give him these concessions: it was congenial not to have to deal any longer with Mrs Thatcher, and there seemed to be a general recognition that the time had come to rein in the headlong move to further integration implied by the 1992 process. For instance on 11 June 1992 M. Delors was reported as having supported a 'steady state Community' in a speech to the European Parliament, and, in contrast to his claims four years earlier, set out a 'vision of a decentralized union'.[3]

---

[2] Marc Wilke and Helen Wallace, *Subsidiarity: Approaches to Power-Sharing in the European Community*, RIIA Discussion Paper, 27 (London: Royal Institute of International Affairs, 1990).

[3] The *Guardian*, 11 June 1992.

Accordingly the concept of subsidiarity was formally enshrined in the Maastricht Treaty in December 1991, which legally constituted an amendment of the Treaty of Rome. That was not ratified until October 1993, but a number of declarations and summit communiques in effect introduced the doctrine. There was constant allusion to the relevant parts of the Treaty, the preamble, and Article 3b, and it is instructive to examine the text directly in detail.

From the Preamble

The objectives of the Union shall be achieved as provided in this Treaty and in accordance with the condition and the timetable set out therein while respecting the principle of subsidiarity as defined in Article 3b of the Treaty establishing the European Community.

The Union shall be served by a single institutional framework which shall ensure the consistency and the continuity of the activities carried out in order to attain its objectives while respecting and building upon the 'acquis communautaire'.

From Article 3b

The Community shall act within the limit of the powers conferred upon it by this Treaty and of the objectives assigned to it therein. In areas which do not fall within its exclusive competence, the Community shall take action, in accordance with the principle of subsidiarity, only if, and in so far as, the objectives of the proposed action cannot be sufficiently achieved by the Member States and can, therefore, by reason of the scale or effects of the proposed action, be better achieved by the Community.

Any action by the Community shall not go beyond what is necessary to achieve the objectives of this Treaty.

A preliminary comment might be made at this stage about the form of words used in this text. It contained reference to both a new principle—only transferring to the Community what could be better done at that level—but also an assertion of the continuity and coherent quality of Community mechanisms and commitments in the form of the reference to the *acquis communautaire*. This was the first time that the latter had been mentioned in a Community text, though it had been in common usage by diplomats and specialists.

This was another example of the duality of Community arrangements which is discussed in more detail below. Assertions of Community, and acceptance of schemes for further integration, had often accompanied assertions of national identity and simultaneously agreeing procedures which protected the separate governments. Now the act was repeated but the lines were in reverse order:

an explicit reference to the protection of the separateness of states had been accompanied by a *sotto voce* assertion of the continuity of the integration process and the inviolability of what had been achieved. Revealingly all the existing member states insisted that any new members must accept the *acquis communautaire* in full: even the British and the Danes did this, despite their various opt-outs in Maastricht and at the Edinburgh Summit.

The principle of subsidiarity was enunciated in the two sentences in paragraph 1 of Article 3b, and that of proportionality was enshrined in the separate, single-sentence, paragraph. These were the key references and after the conclusion of the treaty were the subject of considerable discussion by lawyers and political scientists about what they meant and how they were to be applied. Perhaps the most authoritative text written in interpretation of the principles was that prepared by the Commission of the European Community for the Edinburgh Summit in December 1992, and the following discussion relies heavily upon this.[4]

The Meaning of the Principles

With regard to subsidiarity a key question was that of what was to be regarded as falling within the exclusive jurisdiction of the Community. The point should be stressed that it is impossible to allocate responsibility to the Community or the states on the basis of this principle: such an allocation is determined by the Treaty itself. A distinction had to be made between the formal allocation of powers and the manner in which they were to be exercised. With regard to the *exercise* of competencies 'the Community should do only what is best done at that level, and the burden of proof should be on the Community institutions to show that there is a need to legislate and take action at the Community level at the intensity proposed.'

The introduction to the above mentioned Report puts the main points succinctly.

The first sentence [of Article 3b] underlines that the competencies are given by the Treaty and the limits of these competencies must be respected. Within these limits the Community has an obligation to achieve the necessary results: to attain the objectives which the Treaty assigns to it.

[4] Commission of the European Communities, *The Principle of Subsidiarity*, SECK(92) 1990, Final (Brussels, 27 October, 1992).

The second sentence concerns the areas where the Community has not an exclusive competence and deals with the question whether the Community should act in a specific case. This article requires that the Community should only intervene if and so far as the objectives of the proposed actions cannot be realized sufficiently by the member states. This implies that we have to examine if there are other methods available for member states, for example legislation, administrative instructions or codes of conduct, in order to achieve the objectives in a sufficient manner. This is the test of comparative efficiency between Community action and that of member states.

The factors which could be examined in such cases are the effect of the scale of the operation (transfrontier problems, critical mass, etc.), the cost of inaction, the necessity to maintain a reasonable coherence, the possible limits on action at national level (including cases of potential distortion where some member states were able to act and others were not able to so) and the necessity to ensure that competition is not distorted within the common market.

If it were concluded that a proposal passes the test of comparative efficiency, it would still be necessary to respond to the question 'what should be the intensity and the nature of the Communities action?'. This recalls the principle of proportionality which is already an element of the case law of the Community. It is necessary to examine carefully if an intervention by legislative means is necessary or if other means which are sufficiently effective can be used. If it is necessary to legislate the Commission will as far as possible favour framework legislation, minimum norms and mutual recognition and more generally avoid a too detailed legislative prescription.

The third sentence applies not only to the area of shared competencies but also to the area of exclusive competence. It reaffirms that the principle of proportionality, for which certain criteria are set out above, should apply, but does not alter the attribution of competence.

There are large areas, primarily, but not exclusively, related to the four fundamental freedoms—the free movement of goods, persons, services, and capital—where the Community had come to have exclusive competence. In addition the common commercial policy, the rules of competition, the common organization of agricultural markets, the conservation of fisheries resources, and the essential elements of transport policy, had over time been placed on this list.

But later in the Report the possible variations in such intensity, where powers are shared between the states and the Community, were spelled out. There were *legislative measures*, which were necessary to smooth the operation of the internal market and the common policies, where the Community's powers were very strong; there were *joint measures*, where they were also very strong, which were necessary to achieve economic and social cohesion, and in the future, common foreign and security policy; *supportive measures*, as regards certain social and environmental measures, where the Community's powers might be weaker, and *complementary measures*, where there was only modest political resolve to grant powers to the Community on the part of the states.

The Report also outlined ways in which the separate states might be brought into the process of monitoring the process of applying Community rules within their frontiers. More could be done through annual reports on compliance prepared by the states, or through the work of an ombudsman, which was proposed in the Maastricht Treaty, Article 107d, to check that states and individuals were doing what they said they were doing. Where firms or individuals had not complied with the rules regarding transparency in submitting tenders for contracts governments should have the power to suspend the process. But, to help with transparency, the Report stated that Community legislation should be more accessible, both in terms of intelligibility and in terms of physical availability. It should not need to be reinterpreted.

The Application of the Principles

Writing in late 1994 it was difficult to avoid the conclusion that the discussion of these principles had clarified a number of issues but that it had not led to much alteration in the practice of the Community. But it had served to remind those who were involved in the process of making the rules that they needed to bear in mind the new directions. Douglas Hurd stated in February 1992 to the Foreign Affairs Select Committee that the Commission had in practice been sensitized to the need to act on the basis of subsidiarity, though specific rules and injunctions to this effect were hard to detect, either in the work of the Commission or of the Council of Ministers.[5] But what was important was that the discussion about subsidiarity had focused attention upon the need to find instruments among those available to the Community to distribute competencies in a more sensitive way than hitherto between the states and the Community

[5] Douglas Hurd, in *Evidence* on the implications of the Maastricht Treaty, given to the House of Commons Foreign Affairs Select Committee, Feb. 1992, publ. Mar. 1992 by the House of Commons as HC(1991–92 223–(ii)).

wherever possible, and certainly not to pursue a crude strategy, which sentimental nationalists had found in the integration process hitherto, of transferring powers to the centre whenever possible, and seeing that as a good in itself.

The discussion had indeed contributed to a broad alteration in the course of the development of the Community away from centralist Federalism (the implications of position statements from late 1994 are discussed below). In the course of the discussion in 1992 the Community did acknowledge the primacy of the states in the Community, although paradoxically the Federalists did find some comfort in the prospect it allowed of stronger links between the Community and the regions within the state: if things were to be done at the lowest possible level, even state governments might need to hand powers downwards, and this in turn would facilitate closer relations between the Commission and the regions within states. The British government failed to acknowledge the irony that, although they had prompted the idea of subsidiarity, they had also become in the 1980s one of the most highly centralized states in the Community, and one of the most resistant to the transfer of powers back to local authorities, least of all to regions. Subsidiarity could lead back to London but not to the counties or the boroughs

But that the powers of the state had primacy was now explicitly asserted, one of the very few occasions in the history of the Community when this had appeared in a Community text. At the Birmingham summit, it was stated that the subsidiarity principle concerned purely the exercise and not the conferment of powers, which 'is reserved for the authors of the Treaty, namely the national governments'.[6] In the Report mentioned above, however, the authors stated that the 'conferment of powers is a matter for the writers of our constitution, that is to say of the treaty. *A consequence of this is that the powers conferred on the Community, in contrast to those reserved to the members, cannot be assumed . . . national powers are the rule and the Community's the exception*' (my italics). This seemed to be a considerable alteration in the Commission's public stance compared with a few years earlier, and the lack of any rebuttal of the report by any of the member states in the European Council suggested that it represented the general view. It recognized that the powers of the states were superior, that they were the conferring agency, and that they could de-confer: in other words it asserted the continuing sovereignty of the states.

[6] The *Financial Times*, 13 Oct. 1992.

Indeed the general tone of the Edinburgh Report implied a recognition of injunctions on behaviour of a relatively non-specific kind, or it made explicit that this was already the way of working of the Community. The lawyers had agreed that it could not be otherwise, as the principles were hard to translate into formal rules. Subsidiarity was a political not a legal concept. In a number of countries, however, the primary objective was for the anti-Europeans to be satisfied that something had been done and to stop the trend to Federalism: presentation was the important thing.

This was the spirit of the conclusions at the end of three summit meetings in 1992. The June meeting in Lisbon did little more than acknowledge the issue and to agree that something concrete should be done before the next meeting. This turned out to be the special meeting at Birmingham on 15–16 October 1992, which on subsidiarity produced a text of unexceptional blandness. It was affirmed that decisions must be taken as closely as possible to the citizen, and that making this principle work should be a priority for all the Community institutions without affecting the balance between them. The leaders also agreed at Birmingham that the foreign ministers should look at ways of making the work of the institutions of the Community more transparent. A report on these issues, the Sullivan Report, had been prepared, but attracted little attention. In this the Maastricht treaty had already made a start, as, for instance, when it required that the Commission should inform national parliaments of proposals for legislation on the assumption that they would express an opinion.

According to the *Financial Times* (16 December) just before the Edinburgh Summit a European Commission official had said he expected the EC 'would be able to agree a text sufficiently meaningless to satisfy everyone on subsidiarity', so as to cut through the artificially pumped-up debate on how to divide power between the Community and the member states. The conclusions were that there would be no fundamental changes in the Community's method of working, though members of the Community's institutions would have to demonstrate that action at the EC level was in response to real needs in the member states.

This was in accordance with the main thrust of the debate from the start. The general interpretation among the Eurosceptics had been that Article 3b meant a return of powers to the national level, and indeed the politicians in Britain had rather encouraged this view; that it would allow a clawing back of powers. But at Edinburgh there was no 'bonfire of the 71 items of EC law'[7] which it had been reported would be struck down on the grounds of the subsidiarity principle. Only twenty planned measures from the Commission were modestly affected and there was no deletion of any significant legislation on these grounds. One cynical interpretation was that as the French referendum was now over (4 September) and as John Major had achieved a majority in the House of Commons in favour of the principle of ratifying Maastricht, there was now no need to push too hard on subsidiarity, but merely to do enough so as not to seem to have been duplicitous.

The point should be stressed that the precise wording of Article 3b did not categorically lay down a requirement for preserving the powers of the states, and therefore for protecting their sovereignty, which was what the Eurosceptics had wanted. It could indeed imply precisely the opposite: a transfer of more powers to the Community level for reasons of scale or effect. The Eurosceptics' view implied sacrificing efficiency in order to preserve national competence, whereas the Article actually implied the sacrifice of sovereignty in order to achieve greater efficiency.

Yet there were concessions to the Eurosceptics, though little evidence to suggest that they were acknowledged or even understood. In addition to those already mentioned there was also to be an inter-institutional accord to confirm that all power was vested in the states except where otherwise specified. As the question of the specification of these powers was a matter for the states anyway, and this fact had been stressed in Community documents, the net effect was again a reassertion of the underlying principle that the Community rested upon the separate constitutional orders of the sovereign member states.

The same general conclusions applied to transparency; the appearance of concessions without much achievement. There were minimal changes in the general practice. It was agreed that some Council debates would be televised for journalists, and that votes in the Council of Ministers would be made public (they had in fact been known since 1987). But this could be seen as simply providing further encouragement for the existing habit of making deals in the Council to allow agreement on the basis of consensus, even in areas where majority voting was formally allowed (see below). The standard working practice of the Community of making deals in smoke-

---

[7] The *Financial Times*, 16 Dec. 1992.

filled rooms was not affected. There were no proposals to strengthen the role of the European Parliament beyond those agreed in the Maastricht Treaty itself.

The habit of secret diplomacy was confirmed in April 1994 when the *Guardian* newspaper sought to persuade the Foreign Ministers in the General Council to accept the release of Council documents concerning the governments' positions on proposals for rules governing the employment of children. Despite the initial release of the documents to the newspaper the Council insisted that this had been an error, and that in future no papers about the positions adopted by governments regarding issues before the Council could be released.[8] The furthest move towards a more open approach by the Council was the acceptance that it would be routine to make public a record of the voting of governments.

In the event the debate on subsidiarity also had little to do with the concessions made by the Community to Denmark to allow that country to resubmit the Maastricht Treaty for the approval of the Danish people through a referendum. The Danes did have major concessions, which certainly affected other areas of the Community's business, such as enlargement. Denmark was permitted to opt out of the Maastricht provisions on a future common defence policy, common citizenship, and a future European monetary union, but the subsidiarity text had no specific reference for Denmark, although obviously the Danish 'no' in the earlier referendum had encouraged those who wished to set in place a more specific application of subsidiarity.

Constraints on Integration in the Mid-1990s: The Balance in Empirical Perspective

What explains the appearance of the hesitations which led to subsidiarity, with its implied challenge to Federalist centralization? The Maastricht Treaty was an illustration, not so much of spillover, but of overspill from the period of integrative momentum which culminated in the Single European Act and led on to the completion of the 1992 single market process. But well before this had happened a range of doubts and difficulties had appeared. These took a different form and mix in the different member states of the Community.

[8] The *Guardian*, Mon., 18 April 1994.

There was generally a certain ennui, not to mention disillusion, with the political process in member countries, especially in Britain, France, Germany, and, as always, Italy. There was an impatience with national governments which was easily diverted, sometimes deliberately by national authorities, to a European level. This background contributed to the success of the anti-Europeans in stirring up popular interest, which was readily focused on the evidence of inefficiency and waste at the European level. This may be linked with a realization that things had indeed got to the point at which bonds could be forged between the member states which would be hard to break. For a large number of British, for instance, Maastricht brought home that the choice of Europe was not just a tactical move, a living in sin, which could be revoked at will, but more of a marriage with long-term commitments.

The Maastricht Treaty provoked a vision of stark alternatives: state or Europe. Whether it really demanded a choice between the two was beside the point. The Community never prospered when it seemed to be involved in a zero-sum game with the nation state, if governments pretended that they had to opt for one or the other. Progress was always more likely when it appeared possible, even by resort to some subterfuge, to link the strengthening of the Community with the well-being of the separate states as distinct entities: to present integration as a reinforcement of autonomy! But at a time of recession in the 1990s the alternative routes to recovery—common action through the Community, or competitive unilateralism in individual states—were more widely seen as mutually exclusive and destiny-laden. Clearly neither public nor élite attitudes could support the former without hesitation; there was, therefore, a hankering after the latter.

But this was nothing unusual: the same thing had happened in the mid-1970s, when Europe could have solved the problems resulting from the weakness of the dollar by moving quickly to a joint response in the form of monetary union. The governments simply did not have the mutual confidence to make that jump. Nor did they in the mid-1990s when it came to dealing with recession: measures for joint recovery could have been planned more energetically at the level of the Community, and the more rational technical option would have been to work together vigorously at that level.

Occasionally there were complaints from national governments about the difficulty of doing something in the face of Brussels opposition. Frequently in Britain this was linked with the demonizing and externalizing of the Community institutions. There were Brussels Directives which did not suit our interests—or the interests of some group or other—newly defined as sacred to our culture![9] Such judgements were made without regard to the fact that the national authorities had necessarily been involved in making the Directives in the first place. Feelings of subjugation by external forces which were beyond their control chimed well with the anger of those who were the victims of the recession: unemployment was running at record levels, and even the principle of public welfare itself was sometimes under attack. And governments liked the implication, as they pulled the strings, that they were also merely puppets in thrall to Brussels.

There were also echoes of what Stanley Hoffman had called in the 1960s the *logic of diversity*—the idea that the variety of ways in which the member states related to the outside world necessarily imposed limits upon integration between them.[10] The ending of the cold war, and the uniting of Germany, sharpened a general awareness of a shadow of the past. Germany appeared in an older suit of clothes as a middle European power, and the Kohl government was seen to be struggling to find ways of reconciling a more active Ostpolitik and a continuing active Westpolitik. How would special German interests in Central Europe, and a more active engagement there, affect German commitment to the European Union? The British government began to wonder whether the special relationship with the USA was not preferable to involvement in a European foreign policy arrangement that had failed over ex-Yugoslavia. Greece was clearly following its own line in the Balkans, and Italy was also pursuing its own interests in new frameworks in south-eastern Europe.

It was not just that the logic of diversity was visible: those who were cautious about Europe were ready to develop that diversity further. In Britain Eurosceptics wanted to believe that Europe and the USA were alternatives. But this had never been the case: in April 1994 the US Ambassador to the UK, about to retire from London, felt obliged to point out that ' if Britain's voice is less influential in Paris or Bonn, it is likely to be less influential in Washington'.[11] As President Kennedy had told Harold Macmillan thirty-four years

[9] Melanie Philipps, The *Observer*, 14 March 1994. Bernard Levin, *The Times*, 4 March 1994.

[10] See Stanley Hoffman, 'Discord in Community: The North Atlantic Area as a Partial International System', in Francis O. Wilcox and H. Field Haviland, Jr., *The Atlantic Community: Progress and Prospects* (New York: Praeger, 1963), 3–31.

[11] *The Times*, 20 April 1994.

earlier, so Ray Seitz said to John Major in 1994: the special relationship with the USA and full participation in the European Union should not be seen as alternatives. The special relationship had a future if Britain was an active partner in Europe.

A paradox in the foreign policy arrangements of the European Union becomes apparent if relations between the European states and the United Nations are examined. By the mid-1990s discussions about the future membership of the United Nations Security Council had started under the chairmanship of the President of the UN General Assembly. Among the options being discussed was the admitting of new permanent members to the Security Council, with or without the veto. Germany was naturally one of the claimants, as was Japan, and the question arose of whether the Italians too should not have a closer relationship with the Council. The claims of the states were based on factors such as their great economic power, and their large contributions to the budget of the United Nations, which were indeed greater than those of the existing European members. The confusing factors were that if Germany joined it was very unlikely that the British and French would accept giving up their seats, and indeed the contribution of the two countries to the diplomacy of the United Nations in a large number of crises since the late 1980s would support the view that such action would be undesirable. Another view, therefore, was that there should be a seat for the European Union with a formula, yet to be worked out, to allow appropriate contributions from the member states. But the British and the French declined to accept such an arrangement and insisted upon their right to act individually and separately with regard to business on the Agenda of the Security Council. On these questions they only accepted an obligation to report to the other members of the European Union in New York in the daily meetings. Germany and Italy had accepted this arrangement and, indeed, had agreed to its being enshrined in the Treaty of Rome as amended by the Single European Act and the Maastricht Treaty. The relevant clause in the Maastricht Treaty is in Title 5 as follows. (Other clauses in Title 5 strengthen other aspects of the foreign and security policy mechanisms. They include acceptance of majority voting in a carefully limited set of circumstances.)

Article J.5
1. The Presidency shall represent the Union in matters coming within the common foreign and security policy.
2. The Presidency shall be responsible for the implementation of com-

mon measures; in that capacity it shall in principle express the position of the Union in international organizations and international conferences.

3. In the tasks referred to in paragraphs 1 and 2, the presidency shall be assisted if needs be by the previous and next Member States to hold the Presidency. The Commission shall be fully associated in these tasks.

4. Without prejudice to Article J.2(3) and Article J.3(4), Member States represented in international organizations or international conferences where not all the Member States participate shall keep the latter informed of any matter of common interest.

Member States which are also members of the United Nations Security Council will concert and keep the other Member States fully informed. Member States which are permanent members of the Security Council will, in the execution of their functions, ensure the defence of the positions and the interests of the union, without prejudice to their responsibilities under the provisions of the United Nations Charter [This writer's italics].

Various contradictory trends could therefore be observed proceeding simultaneously. The above extract from Maastricht picks up the trend towards greater unity in the arrangements for European Union foreign policy, which would indicate a strengthening case for a European seat. Some members of the German government said they strongly supported such a common seat, others were more prepared to claim a seat for themselves anyway, especially if there were to be a wide-ranging alteration of the principles of Council membership. But the British and French, though working for a common foreign policy and accepting stronger European Union mechanisms, insisted on protecting their privileges in the Security Council. And the German and Italian governments had accepted, most recently in Maastricht, a formula to protect this situation which could also support their own claims to national seats in the Council.

Such were the delights of the dynamics of the European Union in the mid-1990s: enthusiasts for stronger common foreign policy and defence policies (Germany and Italy) accepted conditions which would make them more difficult to achieve, whilst those who were more cautious, such as Britain, insisted on protecting their right to act unilaterally as a condition of moving towards such stronger policies. One somewhat puzzling result was that there were in the mid-1990s issues on which the British and the French would accept full discussion with EU partners outside the UN whilst limiting it within. With regard to the crisis in ex-Yugoslavia there were, it appeared, full discussions between members of the EPC in Europe, for instance in the tandem EC-UN mechanism in Geneva—the Owen, Vance,

Stoltenberg arrangement—according to evolved EPC principles, but not between the same states in New York where the British and French were only prepared to report.

In the recession of the early 1990s, there were frequent demands for separate and competing national efforts with regard to commercial opportunities in the Far East. It was argued that being over-concerned with European markets had meant that opportunities outside had been lost. Relaunching integration in the early 1980s had been one response to the challenge from the Far East in high-technology products, but ten years later, the limits of that collective response were visible. The markets in the Far East were now to be the target of intra-European competition about market shares. This could only be at the expense of the development of higher levels of trade interdependence among member states, which was one of the more powerful motors of integration. Thus economic take-off in the Far East now helped to limit the integration of the Community.

But there were also factors working in favour of integration, which were if anything stronger than in 1957 and 1974. These were, first, aspects of popular attitudes; second, features of the workings of the institutions of the Union; third, adjustments in the interests of governments and parties; fourth, developments in the ways in which the civil servants of the member states engaged with each other and with officials in the Brussels institutions; fifth, the emergence of an increasing range of common principles, norms, and rules in the economic and social arrangements of the member states, that is, a Community regime had emerged; and sixth, an increase in the level of economic interconnectedness and interdependence, not least, of course, in trade. Each of these developments will now be briefly considered

Changes in attitudes are fundamental to the development of an integrated economic zone. They are discussed more fully in Chapter 3. They affect the mobility of labour. They are also crucial in developing the habit of not balancing the books of one participating state or territory with others: short-term outflows from one to the other are not significant when attitudes have moved towards the pattern found in a socio-psychological community. It is clear that this was not yet the case in the European Union in the mid-1990s, but that there had been some movement in that direction. Without that there could be no redistribution, and continuing complaints by those in areas showing a net outflow of resources.[12]

[12] See figs. in Commission of the European Union, *Eurobarometer*, July 1994, p. A13, Table 3 (contained in Ch. 4).

But there was indeed evidence that public attitudes supported the transferring of competence to perform significant tasks, including the conduct of foreign policy, to the Union.[13] Public opinion on the Union, even in the more cautious states, was much more discriminating than the Eurosceptics would have had us believe. And there was also evidence of the appearance of a *security-community*, as Karl Deutsch called it, among the older core states.[14] In other words citizens of one country were more discriminating in their judgements of the sub-groups forming the population of another; and they were more likely to reject military force as a way of settling differences with them. The Franco-German frontier was not now fortified. Neither were the frontiers separating the other member states.

The institutional arrangements of the European Union in the 1990s were a considerable achievement. It was unlikely that the Community could have survived had the Treaty of Rome been a clearly Federalist document. But it was sufficently adaptable for both integrationists and intergovernmentalists—federalists and statists— each of whom claimed to be its sole legitimate interpreter. By the mid-1990s, however, the view began to emerge more forcefully that the sovereignty of states—the development of their sense of distinctive identity and the consolidation of national autonomy—was, paradoxically, capable of reconciliation with the strengthening of the Community. This was a recognition of the inherent duality of the Community's arrangements, which may be captured in the word *symbiosis*.[15] These points are further discussed below.

The external interests of member states passed through a long period of adjustment and convergence. Governments increasingly agreed about the principles on which foreign policy should be based, and indeed by the mid-1980s there was evidence of the view that pursuing their separate interests, where these diverged, should not be taken to the point of endangering the partnership. This was evident in the wording of Title 3 of the Single European Act called *Provisions on European Cooperation in the Sphere of Foreign Policy.* In Article 30, 2(c), the governments agreed to 'ensure that common principles and objectives are gradually developed and defined'; and that they would 'endeavour to avoid any action or position which impairs their

[13] Ibid.

[14] K. Deutsch *et al.*, *Political Community and the North Atlantic Area* (Princeton: Princeton University Press, 1957).

[15] See Taylor, *International Organization*, ch. 4.

effectivneess as a cohesive force in international relations or within international organizations'.[16]

Even the more cautious states had moved closer to Europe. In Britain Eurosceptics were afraid that in the elections to the European Parliament in June 1994 a massive swing against the Conservatives would be seen as a vote for Europe. Britain had focused increasingly upon Europe and away from the Commonwealth. Similarly the Danes had gone through a period of adjustment of their policy of semi-attachment. The French also became less involved with the francophone zone, and more with Europe, especially under President Mitterand. This gradual consolidation of the underlying philosophy of collective action of the Community had taken a long time and had involved a progressive adjustment of views about the world and related interests.

In the mid-1990s the newly independent states of Eastern Europe could not possibly fully understand this adjustment. As yet these states did not share a similar view of the world, because they had not been in a context in which it had to be learned. The injunctions on behaviour which formed regimes could not be learned overnight. But the philosophy underpinning collective action among the member states was not all-encompassing: it was, as with attitudes, a matter of an increasing unity in diversity. But in the mid-1990s the logic of diversity had to be balanced against a logic of convergence.

The growth of converging economic interests coincided with changes in the working arrangements of national civil servants and in their attitudes towards transgovernmental cooperation. The evidence was overwhelmingly that there had indeed been a Europeanization of the bureaucrats, though arguably this had been at the expense of democracy. Too many decisions were being taken without public scrutiny; despite the stipulations of the Maastricht Treaty, the work of the Council of Ministers was still largely in secret. This problem was not, however, confined to the workings of the Community: it was a feature of modernized democracies in general—despite the delusions of potency among some elected representatives in countries such as Britain! As economic arrangements had become more technical, and more susceptible to international influences, so they had become more detached from the scrutiny of generalist members of elected assemblies. Brussels arrangements

[16] Commission of the European Communities, *Bulletin of the European Communities*, Supplement 2/86, Single European Act (Brussels, 1986), 18.

needed to be more open and accountable, but they were illustrative of a more general problem.

There was also an increasing economic interconnectedness between the member states, shown in such developments as the increasing value of mutual trade, and the increasing value of Community, compared with national, budgetary flows. About a quarter of the British budget flowed through the Union in 1993. In 1994 the EC Budget amounted to a mere 1.27 per cent of Europe's Gross Domestic Product, but 80 per cent of this was administered through member states.[17] Inevitably, and despite the efforts of the more cautious states, this was matched by a greater weight of regulation at the Community level, and an increasing interpenetration of bureaucracies. The changes in the attitudes and behaviour of bureaucrats and politicians alike, and the increasing level of economic connections and transactions, justified the conclusion that in terms of formal rules and in terms of informal conventions of behaviour there had emerged by the mid-1990s a Community-wide system of governance. There was a Community regime.

The Theoretical Setting

In any discussion of the theories relevant to the European Union in the mid-1990s account has to be taken of the different purposes of theorizing. They may be to capture the main elements of the process of integration—what drives it forward?—or they may be concerned with the end-situation—where is the process to end? But this is frequently a matter of stress. The main gradualist process theories had certainly returned to favour by the mid-1990s: neofunctionalism again attracted the attention of scholars in North America and in Europe because of the drive to greater integration linked with the attempts to complete the single market after 1985.[18] But neofunctionalism was relatively unspecific about the end of the process. In contrast, Federalism and Consociationalism, discussed below, focused more on the end-situation, though they had implications for

[17] The *Guardian*, 21 Nov. 1994.

[18] For an excellent reconsideration, and critique, of neofunctionalism see Andrew Moravcsik, 'Preferences and Power in the European Community: A Liberal Intergovernmentalist Approach', *Journal of Common Market Studies*, 31/4, Dec. 1993.

the process itself. As has already been made clear the concern in this essay is with outcomes rather than processes.

Different outcomes posit different relationships between the state and the Community. At least five different kinds of such relationship are conceivable. The first is the traditional hard intergovernmental one, which sees the common arrangements as incidental by-products of the relations between the states, carrying no threat to their continuing primacy. A second sees the Community as involving a set of values which it might be prudent to acknowledge, and, indeed, for political convenience, to genuflect towards, as developments in the Community could conceivably threaten the states; this was arguably the case by the mid-1970s, as is illustrated by the Summit meeting at Paris in December 1974. It implies a softer form of intergovernmentalism. The governments felt able to make concessions towards Europe—direct elections, European passports, and so on—because they felt sufficiently secure to do so, and, indeed, sought to strengthen their defences by setting up the European Council and strengthening the Presidency.

In a third view, the developments in the Community are seen as being essential to the survival of the state: they help the state to adjust to new circumstances in the modern world. Alan Milward's[19] claim that the European Union was merely another mechanism for rescuing the nation state is illustrative of this position. This is a modern version of the Grotian image of international society. It is not, however, the position held in this discussion. This is the fourth view: that the state and the Community had each acquired legitimacy; each of the two levels had a degree of autonomy, and indeed their own politics, and had a *symbiotic* relationship with each other. Each had become essential to the survival of the other. Put differently: there were arrangements at the European level which had become semi-detached from the state, representing a distinctive level of political activity, interacting with national affairs, but containing its own values and imperatives, including that of survival. In this arrangement states retained sovereignty within the transnational system. And finally there is the Federalist position, which sees the Community as being potentially the primary actor, and interprets developments at both levels in the light of this goal. Only in this case is sovereignty transferred to the new centre.

[19] A. S. Milward, *The European Rescue of the Nation State* (London: Routledge and Kegan Paul, 1992).

The task facing the student of integration in Europe is therefore to identify the changes in the *balance* among the states *and* between them and the Community, and to focus exclusively on the nation states is to miss the fundamental changes in the European balance. Although each period produced judgements at the time about likely outcomes of the integration processs, there was a stronger sense in the mid-1990s that the form of the end-situation was more clearly visible. Previously that had not been the case, and whatever stage was reached it had always seemed, to enthusiasts and antagonists alike, that progress towards closer union could continue indefinitely. Indeed the onus usually seemed to be on the latter to oppose rather than on the former to promote.

Any version of an outcome must contain two elements: a view about the relationship between the states and the collectivity, and a view about the relationship between the states. Each of these views has to be compatible with the other. The former is concerned with vertical links, and the latter with horizontal ones. It seems to the present writer that the most appropriate image of the European Union in the mid-1990s, and the one likely to be its end-situation, combined the notions of symbiosis, concerning vertical links, and consociation, concerning primarily horizontal ones.

Consociationalism has been described by Lijphart as having four features, each of which, it is argued here, was reflected in the European Union of the mid-1990s.[20] First, there must be a number of groups which are in some sense insulated from each other, in that their interests and associations are more inwardly directed than overlapping with those of members of other groups in the same state: there are relatively few cross-cutting cleavages, and authority within that state is segmented in relation to such groups. Second, the state is dominated by what Dahrendorf called a *cartel of élites:*[21] the political élites of the various segments are each involved in some way on a continuous basis in the process of decision-making and decisions are the product of agreements and coalitions among the members of that cartel. There is no exclusion from decision-making, as, for instance, in the event of defeat in an election, which would be the case with a majority system. The cartel need not necessarily require that all actors be positively involved in the same way on all occasions:

[20] Arend Lijphart, 'Consociation and Federation: Conceptual and Empirical Links', *Canadian Journal of Political Science*, 22/3 (1979), 499–515.

[21] R. Dahrendorf, *Society and Democracy in Germany* (Garden City, NJ: Doubleday, 1967), 276.

variations on the theme would be an arrangement, as in Switzerland, where it is agreed that each member of the central council acts as leader or president for a specified term, or in the Lebanon before the civil war where there was an agreed division of responsibilities between Muslim and Christian leaders.[22]

The third feature is a logical extension of the cartel principle: it is that all the political élites must have the right of veto over decisions of which they disapprove. In other words the majoritarian principle in the system as a whole, which is characteristic of other forms of democracy, is suspended in favour of the requirement of consensus, though it may be found within the segments, or, on some issues which are contentious, among the members of the cartel.

Finally there must be a law of proportionality, which means that the various segments of the population must have proportionate representation among the major institutions, the bureaucracy, legal systems, and so on, of the state. These features then ensure that the rights and interests of the subordinate sections of society, as interpreted by or filtered through the members of the cartel of élites, are safeguarded. Indeed political arrangements are so contrived that each minority is protected from the dictatorship of the whole. As will be seen each of these features is observable in some form in the institutions and procedures of the European Union.

A central problem of consociation is the maintenance of stability in a situation of actual or potential mutual tension. Indeed the problem implies an irony which is more characteristic of international relations than of stable democracies: the need to generate enthusiasm for stability precisely because of the continuing threat of fragmentation. As Lijphart put it 'The leaders of the rival subcultures may engage in competitive behaviour and thus further aggravate mutual tensions and political instabiltiy, but they may also make deliberate efforts to counteract the immobilizing and unstabilizing effects of cultural fragmentation.'[23] The imminence of mutual tensions is revealed in the determination of the segments' leaders to defend the separate interests of the groups in the common forum. In the more conventional democracies—called Anglo-American systems by Gabriel Almond—in contrast, 'because the political culture tends to be homogeneous and pragmatic, the political process takes on some of the atmosphere of a game. A game is a good game when

---

[22] K. McRae (ed.), *Consociational Democracy: Political Accommodation in Segmented Societies,* (Toronto: McLelland and Stewart, 1974).

[23] Lijphart, *Consociation and Federation,* 211–12.

the outcome is in doubt and when the stakes are not too high. When the stakes are too high the tone changes from excitement to anxiety . . . But in consociational democracies politics is treated not as a game but as serious business.'[24] The leaders are faced continually with the dilemma of acting to preserve the general system whilst at the same time seeking to protect and further the interests of the groups which they represent: again, as in the EU.

With regard to their own groups, therefore, élites must be able to rely on a high degree of homogeneity, and be capable of backing this up on occasion with techniques for the maintenance of internal discipline. This explains Lustick's contention that within segments control may sometimes be so powerful as to appear to challenge the judgement that they are internally democratic. The stability of the whole may require the discipline of the segments, even in ways which move towards the limit of what is acceptable—controls upon the press, limitations upon freedom of association, fixing public appointments, and the like.

Consociationalism tends to the reinforcement of the search for the lowest common denominator at the level of the general system. More precisely, the general interest, in so far as it emerges, is as likely to be a limited consensus among élites as a common interest of segments: consociationalism underlines the potential for divergence between the interests of élites and publics. In contrast the assumption behind federalism in its mainstream form is that the system will over time gradually strengthen the perception of the common interest at the general and élite level. The logic of the consociational approach suggests that élites will strive to promote constrained inter-group rivalry, and will judge that they are victims rather than beneficiaries of developing cross-cutting cleavages.

It follows that in the consociational model the leaders will be activist and politicized in their pursuit of interests in the cartel of élites. As was pointed out above in a consociational system politics tends to be a serious business as the stakes are seen as being high: there is no tendency towards depoliticization. In the federalist process of integration, however, there is an expectation of depoliticization and of the transmuting of politics into a less serious game.

---

[24] Gabriel A. Almond, 'Comparative Political Systems', *Journal of Politics*, 18 (Aug. 1956), 398–9.

Consociationalism as a Way of Understanding the European Union

Consociationalism is useful in that it presents a conceivable outcome of the integration process which differs from those indicated by other theories and allows the identification of aspects in the current situation which could be seen as tending towards that outcome. It highlights the point that integration in the sense of the strengthening of the regional functional systems may be perfectly compatible with continuing cleavages in the existing society of nations.

One reason for this is seen to be that members of the cartel of élites are likely to be faced with a dilemma: they will have an interest in increasing the size of the pie, and the share obtained by their own segment, whilst at the same time protecting the distinctiveness of their segments in comparison with others, since they serve as each member's individual constituency and power base. The process of increasing the size of the total pie, which is the essential condition of larger shares, tends, however, to encourage the development of inter-segmental social and cultural links, alongside the economic ones, which may have a cost in terms of the chances of maintaining the segment's viability in the longer term. Integration may, therefore—apart from committing them to enlarging the pie—also generate in the élites an increasing anxiety about the implications of the strengthening of the horizontal links between the segments since that tends to weaken their constituencies. The status and authority of the members of the cartel are dependent upon their capacity to identify segmental interests and to present themselves as leaders and agents of a distinct clearly defined community.

Consociationalism, therefore, highlights the politics of the relationship between leaders and led, and the way in which the interests of the former may depart from those of the latter during the process. British politics in the mid-1990s is all too reminiscent of this possibility. With Prime Minister John Major, because of the major divisions in his party, attempting to steer a tortuous course between pursuing interests in Europe and power at home.

The theory suggests two ways in which the special interest of the élites may be stressed by them in the integration process. The first is where members of the cartel of élites make agreements together for their own purposes, even when these conflict with those of the segments which they nominally serve. This would be, indeed, the apotheosis of the danger that was advertised by the left wing of the political spectrum in Britain and elsewhere: that European integration was essentially a bourgeois conspiracy of élites and big business—in alliance with governments—against the interests of the mass of the people.[25]

The second is when a particular élite seeks to use the context of the common arrangements to promote changes which suit the interests of their key supporters in their particular segments, so that their power within it is consolidated. In the 1990s the British Government's opposition to the Commission's proposal to introduce a social charter into the EC to protect the interests of workers suggested an intention to make the Community a happy hunting ground for capital.[26] There must be no hindrance in the way of capital's exploiting differences in the cost of labour and the level of welfare provision in the various parts of the EC, even though this also meant keeping social security provisions for British workers at a lower level.

Two sub-themes could be detected in the British position, both of which could be related to its anxiety about preserving its status in its own segment. First, a European Social Charter would enhance the cohesion of labour at the Community level, and therefore had to be resisted; second, reducing the level of social provision would enhance its authority in relation to a key group—business, industrialists—within its own segment, and therefore was to be encouraged. In that it points to the special interests of élites as opposed to publics, consociationalism highlights these points. Integration is seen to have a double effect: it strengthens perceptions of the benefits of collective action, but also creates special incentives for élites to resist the development of 'cross-cutting cleavages'.

The theory is also suggestive, however, about existing élites' attitudes towards minorities in the integrating system and the attitudes of the leaders of those minorities. The appearance of the regional arrangements provides the leaders of dissenting minorities with a forum within which to push for increased specific returns and separate representation. The traditional theories of integration, Functionalism and Neofunctionalism, have no way of coping with this observable political fact.[27] Scots, Welsh, Basque, Irish, and even

[25] See Stuart Holland, *UnCommon Market*, (London: The Macmillan Press, 1980).
[26] Peter Kellner, The *Independent*, 22 Mar. 1989.
[27] For accounts of these various theories see A. J. R. Groom and Paul Taylor (eds.), *Frameworks for International Cooperation*, (London: Pinter Publishers, 1990).

Catalan nationalists have all seen the Community as an opportunity for furthering their cause. The minority seeks to consolidate direct contacts with regional level organization whereas the existing élite cartel members seek to limit such contacts. One test of this hypothesis could be found in the attitudes of governments towards permitting or preventing direct links between local groups and the Community when seeking support from the latter's structural funds.[28] The British government tended to oppose such contacts, and this certainly had implications for the perceptions of folk in the non-English areas in Britain of themselves as forming distinct communities. The British government was also reluctant to allow regions to choose their own delegates to the Assembly of Regions proposed in the Maastricht Treaty. Even more striking in the context of consociation was the strength of the opposition to the free movement of people in the Dutch Parliament in the late 1980s. Segmental autonomy had to be preserved!

Consociationalism provides, however, a small further part of the explanation of the observed pattern of behaviour of the minorities in the European Community. The universal habit was for them to see the Community as the context in which they could obtain a greater level of independence and at the same time increase the level of specific returns to their groups. This suggests that contrary to first impressions the tendency might be for successful integration to sharpen divisions between minorities and the dominant segments, rather than lessen them. In that it stresses the propensity of leaders of the dominant segments to increase their countervailing resistance to minority dissent, consociation theory seems to raise the possibility that integration might serve to exacerbate inter-communal tensions. In the mid-1990s the assertion of the principle of *subsidiarity* contained a fundamental flaw from the point of view of those who simply wanted to use it to resist a further flow of competences to the Community from the national level. The principle seemed to justify a flow of competences down to the local communities within the

---

[28] For instance the British Government sought to protect its position as overseer of applications to the structural funds of the EC from local authorities and other organizations in Britain, and, indeed, appeared to be using EC disbursements not, as had been intended, to increase the size of available funds (the principle of Additionality) but rather as an alternative to what would otherwise have been available from the British Treasury. It was only after the Commission had threatened to withhold funds from a development programme in South Wales in early 1992 that the British government eventually agreed reluctantly to amend its budgetary procedures to reflect the principle of additionality.

state. In Britain it was not only an argument against further flows to the Community, but also an argument in support of the claim by the Scots, the Welsh, and the Irish, for autonomy.

The process of decision-making at the centre of the system is also illuminated by the theory of consociationalism. The theory suggests that in this context members of the élite cartel will become more inclined to insist that they retain an ultimate veto on decisions of which they disapprove and more resistant to decision-taking on the basis of majorities. Decision-making would become more difficult because of the success of the process. At first sight the Single European Act, and the Maastricht agreement, seem to be evidence against the proposition that this was true of the European Community, but the informed reader will at least entertain a rather cynical view about its terms regarding majority voting.[29] The states reserved the right, either explicitly in the Act or in terms of stated intentions, to veto anything which affected their vital interests. The Luxembourg Accord of 1966 which allowed the veto remained applicable.

Of course there was evidence to suggest that majority voting was more frequently used after the amendments and that the Council's work had consequently been speeded up, but the underlying circumstances remained the same: states could veto what they did not like. The success of the French in insisting on the approval of the GATT agreement by consensus in the Council of Ministers at the end of the Uruguay Round of trade negotiations, showed that a member state could still evade the formal arrangement of majority voting.

There were peculiar features of the qualified majority voting (QMV) arrangements which reflected the fact that they applied to relations between sovereign states. Between December 1993 and March 1995, of 283 legislative acts approved in the Council of Ministers under QMV, there were only 72 formal divisions, and of these only 40 involved votes against. Denmark voted against 11 times, Holland 10 times, Germany 9 times and the United Kingdom 7 times.[30] The norm was, therefore, not to resort to formal voting.

---

[29] Paul Taylor, 'The New Dynamics of EC integration in the 1980s', in Juliet Lodge (ed.), *The European Community and the Challenge of the Future* (London: Pinter Publishers, 1989), 3–25.

[30] This evidence from Anthony Teasdale, 'The Politics of Majority Voting in Europe', unpublished MS (Dec. 1995), 7. The arguments here are partly in response to Teasdale.

The President usually acquired a sense of the meeting, and recommended that a proposal be deemed to have been approved or rejected. States were under pressure to concur unless they were sure that they could form a blocking minority. But states, both those inclined to support, and those inclined to oppose particular proposals in draft form, were under pressure to modify their original propositions so that a consensus emerged. In a sense the President cooperated with dissenting states by moving to avoid a vote in which they could be defeated. Indeed the whole of the diplomacy in the committees under the Council, the most important of which was the Committee of Permanent Representatives, was devoted to this end: there was no calculation by those involved in the diplomacy at this level about the chances of obtaining a winning majority, or heading off a dissenting minority, in the Council.

It was accepted that the dictatorship of the majority could not be the routine: attempts had to be made to find the lowest common denominator rather than to push through the maximum of integration by a qualified majority. This situation was predictable from the perspective of consociationalism. Majority voting merely cloaked the continuing need to obtain the assent of all states, though the ways of doing this obviously became more complicated. This is not to deny that cautious states were under pressure to compromise; the habit of disclosing the distribution of votes in the Council of Ministers had increased the embarrassment of governments which were on the losing side. But, on the other hand, the more ambitious states were also under pressure to desist from pushing ambitious schemes to the point of hardening opposition. They also knew that the convoy had to be kept together. As has been pointed out frequently in this discussion, this habit was reinforced by the realization that there was a sense in which the states consented to the voting system used in each individual case: *in extremis* they could still invoke the Luxembourg compromise, and each QMV vote implicitly reflected a decision not to do this. In a system of sovereign states, it could not be otherwise.

There was also evidence of what could be called a federalist dilemma. States which were pro-integration, such as Germany, argued strongly, especially after unification in 1989, that the weight of the votes in the Council should reflect the size of population, or gross national product. The assumption was that this was more federalist and democratic, in that it reflected the need to take account of the views of the majority of individual citizens. The dilemma was that this formula also increased the power of some states, especially Germany. Weaker states were likely to insist that the rights of states and the peoples they represented, regardless of their number, should prevail. Any 'federalist' move to reflect more accurately the views of individuals was matched by an 'intergovernmentalist' claim to defend the equality of states. There was a sense in which federalist strategies promoted intergovernmentalism: compromise between the two positions, taking account of the need to respect the sovereignty and equality of the states, whilst promoting the identity and interest of the collectivity, was always necesssary, and this was what consociationalism predicted.

The introduction of QMV in the Single European Act and the Maastricht Treaty did not mean that the federalizing majority could now impose itself on the more cautious states; it did mean, however, a rather more subtle exercising of national sovereignty. The new arrangements meant that a new balance of restraints and powers had to be found for both the dissenting and the assenting states. The cautious states were as determined to resist the weakening of their ability to form a blocking minority, as the ambitious states were anxious to avoid reinforcing it. With the admitting of Sweden, Finland, and Austria, the UK obtained the concession, at a meeting of Foreign Ministers in Ioannina in March 1994, that the old blocking minority of 23 would normally be necessary. The proposal to increase the blocking minority to 26 was qualified in that it was agreed that, if the blocking minority was between 23 and 25, the old rules would apply. In early 1996 it looked as if the question of the size of a qualified majority, and the number of votes for each state, would be further discussed at the next intergovernmental conference on institutional reform in late 1996 into 1997, but it was very unlikely that the fundamental principle of the right of a state to say *no* on any matter on which it felt deeply, *could* or *would* be abandoned. The continuation of the Union depended on the acceptance by both majorities and minorities that decision-making by consensus was the rule and the imposition of the will of a majority by formal voting the exception.

The members of the Council of Ministers and of the European Council did indeed behave like the members of an élite cartel in a consociational multi-party government, with enormously complex consensus building and a marked tendency to express profound doubts about the others' intentions. Disagreements about policies tended to lead to the disparagement of the others' motives at a very early stage: it was very usual for the complaint to be made that other states were not acting honourably in the Community, or were cheating in some way that would not happen at home. In the 1990s an example of this concerned the scandal of 'mad cow disease' in Britain. Protests by the French, the Germans, the Italians, and the Luxembourgers were immediately treated in Britain as illustrations of the tendency of foreigners to cheat.[31]

The building of consensus in the Community tended to be dominated as much by a fear of being left out, as by an enthusiasm for new benefits. As the consociational model suggests, the condition for retaining the common decision-making system was that the fear of fragmentation was greater than the fear of weakening segmental authority. Traditional functionalism or even neofunctionalism indicates the prospect of greater accord as integration proceeds; in contrast consociationalism promotes a more complicated arrangement which might be better decribed as one of confined dissent.

The implications of this for the central bureaucracy—the Commission—are also worth considering. Consociational theory sees the state apparatus as being an umpire in the serious game of politics among the élites, rather than a promoter of any specific national ideology. Within an existing consociational state the bureaucracy is an umpire in that it must avoid attaching itself to the ideology of a particular segment. This was also true of the Commission of the European Communities, and this of course is not a particularly original point. But there is a more interesting development of this idea which is suggested by consociationalism. It is that integration pushes the central institution to adopt more frequently, and at an earlier stage of the decison-making process, the role of umpire, unless it has entered into an informal alliance with one or more member states. The task of presenting initiatives which reflect the general community interest is by no means eliminated, but the grand designs are more frequently suspected of being part of a conspiracy to promote the interests of one or more segments at the expense of the others.

---

[31] This was a disease found in cattle in Britain in the 1980s which affected the nervous system and which it was feared could be transferred to humans. Some EC governments banned imports of beef from Britain until they were convinced that controls on the slaughter and transfer of meat had been sufficiently tightened, so that infected meat was not imported. A number of politicians and 'popular' newspapers in Britain described this sensible and legal precaution as blatant, unscrupulous opportunism to improve national beef sales at the expense of the British farmer.

In the absence of a hegemonic coalition they tend to be compromised out of recognition. Members of the pro-European lobby held that this was the consequence of the close involvement of government representatives in decision-making at a very early stage in the formulation of policy by the Commission, as in the Committee of Permanent Representatives.[32] It is hard to see how this could be avoided in the light of the way the decision-making process had evolved over the years. The theory suggests, however, first, that pressures to enlarge the role of the Commission as umpire are increased rather than diminished as integration proceeds; and, second, that any escape from this dilemma is likely to be at the risk of appearing to favour some segments over others. As the stakes rise so the members of the élite cartel become more careful to protect their interests and insist that the condition of movement is consensus.

A further insight from consociationalism concerns the staffing of the Commission. Whereas integration theory predicts an increasing preparedness to accept appointments to the central bureaucracy on the basis of ability, regardless of geographical or social distribution, the theory of consociationalism suggests an increasing determination to insist upon proportionality in the central institutions, and indeed an increasing tendency for particular élites to identify their nationals in those institutions as their representatives. In the late 1980s and 1990s the British government took to making a careful count of the number of its nationals in the Commission and of complaining if it judged that it was underrepresented.

The doctrine on the Commission was that it was the supranational body, which was responsible for defining and promoting the interests of the collectivity. But that was only half the truth. The other half was that the Commission was informally representative, in that its members were chosen by governments to promote positions of which they approved, and, as with Lord Cockfield, they were likely to turn against commissioners who failed to do this. Commissioners knew that a careful line had be steered between watching out for the interests of the government of the home state, and promoting the interests of the Community. Beneath the level of the commissioners themselves, there were frequently glimpses of coalitions of nationals devoted to protecting interests sought in their home states. Consociationalism provided a useful theoretical

---

[32] See Fiona Hayes-Renshaw, 'The Role of the Committee of Permanent Representatives in the Decision-Making Process of the European Community', unpublished Ph.D. thesis (London: London School of Economics, 1990).

perpective upon the tendency for the collegiate principle in the Commission to become weaker—dissenting members became much more frequently identified than they had been—and for state governments to act as if commissioners from their states were their representatives.

Conversely the Presidency was superficially an embodiment of the principle of intergovernmentalism: each member, as a separate state, was placed in charge of the affairs of the Community once every six years. Yet states which had the Presidency generally recognized that they could not simply use this opportunity to pursue national interests: they also needed to push for the interest of the collectivity. They became defenders of the Community and upholders of the interests of their own state, a duality of purpose which was partly the result of socialization—the consolidation of the regime's injunctions on behaviour—and partly the result of the rational calculation that to pursue national interests too blatantly would be counter-productive.

Such a duality was, however, a valuable, and indeed essential, aspect of the working of the Community's institutions in the 1990s. It represented a stable relationship between two necessary imperatives which served the member states well. There was at one and the same time both integration and state-building, which is particularly evident in the new democracies of southern Europe, but which is in fact the case for all member states This is a great achievement for the Community's institutions, and one which could be too easily thrown away with over-rapid expansion from the existing core.

Consociation and the Regional System

Traditional international relations theory suggests that one way to view Europe is simply as a segment of international society. In this perspective, Europe is seen as a regional grouping of states, each checking the other through a balance of power, and driven by the larger balances in international society, especially that which existed between the superpowers. However we have seen in the preceding discussion that there is an alternative and more powerful theory with which to understand the dynamics of interstate relations in Europe in the mid-1990s. This sees the European system of states as having a dual structure: the states are held within a consociation, which is one element in the dual structure; this primarily stresses horizontal links between states. The other element in the dual structure is, however, primarily concerned with vertical links, that is, between each state separately and the collectivity. The states are also held in a relationship which is characterized by symbiosis, with states/governments seeing an interest in promoting the Community, and the Community promoting the states. The latter dynamic clearly helps to underpin the autonomy of the segments in the consociation.

But symbiosis also implies a puzzle from the point of view of consociationalism: are the Community institutions about umpiring interstate disputes, as is the case in consociation, or are they about promoting the interests of the collectivity, as is implied in symbiosis, and, of course, gradualist theories of integration like neofunctionalism? The answer is very clear from the preceding discussion: the institutions of the Community, and the history of their development, are themselves likely to be characterized by two paradoxical characteristics. Integration continually needs to be reconciled with autonomy; further steps towards integration help the state; the state continually finds ways of protecting sovereignty as the circumstances in which sovereignty is exercised change; the Commission is both an umpire among states and a promoter of integrative causes. So the Community is not a form of traditional international society, and it is argued here that it is a consociation.

Consociational theory has important implications for the development of international organization at the regional level because it points to the way in which the regional system could develop as a framework for cooperative activity without the implication that the governments' concern to protect their sovereignty, the equivalent of segmental autonomy within states, would be lessened. This is the theme of symbiosis between the participating segments and the collectivity, which is implicit in consociationalism. A concern with sovereignty was very evident in the European Community in the mid-1990s: there was paradoxically an assertion of separateness at the same time as a determined adhesion to the collectivity.

It is not difficult to find equivalents at the regional level of the calculations of the segments within the consociational states. There was the need to promote the common system in order to increase security in the face of both economic and military threats. This need underpinned the drive to a single market, as well as the concern to strengthen a common defence, as revealed in the Maastricht Treaty.

The realization that essential utilitarian/economic returns could only be gained within the common system was evident. This is a point of great importance with regard to the emerging regional superpower, Germany: after unification in 1989 Germany's continuing dependence on the regional system was still evident. And within the system the traditional gradualist integration processes were visible. The neofunctionalist dynamics had certainly re-emerged in the drive towards the establishment of the single market by 1992, and later in the continuing pressures towards monetary union. But this did not in any way weaken the consociational image of the Community.

The political element is probably more important than the economic one: once scope reaches a certain level, states are pushed to accept some constraints in their struggle to promote their own interests by the fear of being marginalized in the common system. The possibility that a coalition could emerge within the cartel of élites which would pursue stronger arrangements amongst themselves to the exclusion of the reluctant partners is a powerful incentive to stay in the game. Hence although Mrs Thatcher may have behaved badly in the cartel of élites she was determined to remain a member. This circumstance encouraged the French in their use of a particular diplomatic weapon against the British, which again reveals the character of the Community as a consociation. President Mitterand was quite prepared to remind the British of the possibilities of setting up a two-tier Europe with the British demoted to the lower tier, if they proved too unreasonable in the context, for instance, of the proposal for economic and monetary union.[33] This behaviour on both sides was as evident in the diplomacy concerning Mastricht in 1989–91 as it had been in that leading up to the Single European Act. On both occasions it was apparent that senior members of the British government, such as Hurd, Howe, Major, and Lawson, were fearful about being marginalized.[34] Both Lawson and Howe resigned at least in part over this issue.

This was not to deny that in a number of member countries there were groups which continued to use the language of federalism: this should not be interpreted as meaning the subjugation of the nation state to an overarching federal structure in which sovereignty had

[33] As on 25 Oct. 1989. This was the lead front page story in The *Guardian*, 26 Oct. 1989.

[34] See The *Guardian*'s lead story 'Cabinet rallies to Howe's EMS Flag', 2 Nov. 1989.

been transferred to a new centre. By the beginning of December 1994 papers outlining attitudes to the European Union, with implications for the next intergovernmental conference in 1996, had appeared in Germany, in a policy paper published in September 1994 by the CDU,[35] in France, in a *Manifesto for Europe* issued by Prime Minister Balladur,[36] and in Britain, in a number of statements by ministers, but especially in Prime Minister John Major's speech in Leiden on 7 September 1994, and in the positions prepared by the Conservatives for the elections to the European Parliament ealier that year. There were clearly differences in stress among the three statements of position, but account should be taken of the domestic political context in which each was made, and of the different linguistic and rhetorical usage in each country. When these factors were allowed for, what emerged was a set of positions that had a surprising amount in common. The main points in the positions of the three may be summarized as follows.

1. Balladur, Major, and Kohl, all wanted the state to survive, and to maintain position in the Council. All three stressed the idea of the 'basic equality of the member states' (CDU paper), though the German view was explicit about wanting more votes in the Council for more people. That is, it argued for stronger representation for itself as a state: 'democratization means striking a better balance between the basic equality of all member states and the ratio of population size to number of Council votes.'

2. All three saw the Council as maintaining a key role in the legislative process, and acknowleged that there was an irreducible core of intergovernmental interests (*intergovernmental field* in the German version).

3. All three admitted the prospect of 'deeper monetary, commercial, cultural and defence cooperation' (Balladur paper) as part of an open list of options. But it was 'open' to Major in the sense that he carefully declined to rule anything out: he avoided positive support, which was the best he could do in the internal political context in the UK in the mid-1990s. He was particularly determined in not ruling out monetary union, the *most* 'federalist' goal, despite constant pressure from the Eurosceptics.

[35] See The *Guardian*, 7 Sept. 1994.
[36] See The *Times*, 30 Nov. 1994. The election of Jacques Chirac to the French Presidency in May 1995 did not signify any noticeable change in the French position.

4. Kohl and Balladur were clear about wanting the positions of national parliaments in the EC system to be reinforced. (Balladur: 'national parliaments must have more voice'. CDU: 'this [strengthening institutions] should be accompanied—not preceded—by efforts to engage participation by national parliaments in the EU decision-making process.') The UK position was distinctive in that there was little call for Parliament's role in the EU system to be strengthened; the UK seemed to want the EU system to be a system for governments, which minimized any direct connections between the Parliament and Community institutions. There was also evidence from elsewhere that leading parliamentarians were hostile to the new assembly of parliaments proposed in the Maastricht Treaty, as something which would dilute Parliament's role.[37] There was hostility to strengthening the role of Parliament in the EU system.

5. All three stressed the importance of subsidiarity: Germany most of all, despite the German usage of the word federalism, which was much more extensive than in the other documents. The UK had the most restricted view of subsidiarity, as it had no implications there of powers to regions, or other areas within the state. The CDU-CSU, proposed in a widely discussed policy paper that the next constitutional confererence on the Community's institutions in 1996 should 'strengthen the EU's capacity to act and make its structures and procedures more democratic and federal'. 'This document must be oriented to the model of a "federal state" [inverted commas in the original text] and to the principle of subsidiarity. This applies not only to the division of powers but also to the question of whether public authorities . . . should perform certain functions or should leave them to groups in society.'[38] A first reading might suggest that this was the same old theme: an advocacy of more powers to the centre. But it should be noted that subsidiarity was stressed, and the words 'federal state' are in quotation marks.

6. The CDU paper was the most explicit about the need for a core of states to go ahead, and not be restricted by the slowest in the convoy. There was strong support for a two- or three-tier Europe, and vigorous rejection of the British proposal of a Europe à la carte. Balladur, in the context of jockeying for position in the lead-up to the French Presidential election—seeking to attract the Gaullist vote—said there should be a 'Europe of flexible circles inside the Union': there would be various circles of members which wanted closer

---

[37] See n. 5 above.   [38] As reported in The *Guardian*, Sept. 1994, p. 6.

union in certain areas. But what areas? It was quite likely that the upper tier would emerge clearly from this—at least in Balladur's text this was not excluded.

Without the domestic constraints the chances were that Major would have said the same: the Hurd/Major statement at the party conference in November, echoing the Leiden speech, was transparantly for home consumption. It was an attempt to assuage the Eurosceptics—a necessary move in view of the government's narrow majority—without explicitly excluding more pro-European policies which might later be preferred. They recognized that they would struggle to avoid being marginalized from a core if that emerged, and avoided—naturally—any indication that they would accept marginalization.

If the three positions are compared, and allowances made for context and usage—the subtext—the differences between them begin to shrink. All three insisted upon the survival of the nation state, all three saw the prospect of more integration. All three supported the principle of subsidiarity. Indeed the German position, which used the word federal most frequently, was adamant about this. The Germans were, however, committed to a constitution for Europe, which by implication would include some kind of final settlement of powers and competences: but they were also explicit about the need for more powers for national parliaments in this constitutional order. The Germans were also explicit in demanding appropriate controls, including democratic controls, for those competences that went to the centre. The French did not exclude further moves towards more integration, but were not specific about the nature of the final order: they wanted to reserve their position about its principles. The British were not averse to more competences going to the centre, but most insistent upon limiting institutional development there. They could not exclude the core idea, but were not prepared to face its institutional implications. It was also arguable that in resisting the core idea, the British strategy was counter-productive: it invited the Germans to positively reject the alternative which they proposed, and to firm up their preference for a core. There was little to suggest that the French, even under M. Balladur, were against this.

The image that appeared from the three positions was, therefore, that the superstate idea had been headed off by the mid-1990s. When examined closely proposals for federation, as in the CDU paper, began to look more like proposals, not for federalism, in the sense of a highly centralized superstate, dominated by a supremely powerful

Commission—the anathema of the Eurosceptics—but more like a rather carefully decentralized association of states, which was a federation only in the sense that there would be some settlement of the powers of the collectivity and the constituents. The various statements by the Commission, and others, in the course of the negotiations about subsidiarity (mentioned above) were confirmed by these images. The point should be stressed: the German image was a federation only in the sense that it involved a formal settlement, embodied in an agreement between states, about what should be done where. It said nothing about ultimate responsibility or the location of sovereignty, though more than was liked by the British about what might be necessary to achieve proper governance, like public accountibility. Indeed such an arrangement even in its most ambituous current versions, though not a form of traditional international society, looked more like a confederation, or consociation.

The major differences between the three concerned the degree of explicitness about the end-situation. Indeed in resisting the German arguments as a start for negotiations leading up to the 1996 Intergovernmental Conference, the British strategy (yet again!) was counter-productive: it meant losing an opportunity to set in place the kind of Europe they preferred, for instance in terms of the location of sovereignty or the ways of managing the system. As it was, their opposition to any discussion of a constitutional settlement on terms such as those in the CDU paper meant that the Europe of which they disapproved remained on the agenda. The state was safe in Europe, but the British were helping to keep the threats to it alive.

Conclusions

Modified intergovernmentalism, in the special form of consociationalism, was, therefore, the most persuasive image of the European Union in the mid-1990s: it was a tightly managed community of states, among which the conventional conditions of sovereignty had been altered. Confederalism had the problem that it tended to undervalue the integrity of the Community system, of the elements which linked the members of the consociation together. A significant alteration was the possibility of separating the performance of functions from the condition of national autonomy. National autonomy was a means of participating in the common decision-making process, and much less an expression of separateness in the performance of specific tasks. But this end-situation also involved a paradox: that the Community did not challenge the identity of the member states, but rather enhanced that identity. The states became stronger through strengthening the collectivity. This perception was inherent in the idea of the European Union and was one of its strengths.

It was indeed remarkable that in Western Europe in the mid-1990s some of the oldest fundamental conditions of sovereignty had been weakened without this being seen as challenging sovereignty. For instance, complete independence in the conduct of foreign policy and defence had in earlier centuries been regarded as fundamental to the idea of sovereignty. There was, however, now an *obligation* to attempt to coordinate foreign policies at the Community level, and the first steps towards a common defence structure and policy had also been taken. It was striking that even in one of the more cautious states—Britain—55 per cent of the population supported the proposition that the European Union should be responsible for Foreign Policy.[39] But these changes took place precisely at the point in the emergence of the European Community when the member states' leaders and publics had been brought to place more explicit limits upon integration.

The obvious conclusion was that the latter was a consequence of having gone too far with the former. More likely, reflecting one of the themes of this chapter, was that the Maastricht crisis was yet another example of the dialectic of the integration process: that there was a symbiotic relationship between the growth of the Community and the nation state. Any assertion of the former was likely, in the pattern of the historical evolution of the latter, to be accompanied by its countervailing development. Thus was the symbiotic relationship between the collectivity and the member states.

---

[39] Commission of the European Union, *Eurobarometer*, Table 3.

3

BEYOND THE PALE: THE EUROPEAN UNION AND NON-MEMBERS

THIS chapter is not about the institutional machinery through which the EU interacts with the outside world. It is concerned with the normative question of what principles should be used in determining which states should or should not belong to the EU in the foreseeable future. It starts from the assumption that the EU has a certain shape and character in the mid-1990s, as described in Chapter 2, and goes on to discuss how it might best be related to the outside world in view of the major features of its likely internal development. In sum: what kind of membership of the EU is most conducive to its making a positive contribution to the well-being of Europe and of the globe?

Any discussion of the European Union in international society in this sense must begin with a consideration of the question of expansion: in the 1990s the question was normally whether there should be *deepening* before *widening* or vice versa.[1] By the time of writing in the autumn of 1995 and early 1996 the European Union had been widened to include Finland, Sweden, and Austria. Norway, again a candidate for admission, had decided, after a negative referendum, not to join. The states that were next in line appeared to be, in Eastern Europe, the Czech Republic, Poland, Hungary, and Slovakia (the Visegrad group), but Bulgaria and Romania, were also interested. To the south, candidates included the island states, Malta and Cyprus, and Turkey. Under the Treaty of Rome, accession was open to any European state, though the implication was that the state had to be democratic. Under the Maastricht Treaty the conditions were

---

[1] See William Wallace, *Regional Integration: The West European Experience* (Washington: The Brookings Institution, 1994).

further tightened to include an explicit requirement for democracy and a demonstrably good record as regards human rights. Under the Single European Act, the power was given to the European Parliament, according to the revised Article 237, to assent to the admission of a new member. The Treaty of Rome also stated in Article 237 that the consent of all member states was necessary in the form of unanimous approval in the Council of Ministers.

Institutional Aspects of Enlargement

There are arguments for and against widening before deepening. The most pressing claim was for enlargement to the East, and what follows mainly concerns that question: but it is more about the principle of expansion, rather than about particular applicant countries. There are some who take a maximalist stance on this: that there should be expansion to the limits of any conceivable notion of Europe. Is the balance of the argument in favour of this? The arguments against seemed to this writer to be the stronger, especially as enlargement does not coincide with the way in which the EU has evolved so far and its desirable direction of development in the future. An attitude towards the limits of expansion in the 1990s is important and necessary.

In previous chapters it has been stressed that the institutions of the European Union are a unique achievement. They emerged as an effective way of governing a set of states which retained their sovereignty, but which had nevertheless agreed to form a system possessing a very high degree of common management. The combination of interests and values which could sustain this system had taken a good many years to evolve, and it represented an achievement which should not be abandoned easily. It involved a long process of learning and adjusting, of socialization in the ways of the Community.

J. S. Mill concluded that the values and habits which sustained democracy in a particular community were acquired with difficulty over a long period of time: they could not simply be introduced overnight from outside, as if, to use a modern reference, an advertising campaign would do the trick.[2] Similarly the values and habits which supported the Community method of working had evolved at

---

[2] See the excellent discussion of these issues in Anthony H. Birch, *Nationalism and National Integration* (London: Unwin Hyman, 1989), esp. 36–74.

great cost of effort and adjustment. The danger in the mid-1990s was that the achievement of the European Union would be undervalued. Every enlargement carried the risk that it would be recklessly and irresponsibly destroyed, as pro-Europeans in the original Six learned to their cost—especially after the enlargements of 1973—to include Britain, Denmark, and Ireland—and 1981—Greece.

The institutions included ways of encouraging the separate states to reconcile their separate interests, but also to reconcile them with those of the Community. Almost all the institutions contained ways of doing this, but the Presidency was perhaps the most striking example. Within it, once every seven-and-a-half years after the 1995 enlargement, states had the chance to act on behalf of the Community and at the same time to promote their own image as separate states. Governments had shown imagination in recognizing the need to promote the interests of the whole, as much as their own, when they occupied the Presidency. But any further increase in the number of member states, beyond the fifteen which made up the Union in January 1995, was very hard to reconcile with the maintenance of this hard won system. An interval of seven-and-a-half years was probably towards the maximum in which states could maintain a sense of involvement and continuity. The intervals between the periods of office would be excessive if the period of occupancy was kept at the present six months. But, if the period in office was reduced, no state would be there long enough to have any impact. Strengthening the Troika arrangement, by which representatives of previous presidencies and future presidencies worked beside the actual presidency—thus easing the transfer of the baton and promoting the sense of continuity—would ease but not solve the problem.

But the other institutions would also encounter difficulties as numbers increased. In the discussions about the offices of the commissioners appointed in early 1995 there was a sense of creating offices in order to appease the new members rather than in order to promote administrative efficiency. Something had to be created for each state, and there was fierce competition for portfolios. With the increase to fifteen members the Commission had to be increased to twenty-one members. This was an artificial administrative accretion to solve a political problem and it made a little too obvious a feature of the Commission that was better left obscure: despite the injunction in the Treaty of Rome that its members should not seek or receive instructions from the member governments (Article 157

(Merger Treaty Article10)), it was also in a sense a representative institution. There was clearly a limit to the extent to which this kind of adjustment could be tolerated as numbers increased, without destroying the delicate balance between representativeness and supranationalism on which the Commission was based, and, as seriously, creating an extremely cumbersome machine.

It was possible to tackle this problem by removing the stipulation that each of the big states should have two of its nationals on the Commission, a proposal likely to be considered at the 1996 Intergovernmental Conference. This would be eminently reasonable if the Commission were solely to represent the states: their sovereignty and equality would be respected in this formula, but even then expansion could not go very far before the problems mentioned earlier arose again. But the Commission was not intended to be a representative of states: it was supposed to be a supranational body, which was required under the Treaty of Rome to promote the interests of the European Union as a whole. As indicated in Chapter 2 it was much more successful in doing this when the President, in addition to his personal resources and inclinations, was also from one of the big states which favoured integration. Examples of this included Presidents Hallstein, Ortoli, and Delors. Similarly the Commission's proposals were more likely to be authoritative if it was believed that they had been backed by a substantial number of the Commissioners from the big states. This was likely to be the case under the existing formula since, although the decisions were in secret, they needed at least a majority of the twenty-one. If, on the other hand, all states had only one member, the chances would be greater that decisions had got through solely on the backing of those from the small states. The Commission's authority would thereby be reduced, and it would be constantly vulnerable to the debilitating criticism that it had become the mouthpiece of minnows.

Once again the interactions between the Commission's representativeness and its supranationalism are seen to be complex. It was not the representative of states, but its ability to exercise its supranational muscle depended upon an unstated faith in some form of input from the powerful. Conversely the inclination of the more cautious of the large states to maintain two commissioners rather than one usually helped the Commission to protect its independent authority. This facility was sustained by the tendency of commissioners, sent to Brussels to protect their government's interests, to convert to the cause of Europeanism. A good example of this was the case of Lord Cockfield in the mid-1980s, but over the history of the Commission there had been many other examples. That such conversion occurred is itself an illustration of the dual purpose of the Commission, which was a desirable state of affairs: Mrs Thatcher could talk of her commissioners as they were in the process of converting to what—from her point of view—was the other side. Confidence that the Commission was in some sense a representative of the states as well as being supranational, and, therefore, beyond their reach, was a feature of the symbiotic character of the Community, and was essential in maintaining the Commission's authority.[3]

The Council, too, revealed problems from enlargement in early 1994. The difficulty was that as numbers increased so the arrangements of majority voting also had to be altered to avoid increasing the opportunities for states to veto proposals. But if this meant making it easier for some states to be outvoted they were unlikely to be very happy with such changes. As reported in Chapter 2 the British objected strongly to changing the weighting of the various states' votes as this would make it slightly more difficult to block a proposal of which they disapproved. Although they eventually accepted a compromise, much to the embarrassment of John Major in the eyes of the Eurosceptics, the British threatened to delay the accession of Sweden, Finland, and Austria unless they retained their ability to create a blocking minority with the support of one other large state and one small state. The problems of how to adjust majority voting arrangements as numbers increased were formidable indeed.

A response to these difficulties, in the arguments of those who supported expansion, in some ways further underlined the scale of the problem. It was asserted that expansion—widening—in fact *required* deepening, that is, that increases of membership forced adjustments to voting systems which made it easier for any one state to be outvoted. This appeared to have been the case with the admission of Spain and Portugal, which had arguably encouraged the move in the Single European Act towards majority voting in the Council and enhancing the powers of the European Parliament. But as an integrative dynamic with general applicability this was rationalist wishful thinking. Very few states were likely indefinitely to

---

[3] For a discussion of the role of the Commission see Desmond Dinan, *Ever Closer Union? An Introduction to the European Community* (Basingstoke: Macmillan, 1994), ch. 7. At the time of writing no substantial general account of the Commission was available.

respond positively to that argument as numbers increased, and a good number of those who supported enlargement did so precisely because they meant to undermine the present system, and to make it easier to resist rather than promote change.

Another argument was that groups of states could agree to hold one or other office together. For instance the small states could hold the Presidency collectively, or could appoint a common commissioner. This again seemed to fly in the face of the realities of the Community to date: that it combined acceptance of the principles of the sovereign equality of states, for Luxembourg as much as for Germany, with the principles of the Community. No states were likely to accept lightly the kind of second-rate citizenship that such arrangements implied. The risks in Europe in the mid-1990s were as much about an intransigent Luxembourg as about a hegemonic Germany: the Quebec syndrome was as threatening as the risk of hegemony.[4]

An underlying problem seemed to be that there was a contradiction in the logic of those who were thinking up ways of dealing with increasing numbers. Arrangements were being proposed which assumed a stronger sense of common identity, and support for a common working philosophy, precisely when that identity was being weakened and the philosophy undermined by expansion. They assumed a strengthening of federalist principles when they were in fact being weakened. The reasons for suggesting the simplifying principles—more diversity, more members, and so on—were the grounds on which the counter-argument, that it could not work, was based. There were echoes here of the classic dilemma of collective security, which goes back to the classic dilemma of federalist approaches to international security, as discussed, *inter alia*, by Rousseau: it could only work in circumstances of international trust and mutual confidence, which were likely to be missing if the system had to be used! But the alternative solution, to increase the degree of intergovernmental representativeness in the Union's institutions, could lead to the opposite problem, as illustrated by the failure of federalism as a political solution to problems of diversity: groups with divergent interests were likely to demand more of a federal government, but that government was likely to perform less effectively

---

[4] See J. I. Coffey and Friedhelm Solms (eds.), *Germany, the EU, and the Future of Europe*, Center of International Studies Monograph Series, 7 (Princeton: Princeton University, 1995).

because it was made up of the quarrelsome representatives of those divergent interests.

In the following sections the consequences of enlargement for two internal tendencies are explored. The first is the tendency towards economic integration, especially with regard to money. The second is the tendency towards greater harmonization of foreign and defence policies.

Problems of Accentuating Economic Divergence

Enlargement would make the bargaining process more difficult, in that it increased the range of interests that needed to be reconciled, especially if the economies and societies of the applicant states diverged. On the one hand it made it harder to reach comprehensive agreements which excluded opt-outs and exceptions, and on the other it increased the pressures in favour of special treatments. On the whole, the original six governments might have concluded, it would have been better to have gone even further towards union before sanctioning British accession. The lesson to be drawn was that it would be easier to reach conclusions among smaller numbers of negotiators rather than larger numbers, and that greater progress towards integration would be likely if a smaller core of states deepened first, and then placed the onus upon the applicant states to accept what had been agreed. Conversely, seeking general agreement between the core and the applicants at each stage would be more likely to lead to a loss of momentum. It was obvious that had the Six insisted upon waiting for the British to agree to the initiatives proposed in the 1969 Summit, before starting negotiations, those initiatives would not have been approved. And the accession negotiations succeeded in 1970–1 precisely because the British did not insist upon detailed agreement upon every issue.

There was some evidence to suggest that in the mid-1990s the idea of the unified area was already weakening. There were pressures for exceptions, derogations, and opt-outs from the Maastricht Treaty, all deriving from the claims of states which had acceded after the European Community had been set up. The Danes demanded and obtained at the Edinburgh summit of late 1992 opt-outs on aspects of the citizen's Europe, on defence, and on monetary integration; the British had earlier obtained opt-outs on the Social

Charter, monetary integration, and so on. As numbers increased further, if such exceptions were demanded and allowed, as seemed likely on past performance, the Union would begin to look more and more like a traditional form of international society, rather than the unique form which it had become. The process of harmonizing interests would be slowed, the diversity of interactions externally increased, and the EU as an international actor made harder to sustain. Enlargement therefore created greater problems in maintaining the integrity of the *acquis communautaire*,—the collective legal and political inheritance of the Union—even though in 1995 this was still defended by the member governments as something which new members must accept in total. It would become increasingly difficult to do so as existing members sought and obtained exceptions and opt-outs, whether before or after accession.[5]

The complaint of the Eurosceptics in Britain that too much had been left open in the accession negotiations reinforced that argument: their implied accusation was that if an attempt had been made to reach a more comprehensive agreement it would have failed. The strategy of the Conservative government of Edward Heath recognized this: he had learned from the experience of the first round of negotiations in 1961–3, when there had been an attempt by the British negotiators to anticipate every eventuality, dot every i and cross every t, that such detailed agreements could not be reached. Even members of the Commission, who largely favoured British entry, reckoned, by the second half of 1962, that the British had taken their determination to cover every exit too far. De Gaulle was reflecting the general ennui when he vetoed the British application, though the other members were shocked by it. It was said at the time that the British, as was their wont, thought that they were irresistible to any club which they offered to join. They overplayed their hand.[6]

There was the danger that any relaxation for new members of the principle that the integrity of the *acquis communautaire* should be respected would also damage the commitment of the existing member states, even some of those in the core. The availability of such opt-outs, chosen, as it were, from a menu, would encourage dissenting elements within them to insist more firmly on what they

[5] For a discussion of the Danish opt-outs and the *acquis communautaire*, see Anna Michalski, *Denmark and the European Union*, unpublished Ph.D. thesis (London: London School of Economics, 1995).

[6] See Kitzinger, Uew, *Diplomacy and Persuasion* (London: Thames and Hudson, 1973).

considered to be their special interests. The context of integration, which had encouraged a bandwagon effect in support of the ideology of Europe, and a focusing upon cooperation, could be swapped for a context in which the search for exceptions would be sanctioned, and new hostilities encouraged. An *is*, reflected in the actual circumstances of Eastern Europe, would be translated into an *ought*, being a concern to cultivate differences in established members of the Union.

The danger of subsidiarity, though as an end-situation it was reasonable, was that it would generate a process of disintegration. Although the theory of *variable geometry* suggested that the core would go ahead and the others would catch up—as opposed to Europe à la carte, which suggested a general *mélange* of arrangements—the danger was that over time in practice this would prove unsustainable. The variable geometry would lead to instability and eventual collapse into the *mélange*. The choice was between: 1) insisting that all new states should accept the *acquis communautaire* as a condition of entry, or 2) risking the erosion of the *acquis* among the existing members. Lessening the demands of entry from without meant weakening the discipline within.

But enlargement complicated bargaining in the Community in other ways. When enlargement was to include states which had poor economies, the prospect of integration sharpened rather than reduced differences of interest about economic issues. Three effects could be noticed. One was heartland pull, which occurred when capital located in peripheral areas was pulled towards the more developed parts of the economic union. This was a reflection within the Union of a more general effect in economic relations between states, which was noticed in the discussion about imperialism. The Leninist theory claimed that capital moved to backward areas and that this was the primary reason for the establishment of empire. In examining this theory, however, economists noted that capital usually behaved quite differently: it moved mainly to the more developed regions of the world in the nineteenth century, as in the twentieth, rather than to the more backward ones. In Europe—other things being equal—capital behaved in a similar fashion: it moved to the areas which were already developed, to southern and eastern England and away from western and northern peripheral regions, and, in Spain, to the areas adjacent to the northern frontier, and then beyond to the industrial heartland in Germany, northern and eastern France, and northern Italy.

Capital was attracted by a fuller range of services, such as transport and communications, better amenities for management and their families, and a larger number of other firms for exchange and support. This effect was noticed in the existing states, and, although detailed economic research was yet to be carried out, it seemed in the mid-1990s highly unlikely that such an effect would not arise in an open system in relations between the comparatively poor economies of the East European states and the Union—unless positive steps were taken to counter this.

A second effect was that further steps towards positive integration, such as monetary integration, tended to be more to the advantage of the stronger economies in the heartland than the poorer peripheral ones. This was not to say that there were not also some advantages of such forms of integration for all states, but rather that more of them arose for the stronger economies. This was particularly clear with regard to monetary integration, where the benefits were seen to accrue mainly to Germany and to the states most closely linked to the German economy. Germany had an interest in preventing the revaluation of the German mark, which would be eased by setting up an exchange rate system. Establishing a more stable currency regime in Western Europe would promote the further expansion of trade with trading partners in the economic community: in effect, the market would be 'internalized' as the exchange rate risk would have been removed. In addition, however, the problem, faced throughout the 1970s and again in the mid-1990s, of either importing inflation from 'weaker' partners, or of revaluing the mark and thus weakening the competitive position of her products, would be avoided; the danger would be lessened that the devaluing dollar would increase pressure unequally upon the various European currencies, tending to push the stronger currencies upwards in relation to the weaker; and it would be easier to persuade the governments of the poorer countries to pursue stability-inducing policies, and avoid more inflationary growth policies. These various effects would tend to keep the stronger industries in the heartland by discouraging policies to regenerate industry in the periphery.

In the 1970s and earlier this imperative was in the form of pressures from Germany to coordinate economic policies more effectively, a strategy which the weaker countries, such as the French, had tried to evade. In the Maastricht programme for monetary integration the equivalent of this was the convergence criteria which substituted a set of performance targets as conditions of joining the single currency for direct coordination of economic policy. These included limits on government borrowing (a maximum of 3% of Gross National Product (GNP) in government deficit and 60% of GNP for government debt); an inflation rate no greater than 1.5 per cent above the best three performers in the system for the previous year; nominal long-term interest rates no more than 2 per cent higher than the three best performing states for the previous year; and stress-free membership of the exchange rate mechanism for the previous two years. The weaker countries, in contrast, would lose the weapon of devaluation traditionally used to improve the competitive position of their products.

The third effect was that different levels of economic performance caused governments to be more determined to protect what they believed to be their comparative advantages, such as capacity to manipulate the costs of production in favour of international capital, by offering greenfield sites, non-union labour, or tax benefits. Economic divergence tended to sharpen the competition among governments for the location of industry. Given the present social circumstances, and the survival of degrees and forms of nationalism, labour was unwilling to move to heartland areas to seek employment, and governments therefore struggled to bring industry to their backward regions.

Arguments about Further Internal Consolidation: The Case of Monetary Union

This was certainly one feature of British policy towards the EU in the 1990s. Resistance to the social chapter in Maastricht was explicable in part as a determination to keep Britain attractive to internationally mobile capital, such as that from Japan. It also helped to explain British opposition to monetary union, as a cheaper pound meant cheaper exports. The problem with these strategies, of course, was that the advantages of improved economic performance for labour were hard to detect, and tended to disappear in the soggy marshland of such notions as the trickle-down effect. And an advantage in the exchange rate was easily lost. In 1995 there were internal contradictions in British policy on this. Escaping from the exchange rate mechanism, on what came to be called *Black Wednesday*, in September 1992, had brought benefits to Britain in the form of a cheaper pound, and correspondingly cheaper exports, and for a while it looked as if the effect on the balance of trade was wholly positive. It was also argued that the failure of Britain to stay in the Exchange Rate Mechanism (ERM) demonstrated the failure of that mechanism.

But if it had failed for other states, such as the French, the British would have lost that advantage. Presumably the British government, and those largely right-wing economists who advised it, wanted the ERM not to work as far as the British were concerned, but to work for everybody else. The rational policy for those who argued that a falling pound was good for Britain would have been not to jeer at the French for staying in, thus becoming, the cynics argued, a kind of German stooge, but rather to support their continued membership. By these means Britain's comparative advantage would be preserved. But this was something which the anti-Europeans in Britain could not do: integration had to be condemned as bad for everybody, even though in the terms of their argument, monetary integration for everyone else would have the benefit that their currencies would be overvalued and their goods uncompetitive.

Unless there was a preference for a pound which was continuously in decline there must come a point at which a value against other currencies would have to be fixed: keeping the pound out of the exchange system suggested to the currency market, as Kenneth Clarke, the Chancellor of the Exchequer, implied in mid-March 1995, that it was expected to fall further, and that speculation against it was therefore a safe option. Alternatively the strategy would involve deliberately using the exchange rate mechanism to gain commercial advantage, in the form of aggressive devaluation, beyond what was required to reflect the level of economic performance. In this case the other members of the common market would be justified in reintroducing forms of protection against British goods. The Eurosceptic case had the difficulty that it was either founded on British weakness rather than British strength, in that it assumed that problems in the economy were such that no particular level of value could be defended; or that the British would exploit devaluation so that the assumption on which it was based, the common market, would be destroyed because partners would retaliate. In arguing against membership in the ERM they encouraged speculation against the pound, though they reflected a further British vice in finding comfort for themselves, and their friends, in the increased benefits for the market in stocks and shares, as a weaker pound benefited exports in the short term. It looked as if British strategy in the long term could not be to stay out of the ERM: there might be short-term advantages in cutting loose, but the long-term costs made it impossible to defend not joining the ERM unless there was a preference for chaos.

Despite the serious problems in the EMU system in the mid-1990s, arising from the shocks of 1992–3, there was still strong support for such an arrangement in the business community throughout the EU. The main difficulties were encountered in resisting the challenges from the currency market, especially for the British and the Italians, when the market became convinced that the value of their currencies could not be maintained in the system. But the overall conclusion must be that the weight of opinion remained that the 1992–3 upsets were exceptional and that the rules developed in the late 1980s, especially the Basle–Nyborg agreement of 1988, had worked extremely well in managing the system in normal times.

The strains placed upon it could be dealt with according to the Basle–Nyborg rules. These were to allow the currencies to move freely within the currency margins agreed; to intervene to prevent undesirably strong fluctuations and to use very short-term financing mechanisms, which should be highly accessible to debtor countries; to use short-term interest rate differentials to abate tensions, and to realign the currencies as a last resort. (The latter was implicit rather than explicit in the Basle–Nyborg rules.) This system should be reinforced with a range of consultative mechanisms, such as use of the EU Monetary Committee and the ECOFIN Council, which had mistakenly not been convened in the course of the 1992 crisis. This would allow more pressure to be generated in favour of budgetary consolidation for the weak currencies and cyclical weakening of budgets for stronger currency countries. 'Outside the turbulent periods that [system] is still likely to be entirely adequate.'[7]

The question was how could such a system be strengthened so that it could withstand shocks, however unusual, such as those of 1992–3. The important point was that the answers to this question were both technical and political. Technical mechanisms could be envisaged, such as making interest rate adjustments faster, and finding ways of placing pressures upon governments to do this. In 1995 the British indicated they may have learned this lesson, in that,

[7] Niels Thygesen, 'Towards Monetary Union in Europe—Reforms of the EMS in the Perspective of Monetary Union', *Journal of Common Market Studies*, 31/4 (Dec. 1993), 447–72.

although indicating any interest in returning to the EMS was political suicide for the government, it nevertheless kept the pound ster-
ling stable against other EU currencies, and preserved low inflation,
by frequent interest rate adjustments. A second improvement could
be to make the central banks of all member countries independent
of their governments, a proposal which was supported by two previous chancellors in Britain in May 1995—Lawson and Lamont.[8] A
concomitant was that the maintenance of low inflation rates should
be the primary goal of monetary policy, leaving promoting lower
unemployment, and economic growth, to other instruments. Third,
greater powers could be given to the EU's central monetary institutions, especially the European Monetary Institute (EMI) to counter
the differing inclinations of richer and poorer states towards managing their currencies within the system, including domestic market
operations.

A major problem was of course the uncertainties about what the
implications of monetary integration would be for the area of policy
discretion of the member states of the Union. The dangers of monetary integration for sovereignty were particulary stressed by its ideological opponents. An important background leitmotif should,
however, be born in mind: that for small and medium-sized states
constraints deriving from the international system on monetary policy and other aspects of economic policy were considerable, be they
in or without the Union. It should also be remembered that monetary integration had a context in a process of integration: much
would also depend on how far other areas of economic activity had
been subjected to harmonization.

Two kinds of argument were distinguishable in the mid-1990s
with regard to this issue. The first concerned the implications of
monetary and economic integration for economic sovereignty. It
was clear that in a monetary union certain policies would no longer
be open to the control of national governments. These included the
option of devaluing or revaluing the currency, interest rate policies
related to the management of the monetary system, and monetary
relations with outsiders. The central institutions would also probably have responsibility for pursuing a low inflation strategy. But the
important question then was what policies remained with governments. In the mid-1990s further research needed to be done on this
crucial question. But the reader should beware of swallowing the

[8] BBC, *World at One*, 12 May 1995.

argument of the Eurosceptics that little or no national discretion remained.

At least two major areas could be identified: taxation and government spending. In the late 1990s, in stage three of the monetary union process, the only specific target left over from the convergence criteria which governments were obliged to follow concerned the level of government borrowing. If that exceeded a predetermined ceiling the Council of Ministers could address policy advice to overspending governments. If that was ignored the Council had the right, under the Maastricht Treaty, Article 104, in effect to impose fines on the miscreant. But as long as it stayed below the ceiling of borrowing a government could alter the level of taxation and spending largely according to its own independent judgement.

The implications of this need to be stressed, as this was not a trivial freedom. It enabled governments to spend, or not spend, on a range of support mechanisms for industry, for instance on training programmes, and infrastructure—transport, leisure and educational facilities, and so on. But it also allowed adjustments in company taxation within broad limits, so that industry could be helped or hindered, the job market expanded or depressed, and exports made cheaper or more expensive. These possibilities were, of course, in addition to more obvious, EU sanctioned, forms of assistance to less prosperous areas such as regional or convergence fund assistance. It was apparent that the range of policy alternatives to devaluation or revaluation was much greater than economists had realized or Eurosceptics would have liked the public to believe. And in any case, was it really likely that the Council of Ministers would be capable of imposing a strict borrowing ceiling on an unwilling state?

Second, reference should be made to other examples of monetary union to consider their implications for the sovereignty of the members of the system. One striking example was that of the Republic of Ireland and Britain. For the period when Ireland and Britain were mostly at loggerheads, over Northern Ireland and other questions, the value of the Irish pound was tied at a rate of one for one to the British pound. Any Irish citizen would have been astounded to be told that this meant that his or her country was not sovereign. Luxembourg and Belgium were also traditionally members of a monetary union: they were sovereign.

One problem for economists was that most of their work had focused on the experience of the USA which had a large number of rather modest-sized states: California was the exception. In Canada, however, the provinces were fewer in number and large compared with the whole. Despite the fact that they were in a monetary union, the provinces were capable of exerting considerable influence upon the budget of the federal government. Indeed by altering their level of spending they could virtually nullify the decisions of the centre. The idea that monetary integration necessarily meant subjugation to the centre in all matters of economic policy, and in areas of policy extending beyond that, again looked questionable.

For all the problems evident in the mid-1990s it looked, on balance, as if monetary union would go ahead, though it was likely to be a postponed and less confident dawn than that foreseen at Maastricht. Certainly it could not be ruled out, as academics and practitioners alike groped their way forward to discover a new balance between monetary integration and national sovereignty which was compatible with the European Union of the 1990s (see Chapter Two). The dominance of the extremists in this debate made it harder to uncover the new balance, though its presence was unmistakable. What problems might arise for non-members?

Enlargement and the Problems of Bargaining

The difficulties in British policy illustrated a number of dilemmas that complicated the bargaining process in relations between countries with diverging economies. The alternative to resisting involvement in policies of positive integration, such as monetary union—which was the British choice in the mid-1990s—was to seek forms of compensation in common arrangements, that in the short term largely benefited the richer states, in the form of side-payments. This had occurred in the late 1970s when the European Monetary System (EMS) was first negotiated. The British, Italians, and Irish then sought side-payments in return for accepting the monetary arrangements.[9] These were agreed for the Irish and the Italians, who in consequence joined the EMS at its beginning, but not for the British who did not join until 1987. In the European Union the normal form of such demands was to request resource transfers from the richer states, or a larger share of the money avail-

[9] For a discussion of the diplomacy about monetary integration in the late 1970s see Paul Taylor, *The Limits of European Integration* (London and New York: Croom Helm and Columbia University Press, 1983), ch. 6.

able through the various funds, the Regional Fund, the Social Fund and the Agricultural Restructuring Fund.

A number of complications in the bargaining process were produced by these effects. Pressures on the structural and other support funds were increased, and the richer states were brought closer to their threshold of tolerance on redistribution from the Community budget. Thus, given that the need for the common arrangement was accepted, the bargaining tended to turn into discussion about how to compensate poorer states in areas which were linked with, but not inherently a part of, the issue under negotiation. Greater support from the regional fund was not an inherent aspect of monetary integration, though it might be related to it. Bargaining in this form was inherently more complicated than bargaining within a closely defined and specific area. It involved trade-offs across areas and the links between such areas might be disputed. This was a characteristic of positive integration policies in various contexts. Negotiations about environmental policy showed similar features, with poorer countries demanding payment in order to accept the standards of the richer. The obvious conclusion was that, where there were economic divergencies, bargaining about further integration was likely to be complicated by the perception that the benefits of further integration would be unevenly distributed, and that therefore some form of compensation was necessary. But the chances of failure to agree were therefore increased.

But the British case also illustrated another problem. The ideology of Thatcherism actually precluded the solution of the problem through side-payments, which was acceptable to Labour in the late 1970s. Side-payments tended to imply a larger Budget and, of course, intervention from the centre. In both these areas there was strong British opposition. Growth of the Community budget had to be resisted, as had any form of stronger regional policy as this tended to lead to more power for the Commission—as was all too clear with regard to the experience of regional policy in southern Europe. Expansion to include weaker countries logically required larger central budgets, and a greater preparedness to accept resource transfers to peripheral areas. But precisely the opposite was likely to be the result. Expansion itself weakened the sense of community, which was one of the conditions of a preparedness to accept larger budgets. One key reason for this was that larger budgets had a very strong political as well as an economic dimension. Money to the centre was readily interpreted as power to the centre, and inspired demands for stronger central institutions. This was a perception that lay behind the reluctance of governments to accept increases in the budgets of other international organizations such as the United Nations.

There are rational arguments in favour of, and against, allowing more money to the EU to pay for the support of backward regions, or to the UN to pay for peace-keeping. But lurking in the political subconscious was a deeper prejudice: the fear that money transferred is power transferred, and that, in the coat-tails of money and power, authority transfer might also occur. Objections to allowing bigger budgets to international organizations were often just the superficial expression of a determination to protect the authority of national governments, loosely interpreted as the sovereignty of the state, and to avoid enhancing the other's authority. Such resistance was likely to be stronger when interests were more divergent and the sense of common identity weaker, which was a likely consequences of enlargement. Two contradictory pressures were released: applicant states placed greater demands upon the common budget, but existing contributors became more resistant to any significant budgetary increases. This was not just a question of rational calculation, but a consequence of the changes in the structure of the Union which enlargement implied. In sum, a more diverse community meant a weaker union and a less federal budget: calls on the common budget were likely to be increased faster than the preparedness of the main contributing states to answer them.

It was ironic that theories and ideologies which had helped to move the collapse of communism, and which had been the source of much advice to the successor states of the Soviet Union, were also a rich source of reasons for placing limits upon aid. The poorer states were encouraged to use the context of negotiations to push integration forward, to seek compensation for the relative costs which they would incur, but the prevailing ideology of the time made it less likely that this would be provided. If this was the case, as the British example illustrated, the poorer countries would be likely to become more resistant to further integration. In sum, features of the Union, some of which would be encouraged by enlargement, were likely to make it more difficult for the candidate countries to bargain effectively if admitted to the Union.

At the same time they would be likely to be encouraged to resist integration, where this reduced their ability to manipulate the costs of production to attract foreign direct investment and resist heartland pull. Being in the Community, in making the common market available to all inward investors, would make the poorer countries more, not less, determined to resist any common policies which had this effect. The candidate states were on average poorer than members. Their admission was likely to add to these problems in bargaining.

The Emergence of the European Union as an International Actor: Relations between Members

A cluster of problems with regard to security were also in the way of enlargement to include the states of Eastern Europe. First, there was the old problem of Germany; second, there was the need to develop a distinctive security identity for Europe; and, third, there was the question of the security architecture of Europe and Eurasia. Under each of these headings the arguments were largely in favour of keeping the European Union smaller for the near future: to deepen first and then widen.

As regards the first issue there was no reason to suppose that the problems of French security with regards to Germany would get any less after German unification in 1989 and the demise of the Soviet Union. The increase in the potential power of Germany after unification increased the potential threat to France, and the prospect of a stronger Germany in a looser framework comprising both East and West Europe was likely to rekindle memories of earlier periods, such as the interwar period, and such policies as the Schacht Plan. The point concerned not just the issue of expansion but more specifically the question of expansion to include this particular group of states which had traditionally been a focus of any expansionist or hegemonist German government that happened to come along. French interest was overwhelmingly in favour of further integration as a way of tying Germany to the West and to a regional framework. Indeed proposals for political union after the fall of the iron curtain can be compared with the proposals for ECSC after its creation in the late 1940s: they were both intended to create frameworks in which the French could reasonably expect higher levels of security. And the experience of the European Union had created a preference for tackling the problem, not through the Little Entente style of arrangement, which had proved so ineffective in the interwar period, but through the functionalist techniques of getting close to your friends but even closer to your enemies.

The point need not be laboured that the problem of security with regard to Germany was not just a French problem: any problem for French security in the 1990s was also a problem for the security of other European states. Fortunately the Germans went along with this view, especially as it linked up with their idea that political union was also a necessary precondition of monetary union. A smaller number of more tightly integrated states was more likely to constitute a suitable harness on Germany than a wider looser system. This was a strong argument against enlargement to include an indeterminate number of East European states, with which the government of François Mitterand not surprisingly sympathized.

With regard to the second issue of Europe's security identity the context was of crucial importance. First was the context of the development of the common foreign and security policy (CFSP) which in the Maastricht Treaty had reached the point for the first time of proposing a common defence policy in the foreseeable future, though without much enthusiasm. 'The common foreign and security policy shall include all questions related to the security of the Union, including the eventual framing of a common defence policy, which might in time lead to a common defence.' It had taken over twenty years for the member states to accept an obligation to discuss with each other the range of their various foreign policies and not just the ones which they separately deemed to be of concern to Europe. In the Single European Act (Title 3) for the first time such an obligation was evident, as was an obligation not to pursue policies which could lead to contradictions with agreed common policies. There was evidence of a willingness to put the presentation of the partnership ahead of the short-term pursuit of separate interests. This was not a legally obliging obligation, but the form of words suggested an extension of the level of mutual commitment. Even Mrs Thatcher was sensitive to this. She was entirely opposed to any tightening of the sanctions against South Africa by the European Community, and succeeded in heading off the more ambitious proposals. She boasted about the small scale of the agreed sanctions, but it was striking that she had nevertheless felt obliged to concede these, when she would have preferred to concede nothing.

The nature of the mutual obligation contained in the Maastricht Treaty should be stressed. The member states declared their support for the principle of a common foreign policy in the kind of ringing terms which would have been unthinkable in the early 1970s at the time of the first steps towards the harmonization of foreign policy. This was a movement of sentiment, but it was real nevertheless. Some of its essence is captured in the European response to the request by President Bush to be involved early on in the members' attempts to reach common positions, a request which echoed that of Henry Kissinger in 1973 as part of his efforts to rescue the year of Europe. The response was that this would be acceptable if the Union in exchange could have a seat in the US Senate: what was revealed was the growing sense of the Europeans that when they dealt with each other they were dealing with insiders, and that even a close ally such as the USA was not one of them!

Title V Provisions on a Common Foreign and Security Policy
Article J
A common foreign and security policy is hereby established which shall be governed by the following provisions.

Article J.1

1. The union and its Member States shall define and implement a common foreign and security policy, governed by the provisions of the Title and covering all areas of foreign and security policy.
2. The objectives of the common foreign and security policy shall be:
   - to safeguard the common values, fundamental interests and independence of the Union;
   - to strengthen the security of the Union and its Member States in all ways;
   - to preserve peace and strengthen international security, in accordance with the principles of the United Nations Charter as well as the principles of the Helsinki Final Act and the objectives of the Paris Charter;
   - to promote international cooperation;
   - to develop and consolidate democracy and the rule of law, and respect for human rights and fundamental freedoms.
3. The Union shall pursue these objectives;
   - by establishing systematic cooperation between Member States in the conduct of policy, in accordance with Article J.2;
   - by gradually implementing, in accordance with Article J.3, joint action in the areas in which the Member States have important interests in common.
4. The Member States shall support the Union's external and security policy actively and unreservedly in a spirit of loyalty and mutual

solidarity. They shall refrain from any action which is contrary to the interests of the Union or likely to impair its effectiveness as a cohesive force in international relations. The Council shall ensure that these principles are complied with.

Article J.2

1. Member States shall inform and consult one another within the Council on any matter of foreign and security policy of general interest in order to ensure that their combined influence is exerted as effectively as possible by means of concerted and convergent action.
2. Whenever it deems it necessary, the Council shall define a common position.
   Member States shall ensure that their national policies conform on the common positions.
3. Member States shall coordinate their action in international organizations and at international conferences. They shall uphold the common positions in such fora.
   In international organizations and at international conferences where not all the Member States participate, those which do take part shall uphold the common positions.

There were a number of related further steps. The distinction between the external relations of the economic community, in which, following the Rome Treaty, the Commission had the right to act on behalf of the Community, and the foreign policy mechanisms among the member states—in what was called the EPC framework—was removed. In practical terms this meant that the Commission was now fully involved in consultations about all questions of foreign policy. In the early days it had been excluded from discussions about EPC, reflecting the concern of some states, especially France, to keep Community external relations in areas such as trade distinct from questions of foreign policy—traditionally defined high politics; next it had been accepted as normally taking part, a principle that was acknowledged in the Stuttgart Declaration in 1983 and formally accepted in the Single European Act, agreed in 1985; later, in the Maastricht Treaty, it was given the right to participate.

Article J.9

The Commission shall be fully associated with the work carried out in the common foreign and security policy field.

As further evidence of the full involvement of the Commission it was bracketed with the other institutions with regard to the discharge of a number of responsibilities.

The Presidency shall consult the European Parliament on the main aspects and the basic choices of the common foreign and security policy and shall ensure that the views of the European Parliament are duly taken into consideration. The European Parliament shall be kept regularly informed by the Presidency and the Commission of the development of the Union's foreign and security policy.

It should, however, be noted that the full involvement of the Commission was part of the process of more fully involving all the established institutions of the Community in the making of the Union's foreign policy. The principles of foreign policy actions were to be decided in the meetings of the European Council, and policies agreed in the Council of Foreign Ministers on the basis of unanimity.

This discussion gives some sense of the significance of the decision to change the name of the Union's policy relationships with the outside world in the Maastricht Treaty. The choice of the term Common Foreign and Security Policy is highly suggestive. There was at least now a formal commitment to a foreign policy of the Union, and not the assertion that this was a harmonized, synthetic composite of the foreign policies of the separate states: that might in fact still be the case, but the understanding of what this meant had moved on. The new nomenclature also indicated the full involvement of the Commission, as well as the other institutions, in foreign policy making, each according to its powers. 'Any Member State or the Commission may refer to the Council any question relating to the common foreign policy and may submit proposals to the Council' (Article J.8). The obligation to consult on foreign policy and to avoid the pursuit of policies or interests which could be in opposition to that was also asserted. And finally the firm insistence that defence was not the responsibility of the Union was abandoned: there was still disagreement about precisely how the Union should exercise its responsibilities in this area, but the principle that the Union now had such responsibilities was accepted. This was the measure of the achievement of the Union under the heading of the Common Foreign and Security Policy.

The limits which still applied to the Common Foreign and Security Policy should however be noted. The policy remained after Maastricht overwhelmingly intergovernmental. It was agreed that joint actions could be decided on the basis of majority voting, but the question of which joint actions should be determined in this way was to be decided in each individual case. Furthermore it should be stressed that the obligation to consult partners about all questions of foreign policy was not a legal obligation, but rather a mutual understanding.

There was also an agreement that citizens of the Union should be able to turn to the representations of any member of the union in a third country when they needed assistance, which would seem to be a small step towards common embassies. It was at least an indication of the move towards a common citizenship. But a system of single EU embassies was still a long way down the road, despite the arrangements for coordinating the positions of the EU members in a number of international organizations, like the General Assembly of the United Nations, and in the capitals of a large number of other states, such as Washington, Tokyo, and Beijing. This was a highly complex coordination mechanism, rather than a single instrument for agreeing a common foreign policy.

There was some underpinning of the movement towards a common defence in a range of specific areas of cooperation among the member states. The British and the French agreed a degree of division of labour with regard to the roles of their air forces, and the French and the Germans had set up a joint brigade, and both of these developments were remarkable by the standards of earlier times. And there was significant cooperation in the area of weaponry development and production. A programme for developing a European advanced fighter aircraft had been running for some years. But, as already stated, this was well short of a common defence policy. And in the United Nations Security Council the two member states which had permanent seats, Britain and France, still insisted that they acted as independent members. On matters before the Security Council they would only report upon developments to the other member states in New York, despite the fact that they held regular meetings at least once a week. They would not accept a mandate from the EU and a joint seat was unthinkable.

Without prejudice to Article J.2(3) and Article J.3(4), Member States represented in international organizations or international conferences where not all the Member States participate shall keep the latter informed of any matter of common interest. Member States which are also members of the United Nations Security Council will concert and keep the other Member States fully informed. Member States which are permanent members of the

Security Council will, in the execution of their functions, ensure the defence of the positions and the interests of the union, *without prejudice to their responsibilities under the provisions of the United Nations Charter* (author's emphasis). (Article J.5 (4))

But for a number of reasons, including the long historical evolution of this policy, the European Union seemed set in the mid-1990s upon further developing their arrangements for coordinating their policies towards non-members. Amongst other considerations this was a product of the accumulation of common interests over a very wide range: involvement in Europe had gone along with retreat from unilateral involvement outside Europe. But there was also something larger and less tangible: the emergence of a shared *Weltanschauung*, or philosophy of engagement with the external world, reinforced by a sense of occupying the same strategic space in international society.

Enlargement and the Security Dimension

Second, Europe was pushed to define its own security identity more positively as a consequence of the changes in the structure of international society in the late 1980s and 1990s, which had seen the demise of the Soviet Union, and an acceleration in the pace of withdrawal of US forces from Western Europe, linked with an enhancement of US interests in the Pacific area. It looked as if there were good reasons for the Europeans to take on greater responsibility for their own defence. This coincided with the internal dynamics, which had evolved stronger economic interests, and the creation of pressures to move beyond being a civil power to being a military power: the logic of integration itself suggested that there would come a time when foreign and defence policy would move up the agenda.

Once again the intellectual and philosophical bases of these arrangements had taken a long time to evolve between the existing members of the Union. They were able to cope with the different perspectives of the governments of the states which had joined most recently, the EFTANS, with their tradition of neutrality, but even this was not without some difficulty on both sides. To expand to include a greater variety of perspectives, especially to include states which lacked the common experience and whose goals were very different, was likely to make it more difficult to achieve a common foreign and security policy precisely when the case for it seemed to be getting stronger, and internal dynamics suggested it might be possible. The achievement of the insiders still rested on intergovernmental agreement: enlargement was always at the risk of introducing an outsider with the power to damage the emerging consensus.

The third aspect of this issue was the question of how enlargement would fit with the security architecture of a larger Europe, and indeed with global security. Would including the states of Eastern Europe help or hinder the security of Europe as a whole? This question may be discussed at two levels. Within the region itself there are many reasons for supposing that the answer was negative. Although there was an opening from NATO to the East through the Partnership for Peace, and the North Atlantic Cooperation Council, the Western allies still stopped short in 1995–6 of offering membership to any East European states. There was much talk of this happening, but there was also considerable stress on the need for any Eastern European applicants to satisfy a very wide range of conditions, of a military and political character, *at their own expense*. These ranged from establishing 'interoperability' with NATO forces, and meeting a wide range of NATO equipment and procedural requirements, to accepting the obligations of membership. It had not been decided in early 1996 whether all of these conditions would have to be satisfied before accession. But the burden of such expensive adjustments on the candidate countries, especially with regard to relocation and new logistics, was so great that they looked like a way of discouraging them, or of setting in place an excuse for inaction if called upon to defend the new members. Whether *in* or *out* it was unlikely that they could be met in full by the East European states for a number of years. It was also significant that the East Europeans were to be separately and individually admitted to membership— they were not to be admitted as a group. The West insisted that the first of the new members should agree that they would not pull up the drawbridge behind them, but it was hard to see how such a forlorn promise could be made to stick. It was probable that the process of admission itself, if it took place, would increase rather than reduce disagreements between the Eastern states.

A further set of problems concerned the reaction of Russia. In 1995 the Russians made it clear that they found objectionable the idea that part of Eastern Europe should join the old enemy, and bring the frontiers of NATO close to Russian soil. This was also one reason for Russian hesitation about the use of NATO forces in ex-Yugoslavia; they also disliked having no impact on NATO decision-making. The point was made in the mid-1990s that the Russians found the membership of the East European states in the European Union more acceptable than their membership of NATO. The assumption behind this preference seemed to be that the European Union was unlikely to develop its own security identity; indeed it suggested that the Russians preferred enlargement as a way of preventing that development. This was not necessarily in the interest of the member states of the European Union! There were also considerable uncertainties about the future direction of Russian policy towards the states to their south and east in the mid-1990s: the rule of President Yeltsin was under threat from a number of directions, one of which very much favoured the consolidating of a Russian realm or sphere of influence in the CIS.

The approach by NATO states to Eastern Europe had developed several distinct components by the middle of 1995. One was the so-called Partnership for Peace, which linked the East European states with NATO in a number of commitments, including to consult on security questions, conduct joint manoeuvres and exchange military information, and for the West to provide economic assistance: it was said that this provided all the advantages of NATO membership to Eastern Europe except the security guarantee. The Russians initially expressed doubt about the Partnership but joined on 31 May 1995 when Russian Foreign Minister Andrei Kozyrev signed the agreement. The Russians had their own individual partnership arrangement. In December 1994 a second component was added in the NATO Summit communiqué which stated that NATO enlargement was expected and that it would be welcomed. US President Bill Clinton had stated in January that 'the question is no longer whether NATO will take on new members, but when and how'.[10]

There was to be a series of reports on the issue in the mid-1990s, but membership was to be subject to the negotiation of acceptable conditions in each individual case, and there was no commitment to accept any specific countries. At the heart of the strategy was an agreement on each side to accept the dissembling of the other. It looked as if only two of the four lead candidates from the Visegrad group—Poland and the Czech Republic—were relatively free of external threats or of major internal dissensions, and from the point of view of security had no need of NATO. But two others, Hungary

[10] Quoted in Michael E. Brown, 'The Flawed logic of NATO Expansion', *Survival*, 37/1 (spring 1995), 34.

and Slovakia, had major disputes over schemes on the Danube, and ethnic questions. Such problems, according to the West, had to be settled before accession. The quid pro quo in this bargain of negatives, was that if the security guarantee of Article 5 of the North Atlantic Treaty were to be called upon by the new members, in the near or medium future, it was very doubtful whether help would be forthcoming.

Politicians in Europe and North America were very divided about whether they would risk the lives of their troops to protect the security of states in Eastern Europe. Discussion about various forms of defence concept, beyond providing help to strengthen national forces in the new states, was pie in the sky. How could the main providers of security, namely the USA and the larger Western European states, accept the kind of commitment implied by a multilateral forward defence strategy in the absence of the scale of military threat and ideological dispute of the cold war period? This had been shown conclusively in the case of ex-Yugoslavia. Indeed the point was made that the irony of NATO's involvement in Eastern Europe was that its main concern in mid-1995 was not how to enforce security in ex-Yugoslavia, but how to get the troops of UNPROFOR out if necessary. Nevertheless the Eastern states remained enthusiastic about joining. When given the example of Bosnia as an example of the limits of Western commitment to the area, one Eastern European diplomat allegedly retorted 'where's that?'.[11]

In 1995 the advantages of membership, even on these dire conditions, were still rated highly by Central–East European governments. The contention was that this was the necessary condition for the survival of their new democratic capitalist systems. 'It is a vital US and Western interest that the gains of the end of the Cold War are not squandered and that democracy in East–Central Europe is not allowed to fail or be crushed.'[12] It would attach them to the strategic space dominated by the USA, and would help detach them from the space dominated by Russia. It would also help their case for membership in the European Union, in that it would draw a veil—however transparent—over the continuing security dilemmas.

Support for this strategy in the West derived from a number of sources. German politicians seemed to be divided about the issue.

[11] Interview with an official, summer 1995.
[12] Ronald D. Asmus, Richard L. Kugler, and F. Stephen Larrabee, 'NATO Expansion: The Next Steps', *Survival*, 37/1 (spring 1995), 27–8.

Defence Minister Volker Ruhe appeared to favour enlargement, but linked it with a strategy for increasing cooperation with Russia in a broader all-European context. This was apparently because it would mean that Germany was no longer in the front line in the East–West relationship. It would also help to protect German investments in the neighbouring East European states, and Germany was the leading investor there. Foreign Minister Klaus Kinkel was more cautious, however, warning of the need to go slowly in order to avoid the risk of reviving East–West strategic rivalry. The Clinton administration was the leading advocate: it involved little real commitment of resources or troops in the short term, but helped to extend the 'civil' space of Western Europe eastward, in which, it was thought, contact and interdependencies could gradually be strengthened and security reinforced by changing attitudes and interests. The Republicans in Congress reinforced the incentive to find a low-cost strategy by threatening in May 1995 to further reduce Washington's miserly direct bilateral aid to Russia of $260 million.[13] Some senior British politicians liked it because it would dilute the European Union, and, at the same time, confirm the special relationship with the USA. The only Western state that showed consistent opposition was France, which disliked what appeared to be a way of enhancing German power, and of weakening the restraints on that power deriving from a deepened European Union, without any real benefits in terms of enhanced East–West security.[14]

The policy was indeed incompatible with any reasonable concept of European security architecture. It had the effect of increasing the fears in Russia of threats or pressures from NATO, which could only help the cause of extreme right-wing politicians, such as Zirinovsky, and the arguments of those who favoured more vigorous and nationalist Russian policies towards the 'near abroad' and the states which had evolved from the Soviet Union. It made it more difficult for the Ukraine to maintain its declared policy of neutrality: it would be under increased pressure to choose between returning to dependence on Russia, or accepting a hollow guarantee from NATO—this when Russian intransigence in their mutual relations was increasing.

Much of the discussion about enlargement in the mid-1990s was about ways of doing it rather than the principle. The assumption was smuggled in that the enemy was Russia, and that therefore some-

[13] The *Independent*, Fri. 12 May 1995.
[14] See Paul J. J. Welfens, 'The EU and Eastern-Central European Countries: Problems and Options of Integration', *Aussenpolitik*, 46/3 (1995), 232–41.

thing had to be done about Central Eastern Europe. But the logic should have been reversed: it made more sense to say that something should be done about Russia in order to put right the problems of central Europe. This could involve providing all the wide range of consultations in NATO and other security forums which Russia could expect, together with every conceivable form of economic assistance and trade liberalization. If the democratic capitalist system succeeded in Russia, then the situation for Central Europe would be completely changed. They would not be caught between two competing camps, entrapped in the rigid constraints of the cold war, but prospering between two supportive partners, the mutual relations of which would be characterized by a low-key conventional balance. This strategy should not exclude planning in the West about what to do if Russia became intransigent. Enlargement should be kept in reserve as a possible response to a new Russian adventurism.

Continuing with the enlargement strategy was likely to increase rather than diminish its undesirable effects. Russia would feel more threatened and the West would be more enfeebled. Once a start was made the difficulty was that of knowing where to draw the line. If the Visegrad countries were admitted why not the next set, say the Baltic states? And what beyond them? There was always a case for the next step for the sake of guaranteeing democracy and capitalism, and chasing the security dilemma it was creating by increasing instabilities further east: it was dangerous to place these arguments ahead of those concerning the best way of providing for the long-term security of the continent as a whole. Other ways for providing for political and economic support for the new states had to be sought, which did not form part of a process of enfeeblement.

There was little or no evidence to support the view that placing the new states of Eastern Europe in NATO or the EU would be essential to consolidate their new democratic systems. Particular political groups or classes might claim that was the case, but where was the evidence? The traditional argument was that democratic forms arose from internal developments, such as the emergence of a general commitment to the values of an open system, which could only arise over a long period of time. Those values were likely to be unique to that community, and could not simply be imported from outside. This was the ancient argument of theorists such as J. S. Mill. A frequent assertion in the discussion about enlargement was that the states of Central Eastern Europe were part of the Western

European experience, and that therefore they belonged culturally with the West. This was clearly not true for a number of the Eastern European states, including the Visegrad countries. That they were Eastern and not Western European states had significant cultural connotations, which were happily glossed over by the proponents of enlargement. In the traditional arguments the only role of external arrangements was to prevent intervention, in the form of military intervention by foreigners or serious economic disturbance with external origins. In the mid-1990s external military interventions for the candidate states looked unlikely, which left the leading capitalist states with an obligation to ensure that the economies of the new states succeeded. This did not require membership in NATO or the EU. Indeed enlargement was either irrelevant to the success or failure of the democracies, or it was likely to attract interventions which would get in its way.

Another aspect of this argument was the assertion that NATO should be expanded to 'avoid nationalist authoritarian regimes . . . caught in a strategic vacuum between East and West'.[15] This was the obverse of the argument about sustaining democratic forms. There were two objections. First, presumably the difference was made by providing economic and other forms of help, and by involving Eastern governments in a wide range of discussion forums. These could be provided outside NATO, or in special arrangements with the EU, and required, not membership, but political will on the part of the providers. Equally puzzling was the question of how a strategic vacuum encouraged authoritarianism. And why was *not* being in NATO *ipso facto* to be in a strategic vacuum? The answers to these questions were not self-evident, and it was ironic that the conditions for joining NATO would impose such large economic burdens upon the candidate states as to increase rather than reduce the dangers of serious social unrest. Second, why was it necessary to include the Central Eastern European states in order to avoid these horrors, but possible to exclude Russia without necessarily promoting them? Surely in both cases mechanisms for involvement and support transcended the formal structures!

The major problem was that precisely when there was an overwhelming need for clarity of purpose and firmness of commitment, in view of the dangers of European chaos, the Western states were uncertain, divided, and irresolute. The NATO enlargement plans of

---

[15] Asmus *et al.*, 'NATO Expansion', 7–33.

the mid-1990s were a part of the problem in that they would produce a larger, more inchoate group of states, less united in purpose, and more likely to be seen as threatening by key non-members such as Russia; drawing a firm line around a smaller Western European economic, political, and economic space would be a part of the solution, in that it would be more likely to contain states which could agree on an effective response to new dangers, working where necessary with the United Nations and the Organization for Security and Cooperation in Europe (OSCE). In the discussions about NATO expansion there was very little about how enlargement would alter the mechanisms of the organization, and the assumption seemed to be that this was the same organization dealing with new problems. In fact expansion meant that the organization itself would change, and decisions would have to be made in different ways, by more states, with different experiences and preferences. This would in fact be a different organization with the same problems. It was preferable for NATO not to expand at all towards Eastern Europe, and to further develop a European Union in which there was institutional effectiveness, reasonable guarantees of security, and an adequate platform for harmonized foreign policy. There was of course a pressing need for clearer policies towards the East to be agreed to contain measures of effective support, and contingency plans for effective action by NATO and the EU, and power projection to underpin defence. 'The Alliance will not need to respond militarily unless a new Russian threat emerges . . . However, even if this happens, Russia is unlikely to regain its military balance for several years. This will provide time to prepare.'[16] In the meantime it would seem more sensible to do everything possible to help Russia to reject a new military build-up, rather than inadvertently encouraging this. This is the argument of the *strategic response* strategy described by Asmus *et al.*, and adopted by Brown.[17]

Enlargement and Global Security Architecture

The development of a low-key balance of power between East and West Europe, with an unattached buffer zone between the two

[16] Brown, 'The Flawed Logic of NATO Expansion', 32.

[17] See Asmus *et al.*, 'NATO Expansion'; and Brown, 'The Flawed logic of NATO Expansion', 34–52.

poles, was a corresponding image of greater European security architecture, which could be a better combination of what was desirable, what was possible, and what was likely. One of the reasons for hesitating about incorporating some of the Eastern European states into the European Union at this stage was the security problems which beset that area, especially concerning the many minority groups which were asserting their rights in various ways, and the irredentist claims of states such as Hungary which had lost around two-thirds of its territory in the Treaty of Trianon of 1920 to Austria, Czechoslovakia, Romania, and Yugoslavia. What advantage could be gained for the European Union by internalizing the violent conflicts which could arise?

Would it not be preferable to work towards greater effectiveness in dealing with such questions through the United Nations, a goal surely better served by a greater degree of cohesion between a smaller number of states in a more integrated European Union? The experience of ex-Yugoslavia was that the EU could not act effectively there even with twelve members, and that when there was a move towards a more active military involvement it was the United Nations which had to have the lead. The arguments in favour of seeking a more effective United Nations were strong, and this would be helped by constructing a more united EU which could act as a key member, rather than a large and more fragmented EU, which contained serious conflicts within itself, and which was less capable of working effectively with the United Nations.

The point might also be made that the larger framework for security maintenance in Eurasia in the mid-1990s was the OSCE, so far a rather rudimentary and ineffectual organization, but certainly worth enhancing. A more tightly organized EU could be more effective within this organization. It was also more likely to be an acceptable partner in the eyes of the Russian Federation if it did not appear to be trespassing into the latter's sphere. It could play a part in implementing the terms of chapter 8 of the Charter, more strictly defined, acting under UN authority, with the participation of the EU, and, under certain conditions, of NATO: the OSCE could properly be empowered under the terms of chapter 8 to ask NATO to act on its behalf within its territory.

A further reason for preferring a smaller EU was therefore that it could play a more effective role in maintaining the security of greater Europe, and also in the United Nations in global security arrangements. There was no reason why the EU should not contribute as much as the USA to the UN, and as the threat to US involvement in the United Nations increased with the return of the Republicans, there was a very good case for enhancing rather than diminishing the EU's capacity for doing this. In 1995 the Republicans in Congress were threatening to reduce the total contribution of the USA to the funding of peace-keeping operations (down to 25% of their costs as compared with the existing 33%), and to insist on the repayment of any US contributions above the assessed sums. As a pillar of global security the EU was better smaller than bigger, if, as appeared probable, smaller was more likely to be deeper, and less burdened by the costs associated with admitting the poorer East European states.

But at the end of the day another argument was decisive: how could a group of states which many EU members would prefer not to admit as full members to their defence organizations, especially NATO, be admitted to their primary economic, social, and political framework? The Europeans had accepted the idea, but very much under US pressure and, with the exception of the British, hoping it would not happen. To consider doing so was to deal carelessly with the achievements of the European Union. Indeed the fact that the USA could lead them in this way if anything reinforced the reasons for opposing enlargement. Its members had gradually accumulated common economic, social, and political interests and on this basis they had been brought painfully to accept a basic Union and a CFSP. But many of the East Europeans, and other candidates for admission, would, for reasons which were connected both with their internal and external circumstances, have great difficulty in adhering to a CFSP and they could not begin to understand the implications of membership of the Union for their new-found statehood. The East European states were in the mid-1990s more divided from each other and more profoundly different from the Union, than had been the EFTANS, or the Iberians, or the British, Danes, and Irish, when they joined. Precisely when the level of unity between the members had risen to a level at which some of them began to hesitate, these were the states whose entry they were invited to consider. They were the opposite of the British, about whom it was said before accession that they did more damage to the European Community from outside than they would within. Theirs was a logic of diversity which for the time being was better kept beyond the pale.

In the mid to late 1990s it was simply too soon to take on a good number of the states which had previously been linked with the Soviet Union. They had only recently adopted democracy, and time was needed to consolidate the new form of government with all the help the West could give. Maastricht implied the necessity for this as a condition of accession, and the European Parliament would be likely to insist upon evidence that democratic forms in Eastern Europe were secure. Not only communism, but also clerical fascism were still too close—notice the Catholic church's rapid enforcement of strict anti-abortion laws in Poland! They also needed to adjust their rules about trade and internal economic arrangements to EU practice, just as the EFTANS did before accession, as well as reach a settlement with their neighbours further east.

But they also needed time to develop the kind of global outlook, a philosophy about the world, which would suit them to membership. There was not enough evidence to suggest they could accept the sharing of management functions of important areas of national life with partners, which had become, after a long period of learning, one of the features of the European Union. They naturally showed a concern with increasing their autonomy, having after all only recently broken away from the Soviet Union. Why should they show integrative tendencies with regard to the states of Western Europe? On the whole the evidence suggested that their attitude, no doubt after an initial enthusiasm, would be a deadweight upon the integration process. In view of this their admittance in the 1990s would be premature. It was not excluded for ever, but Europe needed more time to evolve a final form for itself, and the Eastern states needed time to learn about being states in a cooperative world, and to adjust to the requirements of membership. If they joined prematurely each side could damage the other. There were, of course, some in Western Europe who would rather like that!

Enlargement and Effective Management in the EU

In the mid-1990s there was another set of arguments in favour of deepening within a smaller number of states rather than widening at the risk of deepening. This was essentially that more intense and protected arrangements within regions could provide a defence against uncontrollable movements in the global economy, which was increasingly dominated by international corporations. It was increasingly difficult for individual states to achieve social goals within their frontiers, such as the maintenance of full employment, and this could lead to political and social turmoil. Evidence of higher unemployment and economic problems in Germany, the strongest economy in the EU, in the mid-1990s, illustrated these difficulties, and suggested a bleak future. It was becoming increasingly clear that the uncontrollable economic forces were damaging societies within the developed states, as well as the developing world.

Globalism was not quite the cornucopia which had been expected. A richer transnational élite was becoming detached from confined, less successful—even impoverished—populations that were trapped within local territories. And this kind of social system was likely to provoke mounting local dissatisfaction, and at its worst, was likely to lead to civil disturbance. Some of the Latin American states already showed clear evidence of this: a semi-detached, international élite, sustained by a network of global corporations, facing a confined amd complaining population at home. An open global system, with free trade and a liberal global monetary system, may bring a net increment in the global national product. But it may also bring severe social costs for individual states. Increasing regional differentiation and autonomy offered the best alternative: the prospect of restoring more control of the system to member states, acting together. A deepened EU would be strong enough to impose penalties upon corporations which refused to compromise, by, for instance, market exclusion, or by resisting direct investment. The reactions of multinational companies from the Far East to the prospect of a more exclusive Europe illustrated the possibilities. Overall control of the system by states would be strengthened, and, more importantly, states would find it easier to fulfil social purposes which they still had an urge to follow.

Hitherto EU governments have found it difficult to control their economies, despite increasing regional integration. This was partly for political reasons—they could not agree about how to respond to the international pressures—but it was also partly because of structural difficulties. Each member remained in the 1990s significantly linked with the economy outside, so that the EU as a whole had a much lower level of internal trade between its members than had the individual states in the US with each other. Managing a slice of the global economy within the EU, when the rest was unmanageable, was a difficult task. But with increasing economic interdependence with other states, involving higher levels of mutual trade, this difficulty was likely to decline. Control would be stronger in a deeper but smaller Europe and more difficult in a wider, looser one.

The difficulty may be illuminated by the theory of interdependence. In one way the theory was a form of benign liberalism, finding positive qualities in closer links between the administrations of national states. Such links broke down exclusive forms of national control, and produced greater benefits for individuals in a more open system. Exclusive or national interests in economic terms were perceived as relatively costly compared with international interests, and this was of course an argument in favour of free trade. These arguments had prevailed even though the principles of the GATT had been compromised in various ways in the 1960s and 1970s, and despite the evidence that countries with developing economies had been granted exceptions and opt-outs, rather like those demanded by the poorer members of the EU.

But experience suggested that, even though a free trade system remained the goal, there was going to be tension between the right-wing ideologues, who demanded that all barriers in the way of free trade be removed immediately, and those who reasoned that some exceptions in favour of the developing economies were to be accepted. Some forms of exclusivity seemed to be of value, despite the widespread assumption that greater openness and more liberal arrangements were better. But the problem was to decide how much exclusivity was necessary, and whether departures from liberal openness were permanent or merely expedient. There was no way in economic theory of establishing that either of these views was preferable: it all came down to political, and, indeed, social preferences.

But there was also a pernicious aspect to this mode of argument. Promoting more liberal arrangements implied taking away from the nation state, and challenging the idea of national interest. There was less concern with the evolution of new management centres which in the long term were necessary if chaos was to be avoided. There was ample discussion of what happened within regimes, and between them and other regimes when trade-offs were necessary, but little or nothing was added about the overall overarching methods of governance of such global systems. The behaviour of governments was subject to increasing constraints, and new habits were being formed in particular sectors of activity. But where was the method for coordinating such injunctions so that they served some agreed social purpose? The states seemed to be losing their ability to do this in the face of globalization which involved multiple uncoordinated areas of cooperation, but no alternative was postulated.

A regional organization such as the European Union was likely to be more effective at coordinating sectors of economic, social, and technical activity, so that an overall social purpose was served, than either the separate states or the global system. In the 1990s trade interdependence between members continued to increase, but was still only on average around 60 per cent of the external trade of each state. To this extent the European Union was a part of the international economic system, and because of this it followed that the tendency to concentrate control of crucial functions at the regional level in Brussels was in the face of, rather than because of, the global trends. But there was indeed a trend towards greater trade interdependence, and a very wide range of other forms of interdependence, and this would strengthen the case for more powers for the EU.

An increase in external differentiation, by, for instance, increasing internal trade interdependence, and an increase in internal consolidation, by, for instance, greater regional monetary control, would be likely to enhance the capacity of the regional authorities to follow a wider range of socially beneficial policies internally. There could be short-term economic costs from this, but there would be gains in terms of social stability and safeguarding democracy, and there could be long-term economic benefits. If national parliaments were losing control because of European level interdependencies, so the European institutions, even if they obtained appropriate powers, would lose out if the transnationalization of economies beyond the Union continued. The regional authorities emerged in part because the states were too small to sustain and control their separate economies. Globalization was likely to enfeeble regional authorities in turn, unless they asserted greater control over the constituent units.

These arguments are relevant to the question of the size of the European Union and its enlargement. Increasing size is more likely to create a system which is more difficult to enclose. The whole argument has suggested that enlargement leads back towards a looser form of international society. What is needed is a group of relatively homogeneous units which can accept a higher level of common management, and which do not involve the drains of incompatible or divergent economies.

There were reasons for strengthening regional arrangements which were concerned with internal circumstances, especially a wish for more economic and social welfare than was likely to be produced by global corporations. But there were also reasons for doing this which concerned relationships between the region and international society: the better management of trade arrangements at the global level, so that inter-regional arrangements would remain liberal and protectionism and special trade deals—the new mercantilism—resisted. The argument here depends on the greater weight of the regional economies: a smaller number of larger negotiators would be more likely to agree together about mutually advantageous arrangements, without free riders.

The history of the European Union suggested that as the scope of integration increased so did the tendency to increase membership. The three stages of expansion, in 1973, in 1981, and 1986, all suggested that governments sought to join because they thought that members were completing the phase of negative integration—removing barriers on exchanges between them—and going beyond that to positive integration, namely the setting in place of new common arrangements. In all cases the evidence about political commitment to unification in the states seeking membership was ambiguous. There was little enthusiasm for joining a political union, though there was an anxiety not to be marginalized either economically or politically. On the other hand had the scope of integration remained at a low level there was little evidence to suggest that the British and the others would have been much bothered about joining or that the EFTANS, and others, would have been so anxious to join. So it seemed probable that increasing scope amongst the core of original members set up pressures towards expansion.

The question arises, however, of when that expansion might be expected to stop. The general answer to this question must be that this happens when in the judgement of members the costs of further expansion are seen as being likely to exceed the benefits of not doing so. On the one hand the costs in terms of drains upon the resources of the regional organizations are likely to increase with expansion, because the core states are likely to be richer than later applicants, and because the latter are likely to seek the help of the former with their economic development.

Founding members—core states—have in practice been richer than later candidates for admission but according to Karl Deutsch this is also probable for theoretical reasons.[18] On the other hand the case for further enlargement, from the point of view of existing members, in order to enhance economic security—to provide for

[18] Karl W. Deutsch, et al., Political Community and the North Atlantic Area (Princeton: Princeton University Press, 1957).

economic defensive needs, which were discussed earlier—is likely to become weaker as size increases. These are some of the reasons for resisting further expansion beyond an optimum point; in Europe by the early 1990s a tension had appeared between pressures towards the admission of new members because of what had been achieved within—and what was missing without—and the counter-argument that this might damage that achievement. It was striking that in an earlier period of modest regional achievement, when enlargement would have been less damaging to the achievement, there was less interest in joining and greater stress on the benefits of staying outside; but that with a greater achievement, when enlargement would be more damaging, the wish to join by contiguous states was universal. It was also striking that the advantages of further enlargement tended to be stressed by those member states which were least impressed by the internal achievement, such as the British.

The net increment in the effectiveness of economic defence for existing members is likely to become smaller as size is increased until a point is reached at which costs incurred outweigh any further benefits. An argument in favour of equalizing upwards would be that it reduced vulnerability: the ideal would be to increase in size to the point at which the mutual sensitivity of regions was balanced.[19] It is not denied that other considerations may get in the way of this process in the short and medium term. But rational behaviour on the part of states should be based on the calculation that there was an optimum size which could be exceeded, and that beyond that size the ability to govern was diminished, so that the social purpose of coordinating different sectors of activity effectively could no longer be combined with minimizing vulnerability and optimizing sensitivity to external disturbances. It could not, therefore, be reasonable to continue to expand the EU without any view about a maximum size: expanding beyond the present number could be beyond the optimum.

Another argument for stronger regions was that the superpower condominium of the cold war had gone, and despite involvement in the Gulf War and ex-Yugoslavia, the USA was less willing to intervene militarily outside its own area, and more supportive of the playing of a greater role by other states in their zones of influence. The experience of the European Union suggested that the emergence of

---

[19] The terms *vulnerability* and *sensitivity* are used here in the special sense developed by Robert O. Keohane and Joseph S. Nye in their *Power and Interdependence* (Boston: Little, Brown, 1977).

the region changed the dynamics of the alliance of which it was a member. It used to make sense to say that Europe was part of an American sphere of influence, but by the 1970s that was no longer the case. This was because economic interests and military strategic interests were on a continuum: as governments acquired a wider range of common economic interests it was likely that incentives towards creating a common defence would also increase. Hence after the 1970s the idea that the members of the European Union should strengthen their common defensive arrangements was more frequently proposed and discussed than had earlier been the case,[20] and in the Maastricht agreement the possibility of building a common defence in the future was spelled out for the first time in a Community document. One idea which had become current in the mid-1980s, and which was incorporated in 1991 in the Maastricht Treaty, was that the West European Union should be reactivated—thus ensuring a link with NATO—but there were other proposals for giving the Community itself a more independent defence capacity, so that it would become a military power rather than being merely a civil one. This again was a logical outcome of the expansion of the scope of integration; it was likely that any region would be more liable to seek a stronger common defence as its range of common economic interests expanded.

In the major alliance of the developed world, NATO, the dominant power, the USA, began in the 1980s to push much more vigorously the idea that the junior partners, the Europeans, should, given their greater economic prosperity, contribute more to their own defence within the alliance. There should be a more equitable burden-sharing.[21] At one and the same time, therefore, there appeared at this particular stage in the development of regional integration in Western Europe incentives from within and from without to emerge as a regional military power. Of course the US Government and some commentators had seen such a prospect as not damaging the NATO alliance but rather as a way of getting the Europeans to play a more active role within it. It was, however, difficult to see how

[20] Hedley Bull, 'Civilian Power Europe: A Contradiction in Terms?' in Loukas Tsoukalis, *The European Community: Past, Present and Future* (Oxford: Basil Blackwell, 1983), 149–64; Bernard Burrows and Geoffrey Edwards, *The Defence of Western Europe* (London: Butterworth, 1982).

[21] David Calleo, *Beyond American Hegemony: The Future of the Western Alliance* (Brighton: Wheatsheaf, 1987); and Andrew J. Pierre (ed.), *A Widening Atlantic? Domestic Change and Foreign Policy* (New York: Council on Foreign Relations, 1986).

encouraging Europeans to pay more to the defence budget would do any such thing: they would be more likely to be encouraged to consolidate their own distinctive arrangements and pursue more actively their own distinctive interests. There was a greater tendency towards bifurcation in NATO and the idea of an American sphere of influence extending over the Atlantic looked distinctly less credible by the mid-1990s.

The reasons for being very careful about the further expansion of the European Union have now been considered. They included arguments concerning the adjustment of the institutions and established ways of working, to cope with enlargement; the economic problems that could arise; the problems concerning defence arrangements and the relationship between defence and economic cooperation; and arguments about the best relatationship between the European Union and the international economic and strategic systems. These points are discussed further in the concluding chapter, but the conclusion is obvious: enlargement should not be undertaken lightly, and though not excluded for all time, is full of dangers for the short and medium term. The costs of enlargement greatly exceed the benefits.

4

NATIONAL IDENTITY AND PARTICIPATION IN THE EUROPEAN UNION

THE theme of this chapter is the way in which European integration has affected the identity of people in the member states of the European Union, and the manner of their involvement in the arrangements of that organization. What happened to that sense of identity in the time between the establishment of the Community in the late 1950s and the mid-1990s? The founding fathers certainly had the intention of establishing what was called in the preamble to the Treaty of Rome an 'ever closer union of peoples'. And the institutions of the European Community were designed to reflect that particular goal (see Chapter 1 above). This is one of those quixotic exercises which the student of the Community has to undertake: it is necessary to assess the balance of national and European identity because, to be viable, the European Union, like any polity, has to be solidly rooted in popular attitudes. The point should be stressed: the only real test of the success of the European Union, as with any other system of government, is that it has attracted the support in some sense of the people. The Eurosceptics in Britain claimed that this was not the case. Their argument needs to be examined.

As already pointed out, at the core of the Community's decision-making system were two major institutions, one being the Commission, which was headed by people appointed by the member governments, but which was intended to reflect not just the common interest of the member states of the Communities, but also that of the peoples; and second, the Council of Ministers, which was made up of Government representatives. It was in the Commission that the European interest was to be identified: it was the supranational institution of the European Community, and was to be a major source of pressure towards the formulation of an 'ever-closer union of peoples'.

It was expected that the interests of the Community, expressed through the Commission, would slowly impinge upon, and increasingly dominate, the separate interests of the states, and that this would drive the creation of a sense of common European identity. At the beginning of the integration process—taking that as starting in the mid-1950s—a condition would be found which had existed in Western Europe, certainly for two centuries and possibly for much longer, and the design and method of work of the institutions in a sense represented that condition. It was summed up in one of the great insights about Western European identity penned by Montesquieu in the eighteenth century: that it contained an inner dialectic, 'unity in diversity', or 'diversity in unity'. In the mid-1990s this was still the essential condition of European attitudes, though, as will be shown, the balance between the two elements had changed.

On the unity side were a number of transcendent elements in the attitudes and values found in the various member states. Though there were numerous variations, certain principles were both key and common, in that they generally formed the starting-point of thinking about society and recurred in various national contexts. These could often be traced to the inheritance of the Renaissance, and the experience of the industrial revolution, which led to a preference for rationalism as a mode of thinking, a tendency to draw a line between the religious and the secular aspects of society and to reject too close an involvement on the part of the church in civilian arrangements.[1] We can add to the list a concern with parliamentary institutions, and, in more recent years, a belief in a rather special mixture of capitalism and socialism. This contributed to the evolution of the welfare state in Western Europe in a form which leaned more towards socialism than in the USA, but not as far as in the states further east before their emergence from the Soviet Union.

Despite the move to the right in most member states in the 1980s the welfare states survived in their major principles. Even the most conservative of governments hesitated to abandon its responsibility for the general welfare: no government could have survived the public wrath which would have followed its abandonment of ultimate responsibility for the welfare of its citizens, despite the wishes of

[1] See Anthony D. Smith, 'National Identity and "Europe" ', *International Affairs*, 68/1 (Jan. 1992).

some right-radical politicians and intellectuals. In Britain, despite the wishes of anti-welfare politicians, such as Michael Portillo, spending on welfare went up rather than down under the Conservative government in power since 1979. This was, however, mainly because of the increase in the level of support for unemployment: even the right in Britain could not bring itself to abandon that. The list of unifying factors could be much extended but enough has been said to make the point.

On the other side, however, were the elements of separateness. Each of the member nations had its own separate myths, its own sense of identity, and each of the nations tended to make very clear distinctions between itself and the other nations in Western Europe. There were symbols, ceremonies, and special histories that were unique to each. There was also a particular view about the kinds of things that should be done within the nation in order to ensure national autonomy. The range of these national tasks was very much a product of its time, and if they could be precisely counted, it would be found that the range was wider in the 1950s than it was in the 1990s. It would also be found in the 1990s that the range was wider in the newly independent states of Eastern Europe than among the member states of the European Union. This point will be considered further below.

How did the experience of the European Community affect this pattern of unity in diversity? There were developments which reflected the gradual strengthening of the web of unity, and which could also further promote it, such as the introduction of a European passport or the gradual extension of the use of the European flag and logo. These were icons which indicated a stronger sense of being European, of belonging to an in-group, and sharpened the perception of differences between Europeans and outsiders. Some of these influences were subtle: the appearance of the common market encouraged the wider distribution of food stuffs which had previously been local, confined very often to the Mediterranean countries. Green peppers and wine were no longer unusual in the shops of North Wales, where they had been less widely available in the 1950s. A process of increasing awareness of, and interest in, the cuisines of other countries was certainly further encouraged by the 1992 process. The Market also encouraged the retailers of particular countries to set themselves up in other member states, such as Marks and Spencer in Paris, which in the mid-1990s astounded everyone by successfully selling a range of British food products to the French. In clothing and personal style, too, there was a certain convergence among Europeans, particularly among those born since the Second World War. It became easier to confuse British, German, and French, Italian, and other EU youth; and although they had in common the influence of American fashion, it was striking that Americans increasingly looked different from the Europeans—even the British.

From time to time the European Community made conscious efforts to encourage the appearance of a sense of common identity among its populations. In the first years of its operation, perhaps going up until the mid-1960s—the time of the crisis generated by Charles de Gaulle (see Chapter 1)—there was some evidence of the belief that it would be possible to move the sense of European identity in the direction of a single nation. Among the enthusiasts for integration there was a more conscious focusing on nation-building. Many of those who studied the formation of popular attitudes in Europe had also been interested in the prospects for creating nations in newly independent states in Africa and other parts of the world.[2] The irony was that a concern with the difficulties of nation-building in new states was sometimes associated with higher expectations about what could happen to national identity in Europe. Disappointment about what was happening in Africa led to lower expectations about what was possible in Europe.

Concern with encouraging a sense of common identity, both as a measure of integration in itself, and as a way of underpinning the work of the institutions, was evident from early on. The Commission followed until the late 1960s a policy in its dealings with interest groups of preferring discussions with the European-level federations.[3] This was to promote the convergence of national institutions, interests, and attitudes, and the development of supranational non-governmental organizations. The Commission also supported a research organization—Eurobarometer—which examined the changes in public opinion, particularly with regard to identity, on a half-yearly basis: indeed the citizens of Europe were to become the world's most intensely questioned public.

[2] See Amitai Etzioni, *Political Unification: A Comparative Study of Leaders and Forces* (New York: Holt, Rinehart, and Winston, 1965); and Karl Deutsch and William J. Foltz (eds.), *Nation Building* (New York: Atherton Press, 1963).

[3] See Dusan Sidjanski, 'Pressure Groups and the European Economic Community', in Michael Hodges (ed.), *European Integration* (Harmondsworth: Penguin Books, 1972), 401–20.

There were occasions when the attempt was made to promote the human face of Europe and its development into a great society. These were in the early 1970s, and later, at Fontainebleau in June 1984: the member states, at the invitation of the French, agreed to set up the Adoninno Committee on a People's Europe to examine ways of making the visible symbols of Europe more varied and more attractive, with the intention of enhancing public attachment to the Union. There was evidence of movement in that direction, which is examined in more detail below, although the public relations exercises must be seen as being only one of the considerations which explain it. Even in Britain, which had been particularly cautious over the years in its approach to the Community, the people had begun to acquire a sense that Britain was in the Community, belonged there, and would probably stay. This was reflected in an increasing impatience with the party of power, the Conservatives, in its carping and negative view of the Community, as was revealed in both the 1989 and 1994 elections to the European Parliament in Britain. In 1994 the Conservatives adopted rather negative policies towards the EU and this was one of the explanations of their loss of a large number of EP constituencies. This was not to suggest that the European Union was without its critics in the UK, but rather that, though there was tactical opposition, there had emerged a measure of strategic support. It was not opposing EU proposals on specific issues to which the British public objected, but rather the tendency to treat any proposal emanating from Brussels as anathema.

The British government realized this, of course, but was faced with a difficult choice between the need to placate the anti-European zealots in its own party, and the need not to alienate the public by being overtly over anti-European. In the mid-1990s British Prime Minister Major was desperately trying to find a style of tactical opposition to the Union, which would be interpreted by the anti-Europeans as profound anti-Europeanism, and by the pro-European electorate as being constructive criticism, whilst at the same time trying to retain his reputation as a man of principle. This difficult trick explained the hopelessly confused signals sent out at the time of the British Presidency in 1993: impressive and expensive logos and other public relations devices, which conveyed a positive image for the Union, whilst in practice remaining obdurate and negative on a number of policies which were supported by the continental partners.

But these dilemmas existed for the British because there had been a long-term reconciliation with Europe on the part of the public, for all the attempts of the anti-Europeans, including much of the British press, to talk up Europhobia. The real doubts and hesitations which arose at the time of Maastricht, and which were revealed in the anti-Maastricht vote in Denmark, and the narrow approval in France, were blips in the progress of pro-European sentiment, qualified though it was, as is shown below. Indeed it was a tribute to the strength of pro-European feeling that the difficulties over ratifying Maastricht were not greater than they were. In France, for instance, President Mitterand approached the referendum with the hope that in supporting it he would be able to capitalize upon the strength of pro-Europeanism in France to garner support for his Socialist Party in the forthcoming election and for his own candidature for re-election as French President. In the event it worked the other way round: the unpopularity of the Socialist government, and an increasing distrust of the President, led French citizens to vote against Maastricht. Given all the reasons which may be adduced from internal political and economic circumstances for the French to vote against the government, and, as a consequence, against ratification, the small majority in favour was a measure of the astonishing strength of pro-Europeanism in France. In Denmark, of course, ratification was extremely uncertain: even there, however, the favourable outcome of the second referendum marked a public realization that a semi-detached relationship with the Union was unthinkable. With all its demerits it was the only place to be.

But it should not be supposed that throughout the Union there was a uniform strengthening of the sense of common identity. There were various degrees and kinds of support. National symbols remained of overwhelming importance in all the member states, and particular symbols had no equivalent in other states. The French had no Armistice Day; the British had no equivalent of 14 July, because the British state was not born in the manner of the French. Examples of such symbols can be multiplied. And in the newer states, the pattern of support was different from that among the core. In Ireland support for membership was strong, but this turned out to be support for a system which provided 6 per cent of GNP through subventions and grants from the EU—the highest rate of per capita financial support in all the member states:[4] it did not translate into support for supranationalism and more powers for the central institutions. The highest level of support for greater powers for the

---

[4] See data in Paul Taylor, *The Limits of European Integration* (London and New York: Croom Helm and Columbia University Press, 1983), esp. 182–5.

Brussels institutions was to be found among the original six member states. The Community regime had been consolidated in their national systems to a much greater extent than in the newer members. One measure of this was that the question of membership had not been an issue in national elections since 1965: it then figured in the presidential election in France in December 1965, when de Gaulle had defeated the more pro-European candidate, Francois Mitterand in the second ballot.

In the preceding discussion it was assumed that the development of a stronger sense of European identity was in some sense a linear process. Indeed this assumption was often made in writings about the development of forms of identification such as nationalism: that their development was a matter of the weakening of one set of loyalties and their being overtaken by another. But it is necessary to add further dimensions, if a picture is to emerge which avoids this oversimplification, in that it is not constrained by a hidden assumption: that the end-situation was a new and larger nation state.

How do we look at identity without in some sense fixing the argument to suit this outcome? The answer is to identify distinct facets of the nation state, in the sense of the way in which the nation state is supported by public attitudes. What emerges is accounts of changes in identity along three axes: one in a direction which supports the transfer of *sovereignty* to a new and larger centre; a second which underpins the performance of an increasing number of tasks by centres which are at the higher level, that of the Union, rather than the states—there is a transfer of *competence*; and third, are changes in identity which support movement towards the appearance of what Karl Deutsch called a security community.[5] There can be movement in terms of the weakening or strengthening of loyalties, and the refocusing of expectations, along any one of these three axes without any necessary implication for movement along any of the others. This method of analysis also allows for the possibility that the functions of the nation state could be disaggregated and distributed between various levels of organization.

The development of identity was not a linear process, in the sense that it either moved towards support for the European state, or remained focused on the existing nation states. Not only was it possible, and indeed usual, for there to be multiple identities, with loyalties to a particular group coinciding and being continuously

[5] K. W. Deutsch, *et al.*, *Political Community and the North Atlantic Area* (Princeton: Princeton University Press, 1957).

reconciled with loyalties to other groups, each with their associated symbols; but identity might also evolve in such a way that it supported the redistribution of responsibility for performing basic tasks and fulfilling basic human needs, without this necessarily having direct implications for sovereignty or security. The traditional view, dominated by arguments about the nature of the nation state, was that sovereignty coincided with responsibility for performing key tasks, such as protecting security, and ensuring the welfare of the citizens.

But does this have to be the case? Sovereignty and the performance of key tasks may in these modern times, as human attitudes and values evolve, become disconnected from each other: security may be provided beyond or above the state, and so might a number of other basic human needs. The perception could form that key tasks, even those concerning foreign policy and defence, previously seen as essential to sovereignty, need not be performed by national governments. Expectations and loyalties may support the performance of tasks at level *A*, whilst sovereignty, in the sense of the location of ultimate responsibility is at level *B*, whilst security, it is expected, derives from what happens at level *C*. The question then becomes: how far does data about public attitudes in the European Union illustrate this possibility? If such a pattern is evident, the uniqueness of the European polity is confirmed—neither nation state nor international society—and we are alerted to the changing relationship between sovereignty and competence.

There was in the European Community between the mid-1950s and 1990s a degree of movement in the direction of a sense of common destiny, but a very long way to go before it would make any sense at all to talk about a European nation. The patterns were far more complicated than had been envisaged in the mid-1950s, and, as indicated, these may be discussed under three major headings, linking identity with, in turn: sovereignty, competence, and security–community. There can be changes in public attitudes with regard to each of these issues.

Identity and Sovereignty

One of the statements made by Charles de Gaulle in the mid-1960s about the institutions of the European Community was that they were an extension of the juridical and administrative arm of the state.[6] What Charles de Gaulle was anxious to stress was that governments in Europe were obliged to the nations in the separate member states: as there was no European nation, there was no basis in popular attitudes for the view that the institutions of the Community had acquired any authority, other than that borrowed from member governments. In practical terms what that meant was that in extremis the people of the various member states still expected national governments to accept responsibility for their fate. There was no evidence in public attitudes of the kind of support, or focusing of expectations, which could be the basis of the claim that the Brussels institutions were now responsible. They could not be regarded as having taken over, or as sharing in the sovereignty of governments.

By the mid-1990s it was still hard to discover any evidence that pro-European sentiment had grown to the point at which this view could be abandoned. The European nations remained the primary political reality of Europe. This may be demonstrated by reference to a variety of factors. Of course the primary one was the pattern of public attitudes as reported in poll material, which is dealt with below. Another was the reflection of those attitudes in what might be called the primary locations of power in the West European democracies, namely the political parties.

A further reflection, however, was the reactions of decision-makers to public attitudes as revealed in the working procedures of the Community, though they often selected or even distorted attitudes in order to justify policies or ways of working which they preferred, and their actions helped to shape them in the first place. But when politicians talked about the need to take more account of the public mood with regard to Europe they were acknowledging the reality of that mood. That they may also have been seeking to exploit it for their own ends, including the preservation of their own power, should not be taken as evidence to the contrary. Indications of the nature of identity in Europe in the mid-1990s might, therefore, be found in three contexts: parties, procedures, and polls. These are examined in that order in what follows.

The basis of political power in the European Union remained the national parties and the national constituency: there was no European-level constituency. There had been, it might be argued,

[6] See Leon Lindberg, 'Integration as a Source of Stress on the European Community System', International Organization, 2 (1966), 233–63.

some movement towards the development of European political parties. Party coalitions in the European Parliament cut àcross national party groups and were the primary organizations in the Parliament's work, both in the plenary meetings of the Parliament and in its committees. Indeed the growth of such groups had been one of the great achievements of the European Parliament in the period before it acquired greater power over the Union's budget in the early 1970s and later, in the Single European Act and the Maastricht Treaty, over legislation. It looked to some as if such groups could be the forerunner of supranational parties in Europe.

But in the mid-1990s the party groups outside Strasburg remained rudimentary, and, despite the appearance of trans-European frameworks for discussing policy, links between the national party groups before the elections to the European Parliament in 1989 and 1994 were undeveloped.[7] Indeed each national party fought its own campaign, and made minimal acknowledgement of its relations with parties of similar political idealogy in other member countries.

The conclusion must be that European elections in the mid-1990s were still primarily about national issues and they were fought by national parties. In other words national parties were the focus of public attention and it was through them that governments at the national level acquired responsibility and power. European elections, despite the best efforts of pro-Europeans, were another occasion on which the power of national governments, not the prospective European one, was reconsecrated. They confirmed the pre-eminence of national over European identity, and at the same time revealed the weakness of the claim to authority of the institutions in Brussels, which simply had no power base, except through the mediation of national governments. Indeed it was revealing in the mid-1990s that governments retained the option, because the national parties which sustained them also retained their identity in the European Parliament, of managing their representatives there in order to block legislation of which they disapproved.

This was despite the extension of the powers of the European Parliament with regard to legislation in the Single European Act and in the Maastricht Treaty. The problem was that in developing the powers of the European Parliament there was a Community dilemma which was rather like Alice's approach to the mountain in *Through the Looking Glass*: the more you tried to create Community

[7] See Francis B. Jacobs, *Western European Political Parties: A Comprehensive Guide* (Harlow: Longman, 1989).

powers the more you risked strengthening national powers over the Community.

Take for instance Article 189b of the Maastricht Treaty! In one way this article seemed to strengthen the powers of the European Parliament in that it allowed it an unconditional veto in certain stated areas. The Council of Ministers and the Parliament each had to agree to act in this context: if there was disagreement there had to be resort to conciliation procedures, reminiscent of those of the Senate and the House of Representatives in the United States Congress. It seemed to go beyond the terms of the cooperative procedure of the Single European Act—later incorporated in the Maastricht Treaty as Article 189c—which only allowed the European Parliament a conditional veto with regard to ten stated areas, including many aspects of the single market process: the Council of Ministers could overrule the views of the Parliament.

But apparent concessions to integration must be balanced against apparent reinforcements of the reserve powers of the governments. Much depended, as was mentioned in Chapter 1, upon the interpretation of the significance of the various uses made of articles 189c and 189b. The evidence of the Agreement suggested that this was a matter of fine judgement by the negotiators at Maastricht, with broadly speaking 189c being preferred if the question was one of importance to the members of the Council who wished to get their way in the positive sense of getting something done, and 189b being preferred if the members were less enthusiastic about an issue and were prepared to put up with a veto by the European Parliament.

The latter procedure also allowed for a kind of double block by states which opposed the policy proposal under consideration. If it was outvoted in the Council where qualified majority voting applied, then it could seek to mobilize opposition in the European Parliament in order to create a majority of members against its acceptance there. This would naturally tend to encourage the more hesitant governments to whip members of their party in the European Parliament into towing the party line, and would tend to weaken the development of European parties, despite the lip service paid to this in Annex 1 of the agreement. This was another instance of a well-established doctrine about the development of the European Communities: that apparent concessions to supranationalism were more likely when intergovernmentalism had been bolstered. The paradox should be noted, that 189 which appeared to give more powers to the European Parliament could be interpreted as helping the more cautious states.

The 189b procedure was introduced in some areas where 189c had previously applied in the form of A.149 of the Treaty of Rome. This was true for Title 111 legislation on the free movement of persons, services, and capital, and also for Article 100a legislation under Title 4. Decisions on the Multiannual Framework programmes on research and technology cooperation under A.130i were to be taken under 189b, though they were previously to be taken under the terms of the SEA by unanimity in the Council. Decisions on cooperation in public health matters, and in consumer protection, both brought in as specific Community policies under their own heading, were to be based on 189b.

It was particulary interesting to note the discrimination between the use of 189b and c, and it was difficult to credit the nuanced reasoning used by the negotiators in achieving such an arcane giving and taking of powers. Read quickly it looked like a litany of jokes! On transport, policy guidelines were to be on the basis of 189b but decisions on implementation, on establishing interoperability in transport, and on agreeing technical standards were on the basis of 189c. Under the general heading of Social Policy, Title 8, decisions to promote cooperation on matters of education were to be taken by the 189b procedure, whilst under the same heading decisions to promote vocational training to adapt to industrial change, facilitate mobility, and cooperation on training, were to be taken through 189c. With regard to research and technological development, the overall programmes, as already indicated, were through 189b, but specific programmes were to be approved by majority vote in the Council, that is, not even by 189c, the equivalent of which, the procedure introduced by the SEA through A.149, had previously applied. (Here was a case of regression.) Decisions on the tasks, primary objectives, and organization of the structural funds were to be taken on the basis of unanimity—no change from the SEA—but implementing legislation with regard to the Regional Fund and the Social Fund were 189c, whilst decisions on the guidance section of the Agricultural Fund were somewhat oddly to be taken solely by qualified majority vote in the Council of Ministers.

The reservation of unanimity in some questions was also interesting. Article 189c procedures could be used to decide the actions to be taken to implement environment policy, but unanimity was to be used for provisions under this heading of a fiscal character, for measures affecting town and country planning, and for measures '. . . significantly affecting choice between different energy sources' in member states. On Title 14 questions regarding industry, cooperation between undertakings to promote innovation, and adjustment to structural change were on the basis of unanimity in the Council.

There was also an extremely interesting innovation in giving the Communities a role in a common policy on entry visas, under A100c, but decisions on this were to be on the basis of unanimity—to establish guidelines—until 1996, when qualified majority voting in the Council was to apply—not 189b or c—with states reserving the right to act alone with regard to law and order and internal security questions. On decisions which could facilitate exercising the rights of citizenship, unanimity was to apply. With regard to the establishment of a Community role on education, decisions concerning the harmonization of laws and regulations of member states were not to be subject to 189b, but unanimity in the Council.

What appeared here was a very careful allocation of competencies to European institutions, with formulae for voting being applied on the basis of principles which were often obscure. But the dominant motivation appeared to be to retain control over important questions in the hands of governments. Two points of relevance to the powers of the European Parliament emerge: first that 189b applied to areas which were of lesser importance, and they were often carefully ring-fenced: the area within which they were to apply was carefully delimited. Second, 189b could be interpreted as allowing governments a second bite at the cherry: if they were outvoted in the Council on first reading they could block action by constructing an opposing majority in the European Parliament. To see these acts as representing a programme of federalism, be it favoured or opposed, was misleading.

The Council of Ministers moved towards majority voting in the Single European Act and this was taken further in the Maastricht agreement. But it was a very peculiar form of majority voting, and should not be confused with majority voting in the parliament of a democratic state! Its main purpose was to achieve goals that had already been agreed on the basis of unanimity. It was a mechanism to ease the process of implementation, rather than a way of agreeing upon major issues of principle. The 1992 goals had been agreed on the basis of unanimity in the Single European Act in December 1985, and the programme for the 1990s, especially on monetary integration, in the Maastricht Treaty in December 1991.

There were three arguments against the view that majority voting had fundamentally eroded government's powers to veto action of which they disapproved.

1. The first was quite simply that the national systems, in their various ways, could nullify acts which proved objectionable. Such a course might damage relationships with the Community, but that political or economic costs might arise was irrelevant to the constitutional and legal possibilities.

2. Second, the governments retained, even in areas where the formal arrangement was majority voting—because they spoke for a sovereign state—a *reserve power* in the Council to veto any *proposed* legislation of which they disapproved. Although it was highly unlikely that this would be a part of the routine arrangements of the Community after the Single European Act and the Maastricht Treaty, it nevertheless remained as a power to be used *in extremis* by member governments which objected to a particular course of action.

There was little likelihood that a sovereign state would be regularly outvoted on issues which it regarded as vital to its national interests. Even in areas where majority voting was a formal possibility every effort was made to reach consensus. (This question is discussed in Chapter 2.) Indeed its main effect was to put greater pressure on states to compromise so that a general agreement could be found. No government liked to be outvoted, and would do everything in its power to avoid this. When formal voting was used it was likely to concern technical issues, where major issues of principle were not at stake, and in this sense majority voting, when it took place, was usually not about first order questions.

3. Third, governments had another kind of reserve power. Even though it might be accepted that a particular institution should have the power to act in specific areas without being subject to instructions from government, governments retained the right to negotiate a different set of powers for institutions in other areas. They were not subject to any general principle, for example, a federal principle, according to which the powers of future institutions were to be allocated. Indeed, as shown in Chapter 1 the opposite principle, that of subsidiarity, was asserted at Maastricht: powers were to be kept at the lowest level possible. That governments retained the right to pursue their own strategy in these matters meant that they could seek to balance the loss of powers in one realm against the gain or retention of powers in another: supranational powers to the Eurofed

could be balanced against unanimity in the area of economic coordination.

It might be argued that, even though they might continue to seek such countervailing powers, they would be increasingly condemned to accept supranationalism: there was a federalizing process. As has been argued at various points in this book there was little in the Maastricht Agreement to substantiate this view, and this writer sees little evidence to support it. The availability of this strategy was another indication that states had retained their sovereignty. Neither accession to the European Communities, nor the terms of the Single European Act or the Maastricht Agreement, had altered the underlying legal and constitutional circumstances of national sovereignty. Indeed, the fear that this had happened was strikingly absent in most member states.

Is the above picture reflected in the views of the European publics in general. What does the poll data show about attitudes towards the Union? The main source of such data is the series of six-monthly reports published by the Commission as *Eurobarometer*.

In this section those public attitudes which are relevant to the question of sovereignty are particularly sought. It is not always easy to select poll materials which are explicitly and clearly related to this issue: usually it is a question of indications of a preparedness to accept the European or the national centre as having ultimate responsibility. This is difficult to pin down because frequently those asked strongly favoured increasing responsibility for the centre, without being clear about what that meant. Sometimes this was merely an expression of annoyance with national performance, rather than a wish to see the national centre superseded. On other occasions support for developments which were expressed in general terms, like a stronger European government, was conditional on terms that in practice could not be accepted.

The editorial of the *Eurobarometer* (EB) published in December 1992 was worth noting as it marked a threshold in the development of public opinion in the European Community. It pointed out that public opinion regarding Europe had been accurately described as a *permissive consensus* for many years.

As we wrote in 1987 (*Eurobarometer*, 27, p. 42): Consensus about 'Europe', and about 'more of it', was more permissive, acceptive, benevolent than demanding, challenging, pressing or pushing. Approval and support were high, but not deeply felt by many. Political leaders, and governments, had a remarkable margin of manoeuvre. 'Europe' was peace, friendship and

mostly beneficial economic cooperation. Up to 81% were for the unification of Western Europe. But 'Europe' was not extremely salient for many:
the percentage of those 'very much in favour' of European unification
never was higher, on EC average, than 38% (EB27). There were never
more than 24% (EB26, 1986; EB4, 1975) or 26% (EB3, 1975) who said they
were 'a great deal' interested in EC affairs.'[8]

The point relevant to sovereignty was that such a consensus,
being permissive, could not be interpreted as a transfer of expectations to the new centre: 'permissive' required that there be some
other primary player, like the national governments.

The *Eurobarometer*, 38 editorial also had some important points to
make about the changes in that permissive consensus around the
time of the Maastricht Treaty which strongly support the general
theme of this book. It pointed out that there were many signals
pointing to a change in the nature of public attitudes towards the EC.
The consensus that remained had become less and less permissive.
But there was no evidence that the EC was likely to fall apart because
of lack of public support. There was evidence, however, that a significant proportion of the public in several member countries—
although still being for Europe—wanted an explicit say in the debate
about 'which Europe' and 'how much of it'. The editorial made the
point very strongly that evidence of this change had appeared before
the main debate about the Maastricht Treaty, and that it was attrib-
utable more to the sensitizing of the public to European issues
because of the 1992 process, the downturn in the economies of the
European states, and the major political changes in Eastern Europe,
and Germany, in the late 1980s. The data revealed that

many who said that they did not agree with the EC, as they saw it currently
working—and often agreed even less with what they read into
'Maastricht'—wanted or preferred in turn an EC that was more or less the
one we currently had, and often preferred an EC as 'Maastricht' foresaw it
actually becoming. *But they were simply not aware of the reality.*[9]

Questions asked in the context of the Maastricht debate were
more directly relevant to the question of sovereignty. One type of
question addressed the respective issue (a European Government, a
common foreign policy, a common defence policy) in such a way as
to not remind the respondents of the essential role member states'

[8] Commission of the European Communities, *Eurobarometer*, 38, Dec. 1992, p.
vii.
[9] Ibid., p. viii.

governments played in the EC and EC decision-making. Another type of question addressed the same issues with an explicit reminder of the member states' role. In most cases in most member countries, majorities in favour of the respective proposal were significantly stronger—and in any case, opposition very significantly weaker—when the member state governments' role was explicitly referred to.

When the question was of 'whether citizens were for or against the formation of a European Union with a European Government responsible to the European Parliament', 51 per cent on average were for this, 28 per cent against.[10] (By the autumn of 1993 this figure had fallen to 47%,[11] but by July 1994 had gone back to 50%.[12]) When the question was whether people were 'for or against the European Community having a European Government responsible to the European Parliament and the European Council of Heads of National Government', 56 per cent were for it and only 16 per cent against.[13] The picture obviously varied somewhat from country to country—the UK public had the lowest support for the EC's taking over responsibility for foreign policy—but even there 55 per cent was in favour.[14]

This evidence did not suggest any tipping of the balance of views in favour of the ultimate responsibility of the European institutions in the period following the erosion of the permissive consensus in the early 1990s. The national governments were still perceived as carrying main responsibility for the welfare of the publics. The July 1994 figures on attitudes towards membership of the European Union and on the balance of benefits and costs from membership contained some evidence of a recovery in pro-European sympathy following the erosion since 1991.[15] There had been a decline in the number of those agreeing that membership was 'a good thing' since summer 1991, but only by 3 per cent. But the gap between these and those who thought it was 'a bad thing' was comfortably wide in all member states. The gap was narrowest in Britain at 22 per cent, and Denmark at 27 per cent, and widest in Italy, Greece, Ireland, Luxembourg, and Holland where it exceeded 60 per cent. With regard to the perception of 'benefiting' or 'not benefiting', however,

[10] Commission of the European Communities, *Eurobarometer*, 38, Dec. 1992, Table 48, A45.

[11] *Eurobarometer*, 40, Dec. 1993, Table 20, A33.

[12] *Eurobarometer* 41, July 1994, Table 16, p. A28.

[13] EB, 38, Dec. 1992, Table 24, pp. A28–A29.

[14] Ibid., p. A29.   [15] EB, July 1994, pp. 11–24.

in most member countries the gap significantly narrowed after 1990, and in Spain, France, and Britain 'not benefiting' exceeded 'benefitting' for a while before July 1994. In Britain and Spain the perception of a net loss of benefit had lasted longest: since early 1992. What was striking, however, was that by mid-1994, the number seeing 'benefit' in membership once more exceeded in all countries the number of those seeing 'no benefit' in membership.

These figures indicated that there was a measure of identification with the Community: support for membership, though slightly eroded in the early 1990s, remained at a high level despite a weakening in the perception of benefits. Had there been no identification with Europe, had membership been merely a matter of utilitarian calculation, support for membership would have declined in correlation with the decline in the perception of benefits. The general situation, however, even in states where there was for a while a perception of negative benefit, like the UK, was that the number of those supporting membership continued to exceed comfortably the number of those opposing it. Indeed the one country where net support for membership was less than net perception of benefit in the early 1990s was Denmark: in July 1994 net perception that membership was a good thing was 27 per cent (difference between the percentage saying it was a good thing and those saying it was a bad thing) but net perception of benefit exceeding no-benefit was 38 per cent (difference between the percentage saying Denmark benefited and those saying there was no benefit). This suggested that Danes then had a weaker identification with the EC than the people of other member countries.

In general, however, the figures indicated a degree of identification with the Community which was ahead of the perceived level of utilitarian reward. The poll materials overall reinforced the conclusion drawn from the other two contexts of analysis—parties and procedures—that the publics still identified primarily with the nation states, though there was also a degree of identification with Europe. They suggest a preference for the exercise of joint sovereignty in the common enterprise, but doubt about anything more ambitious.

Identity and the Allocation of Competence

The Editors of *Eurobarometer* 38 summarized the views of the European publics towards the European Union after the Maastricht Debate as follows. They wrote that:

A notable part of the public is in favour of European unification but against a certain type of Europe which they believe is represented by the Maastricht Treaty and even by the current EC as they perceive it.
They are against a Europe:

- which threatens national identity and cultural diversity.
- which gives citizens insufficient democratic influence;
- which gives their country and its governments no say in European decision-making;
- which centralises 'everything' in 'Brussels'; and
- which is run by an enormous Brussels bureaucracy that is out of touch with the real world of citizens.

They are, however, in favour of a United Europe

- where national and regional identities and cultural diversity are respected, protected and defended;
- where democratic channels of citizen influence exist and visibly function;
- including their democratically established national government having an important role in common decision-making
- where sovereignty is pooled and exercised through common institutions only in such policy areas, where national or regional governments can no longer solve problems effectively;
- where such policies are prepared and executed by an administration of adequate, limited, size which is directed by a body (the Commission, or later European Government) responsible to a powerful democratically elected European Parliament, and to the European Council consisting of the democratically established national Heads of State and Government.

The type of Europe rejected clearly is neither foreseen in the Maastricht Treaty nor is it represented by the current EC in spite of many a shortcoming.

The type of Europe favoured, acceptable and supportable, on the other hand, is the very Europe designed by 'Maastricht' and in many respects already existing and functioning as the European Community. But the public, and the Euro-sceptical part of the public in particular, *does not know*.[16]

---

[16] *Eurobarometer*, 38, pp. ix–x.

This overview brings out a unique feature of the European Union in the mid-1990s. That the publics had begun to accept a new version of the implications and corollaries of national autonomy. What was detected was a continuing concern with autonomy and, by implication, sovereignty, but a willingness to reconcile that with collective action. Competence for performing tasks could be extended to the European level, according to the requirements of efficiency and effectiveness—the subsidiarity principle in Maastricht—but responsibility was to be retained by national governments and national representatives. Over the years the range of tasks which could be relocated was extended, though there were always some which the publics insisted should be dealt with locally. And there were, not surprisingly, major differences between the states. But it was striking that overall the publics were generally happy to see some functions managed at the European level, especially foreign policy and defence, which had traditionally been regarded as the prerogative of the nation state. Renouncing an exclusive control over these areas had been tantamount to losing sovereignty.

These points are illustrated in tables at EB, 41, July 1994, p. 32; EB, 37, June 1992, p. 28; and EB, 35, June 1991, p. 19 (see below for the question put in these three tables). The evidence suggested that, broadly speaking, the nearer to home the issue, the more people preferred national governments to handle it. There was a core of issues which seemed to be especially closely linked with the sense of personal security, and where the suspicion in some sense of non-insiders was all too evident. In the period from spring 1991 to July 1994 there was consistently a strong hostility to transferring responsibility for education to the Union, and only slightly less opposition with regard to an enhanced European role on health and social welfare, and cultural policy. These questions might be thought to be closely related to the sense of national identity, and mark the limits of identification with citizens of other countries. Some things you could simply not trust to outsiders! For instance European Union citizens were deeply convinced that other EU national doctors and medical practice were not to be relied upon!

But there was also a surprising range of issues on which Europeans were prepared to accept joint European Union decision-making, though it was noticeable that there had been a small decline in support for this since 1991. A few preliminary points should be made. The question to which people were invited to respond was the same one in each of the tables, despite the difference in the wording of the captions: the earlier ones might be thought to be asking for a clear choice between national and European control, rather than national and joint control; the latter form could have encouraged a greater willingness to agree to a European involvement. The question was:

Some people believe that certain areas of policy should be decided by the (national) government, while other areas of policy should be decided jointly within the European Community/European Union. Which of the following areas of policy do you think should be decided by the (National) government and which should be decided jointly within the European Community/European Union?

Despite the longer list of items on the July 1994 list than on that for spring 1991, it is useful to compare the main features of each. In both there was a strong sense of the appropriate level of competence for action, a much stronger preparedness to do things at the level at which for technical reasons they could best be done than was often found among political leaders, where questions such as the retention of personal power at the cost of effectiveness might be expected to play a part. The 1994 evidence was particularly striking in that it foresaw a joint European role for science research, for the protection of the environment, for immigration policy and fighting unemployment, as well as the management of currencies. In view of the adverse public comment on the chances of monetary union the clear majority for doing this at the European level was impressive. There did indeed seem to be cases where the current judgement by politicians—that they had moved ahead of the public—was in need of some refinement. The public was prepared over the Union as a whole to accept a rather higher level of joint control than politicians pretended.

But on issues other than those with a clear technical element there were also striking developments. The 1994 evidence showed an overwhelming majority for managing foreign policy at the European level, despite the failure of the European Union's policies with regard to ex-Yugoslavia. There was also a more modest majority in favour of a joint defence: when security and defence were linked together, the judgement was evenly balanced, presumably because the public interpreted this as a reference to civil police activities, which they preferred to keep at the national level. But note that the majorities in the July 1994 evidence were generally somewhat down on those of 1991, for reasons that need not be explored again here, and that even though security and defence were not distinguished from each other in the 1991 evidence there was nevertheless a clear majority in favour of joint action.

A few caveats should be entered however: the majority in favour of joint European foreign policy was the narrowest in Greece, probably because of the Greeks' feeling that they were on their own with regard to the question of recognizing Macedonia. (See EB 41, Table 3, p. A13.) The British and the Danes were together in preferring national control over the granting of political asylum and on immigration policy (the Greeks and the Irish were evenly divided on these issues); on the currency issue there were majorities in favour of joint action in eight countries, with Danes and Portuguese divided, most Germans unhappy, and most British resolutely against. But note that even the most reluctant of the publics—the British—had a majority in favour of European-level action on the environment, cooperation with the Third World, research policy, and most interestingly, on foreign policy towards non-EU countries. They also favoured the setting up of a European Central Bank. Furthermore the Danes and the Luxembourgers had both increased support for joint action on environmental questions by 11 per cent compared with six months earlier. (See EB, 41, Table 22, July 1994, pp. A34–5 and EB, 40, Table 41, Dec. 1993, pp. A53–4.)

Taken as a whole the evidence showed a public preparedness to accept the transfer of functions to the higher level if there seemed to be good technical reasons for doing so. The original six countries were most supportive of extending EU competence, but there was little evidence to suggest that the citizens of Western Europe in general wished to hang on to the control of everything because that was crucial to their sense of national autonomy. Indeed politicians, in the cautious states, but also in the mid-1990s in the original six members, often pretended that public resistance was greater than it was for reasons of their own, presumably because losing competence would lose them power. The conclusion on this was that attitudes among the publics of the European Union in the mid-1990s had changed to the point at which the relationship between competence and autonomy had been considerably relaxed compared with that in earlier years, and that which still existed in more primitive nationalisms such as those in Eastern Europe.

As Hugo Young noted, the situation in Britain regarding the media and Euro-sceptic views on Europe in the mid-1990s was little short of scandalous. The views of the British public, as reported in this chapter, were ignored and there appeared to be a conspiracy to hide the truth from the public and to talk up the extent to which public opinion was opposed.

The tabloids appear to have become physically incapable of alluding to Brussels without epithets of ridicule and hatred. If a pro EU group dares to raise its head with modest and balanced, albeit favourable, opinions on the single currency, as Lord Howe did last week, depend upon this Tory press to depict him as a treacherous lunatic whose actual words do not deserve the smallest effort at accurate reporting. Yet this performance rests on a false account of public attitudes, which are closer to indifference than hostility. It's another case where the media seem to be the aiders and abetters of powerful untruth. The media line, as exemplified by these Tory papers, does not speak for public opinion at large. It's the driving obsession of a handful of editors, mostly appointed by semi-absentee proprietors. Combined with another handful of ultra-sceptic Tory MPs, they together prove it doesn't take many minds to compose a critical mass sufficient to intimidate alternative voices, and silence them in the name of public opinion.

Young also reported that

when Gallup polled a national sample for Channel Four News last month (May 1995) the result suggested first an extraordinary imperviousness to the one-sided assault now coming out of the ether, and second the falseness of a political strategy based on the presumption that public opinion no longer tolerates the European idea. Asked the most basic question, which is whether they wished to stay in or get out of the Union, 61% said they would vote to stay—just as they had done in the referendum, 20 long and passion-filled years ago.[17]

The evidence contained in this chapter shows more pro-Europeanism in Britain than was found in the Channel Four report. This strengthens rather than weakens the points made by Young.

A distinction could be made between *hard* public opinion and *soft* public opinion. The former was enduring and included core values and immutable preferences; the latter was changeable, and was capable of being led and persuaded. The evidence discussed here suggested that public opinion on the distribution of competencies between the Union and the nations was of the latter kind. It was one of the hypocrisies of the Eurosceptics in the mid-1990s, and those who were prepared to play their games, that they pretended it was

---

[17] Hugo Young, 'Nothing could be further from the Truth', The *Guardian*, Thurs., 15 June 1995.

the former. And, of course, the public was vulnerable to the mis-leading advice of the Eurosceptics, because, as has been pointed out at several points in this chapter, they were often ignorant. Again, politicians and their media allies were frequently anxious that this situation should be maintained: if they initiated a campaign to edu-cate the publics in the dissenting states about, say, monetary union, it would appear very quickly that they were not fundamentally opposed.

This picture was confirmed by the data in EB, 41, Table 3a, A14 which contained evidence about who the Europeans thought should exercise this competence. (Note the question asked to elicit these responses on p. A12.) This information again brought out the limits which the European publics preferred to place upon their involve-ment with the European Union: it helped to measure its distance from federation. Note in particular the nuancing of judgement about who should be allowed to vote and stand in various elections. European citizens agreed that the citizens of a EU member state residing in another EU country should be allowed the right to vote at Euro-elections—as indeed they were for the first time in June 1994. Support for this had in fact increased after it had been agreed at Maastricht! Two-thirds of European citizens also said that EU non-nationals should be allowed to stand as candidates at European elec-tions—this was 3 per cent more than in EB, 40 from December 1993 (see EB, 40, Table 40, Dec. 1993). The line was drawn, however, at allowing EU non-nationals to stand as candidates in local elections: there had been a move in favour from December 1993, but still a clear majority against. This was despite the acceptance of EU non-nationals' *voting* in these same elections! These were the points at which the identities were revealed as multiple; but quite often, even where the overall majority was against, the movement was in the direction of European identity.

A similar fascinating nuancing of opinion was revealed in the evi-dence about European citizenship from December 1993 (EB, 40, Dec. 1993, Figs. 5.1–2, p. 84 and Table 64, A73). This was particularly striking in view of the media perception that there had been a dra-matic rise in nationalism. If this had happened it was not brought out in this evidence. At the EU level nearly 45 per cent reckoned they were both of their nation and European, whilst 40 per cent said they were only of their nation: very few said they were European first and of their nation second. The Italians were the most European, fol-lowed by the French, Belgians, Luxembourgers, and Dutch. The

Irish and Danes were divided between the two, while the British public was unique in that there was a massive majority claiming to be solely of the nation rather than of the nation and Europe, or of Europe. It was indeed the case that 'national only' feelings had grown, particularly in Luxembourg, East Germany, and the United Kingdom. Against this, feelings of nationalism had declined in Belgium. Overall, this change, though measurable, was hardly such as to justify the bleak picture often gleefully welcomed by the right and the Eurosceptics, that there had been a reassertion of nationalism.

Even in the European Union what had happened was that the conditions of sovereignty had changed rather than that sovereignty was under threat. People accepted the need to manage common problems together as and when necessary, and this could mean relating to outside actors through joint mechanisms. There was, in other words, in the Community a tendency towards policy harmonization and the exercise of competence jointly amongst the group of states, but not to the extinction of their sovereignty.

In one important respect Western Europe may be regarded as signifying a significant change in thinking about the conditions of sovereignty. In that small region a new version of the idea of national self-determination had begun to emerge by the 1990s, which was not evident as yet in other regions. What had happened was that the utilitarian aspects of sovereignty had been semi-detached from the principle of national self-determination. It was now possible in Western Europe to allow crucial tasks to be managed at the larger level, without this being seen as a challenge to the principle of national autonomy. For example by the early 1990s the Scottish nationalists had come to see the European Community as a support for their claim for national autonomy: autonomy had become a way of relating to the outside world, whereas in earlier years claims for autonomy amounted to a means of withdrawal into an introspective concern with national issues, and a form of detachment from the larger entity. In it was noted that the Scottish and Welsh were significantly more often 'also European' as compared to the English.[18] But this was only one case of a general tendency to accept that within the territory of the European Union tasks should be performed at the most appropriate level determined in the light of technical criteria rather than exclusive nationalism.

<hr/>

[18] EB, 40, Dec. 1993, 83n.

One might speculate about the reasons for the trend in Britain to be not quite in conformity with this general principle: as already stated, extension of competence to the appropriate level, as advised by the doctrine of subsidiarity, did not extend down to the regions within Britain, which had become under Mrs Thatcher a highly centralized state. (Perhaps Welsh and Scottish pro-Europeanism was a function of this!) But even foreign policy and defence, previously judged to be at the heart of sovereignty, seemed amenable to semi-detachment from the principle of national autonomy. What remedied the situation, of course, was that the states could be said to have pooled their sovereignty rather than abandoned it, and they sought increasingly sophisticated ways of managing their common enterprise to protect this principle.

In Eastern Europe and elsewhere, however, there was a much more primitive version of the principle of national self-determination. There was still an insistence upon keeping what were regarded as essential tasks firmly attached to the emerging nations: they wished to establish national currencies, armies, economic policies, and the like, when there were signs that the countries in Western Europe had begun to feel that exclusive controls over these were not part of the necessary condition of sovereignty. Again the long cycle is interesting: Western Europe was the homeland of the principle of national self-determination and the connection between retaining control of key tasks and national autonomy used to be stressed there; perhaps Western Europe was once more ahead of the pack in the early 1990s, in demonstrating that national autonomy did not necessarily involve an exclusive utilitarianism. It could become a way of relating rather than of excluding.

Identity and Security

In the previous sections attention was focused upon the attitudes of the European peoples towards the European Union. The concerns were with the question of which level was thought to be ultimately responsible for the welfare of the publics—which institutions incorporated sovereignty—and with the level at which it was accepted that competence with regard to particular tasks could be exercised. There was, however, a third facet of identity which was not considered in the discussion hitherto and which was arguably the most important of all: the way in which the attitudes of the publics towards each other had developed in the Community/Union. How far had they moved towards a sense of mutual sympathy and understanding? This, after all, was at the heart of the security of these publics in their mutual relations.

In the development of the European Community the key question was obviously how far had the Germans and the French changed in their views of each other? After all they had fought each other three times since the 1860s. Was there a widespread distrust and expectation that future disagreements could lead yet again to the use of violence? Or had attitudes changed to the point at which there was no expectation that violence would ensue, and no military planning for defence against the other?

Were the attitudes of the French and Germans towards each other in the 1990s quite different from the 1930s, or, indeed, from those in the early 1950s? In the mid-1990s there was evidence to suggest that this was indeed the case. In the 1930s the French had felt it necessary to build major fortifications along their frontier with Germany—the Maginot line—and it was noticeable that no such fortification had appeared by the 1990s. And the *Eurobarometer*, one of the key sources of opinion materials about the progress of integration, contained only a modest range of information about this question; the improvements seemed to be so self-evident that they could be taken for granted. Of course the German and the French would not fight each other again!

How could this extraordinary conclusion possibly be supported? There was a body of writing in its favour, though, of course, it could not possibly amount to proof. Much of this derived from the work of Karl Deutsch who had been interested in the way in which nations developed. As an aspect of this work he developed the notion of *security-community*.[19] There were, he proposed, both amalgamated and pluralistic security communities, amalgamated being where there was a reliable expectation of peace within a state, and pluralistic where such expectations prevailed in relations between states. The latter was perhaps more interesting: examples included Scandinavia since the nineteenth century and the Canada–USA relationship. The question became: why did these states constitute security communities and how far was the European Community/Union moving in that direction?

[19] Deutsch *et al.*, *Political Community and the North Atlantic Area*.

There were a wide range of indicators of security–community: a preparedness to discriminate between the citizens of the other group, so that characteristics, good or bad, were not attributed to them in general: the belief that the behaviour of the other was predictable; that lifestyles were similar; that interests overlapped and showed cross-cutting cleavages; that there was a move away from seeing the other as the *out-group*, to accepting it as part of the *in-group*. The attitudes of the Germans and the French in the early 1950s showed numerous illustrations of such distinctions. These included the making of broad generalizations about the character of the other peoples: the Germans saying the French were charming but lazy, that they didn't work hard enough, and were untrustworthy. Their lifestyles were also seen as being quite different from that of the Germans. The Germans also believed that the French were right to believe that the Germans would probably take over control of the European Defence Community, and they found it impossible to accept that the EDC could be commanded by a French general. Behaviour could not be predicted, interests did not overlap, and French incompetence and distrust was such as to make this appointment unacceptable.

Contemporary poll materials reveal that there were in the early 1950s clear limits upon the extent to which German citizens were prepared to go in considering their own interests as identical with those of the French. These limits were indicated particularly in the context of sensitive political issues, such as that of the future of the Saar, but they were also revealed in the sort of qualifications with which German citizens surrounded their general approval of European goals. There was also some evidence of a surviving preparedness to view the French people as a whole as a single out-group which should be treated with some caution by German citizens.

In the period from the end of the Second World War until the autumn of 1954 there had been considerable speculation and interest about the fate of the Saar in both France and Germany. Before the Paris agreements at least established the method by which the future of the Saar should be decided several alternative solutions seemed possible—independence, adherence to France or Germany, or some form of 'internationalization'. Amongst the various solutions being discussed at the beginning of 1954 was the establishment of some form of joint Franco–German responsibility for that region. It represented a potential joint undertaking for the Germans and the French, and the reactions to the proposal of the joint administration of the Saar provided a useful example of the limits of acceptability of European solutions for Germans at that time. The Saar issue, concerning an area which was predominantly German in speech and outlook, aroused strong feelings in the Federal Republic. The issue would become increasingly sensitive, arousing more anxiety and bitterness, in direct proportion to any decreasing willingness to accept joint action, or perceive of the interests of the French and the Germans as identical.

In the course of a series of questions about the evolution of Franco–German relations from 1947 to early 1954, 47 per cent said that relations had improved whilst 20 per cent said they had not improved.[20] When questioned about the state of the relations at the time of the enquiry, however, 5 per cent said that relations were very good, 11.5 per cent said they were good, 48 per cent said they were not very good and 10.5 per cent said that they were bad.[21] (It is interesting that the most favourable answers to both the first and second questions were those of younger men.) Of the sample, 59.5 per cent therefore felt that relations were either not very good or bad, and it may be presumed that this was in part an expression of anxiety about the way that certain issues, including the Saar, might be handled as a result of any greater Franco–German cooperation. The following question was put to those who thought relations were 'not very good' or 'bad': why are relations between France and Germany bad/not very good? The response (as a percentage of those asked), sub-classified according to age group, was as follows.

	Less than 30	30–49	Over 50
Envy, fear, hate	43.5	53.5	52.5
The Saar issue	28.0	27.0	27.0
Past	21.5	19.5	14.0
Non ratification of Treaties of Brussels and Paris	9.5	8.0	8.0

This evidence suggests that fear about the future of the Saar was related more to a general fear of what might happen, than to a reaction against what had actually happened about the issue. The preference was based more on general sensitivity than on discussion and evaluation of the proposals put forward by the German and French

[20] Gessellschaft für Markt und Meinung Forschung m.b.h., *Image de la France. Un Sondage d'opinion publique allemande*, winter 1953–4 (unpublished) (Frankfurt-am-Main, July 1954). Carried out for the Institut für Sociale-Forschung of the Johan Wolfgang von Goethe University, Frankfurt-am-Main.

[21] Ibid.

governments. There was a lack of knowledge about what solutions had been proposed, and uncertainty about preferences amongst various given solutions.

(a) *Lack of Knowledge* In order to test knowledge about the proposals put forward as 'solutions' to the Saar problem, a question was put to discover what people thought the German government had proposed. The answers, set out below, are again given according to age group (as a percentage of those asked):[22]

	Less than 30	30–49	Over 50
Ignorant	41.0	43.5	35.5
The Saar would go to Germany	27.0	19.0	13.0
The Saar would go to France	—	1.5	—
Europeanization	10.0	6.0	8.0
German Government has not decided	10.0	11.5	10.0
No answer	12.0	20.0	32.0

Respondents in general preferred return to Germany, and believed that their government was following this end. 'Europeanization' was the next best solution, and return to France the one least favoured. It seemed that although some could envisage the Federal Government allowing the Saar to be 'Europeanized', none could face the prospect of its return to France. The results of this enquiry reflected more an element of wish-fulfilment and varying degrees of faith in the government, than detailed knowledge of solutions proposed. Further indications of this were to be found in an exaggeration of the Saarlander's wish to return to Germany and the feeling that cession of the Saar would undermine the German case for the recovery of the territories in the East.[23] The Saar issue became related to a much deeper anxiety in German minds—the anxiety about reunification. It will be noticed that the group having the highest percentage of 'no answers' and the only group which felt that the Saar might return to France, was that aged 51 and over, the group most likely to be disillusioned and either indifferent or cynical about their government's chances of recovering the Saar.

(b) *Preferences* Evidence about preferences derived from a more direct question about the strength of the preference for a return to Germany, and of the higher priority attributed to this solution than to the amelioration of Franco–German relations. A question was put in the following form: which is the most important, return of the

---

[22] Ibid.   [23] Ibid.

Saar to Germany or amelioration of Franco–German relations by 'Europeanizing' the Saar (response as a percentage of those asked)?

	Less than 30	30–49	Over 50
Return to Germany	39	35.5	26
Amelioration	34	29.5	26
Neither	2.5	1	5
No decision	14.5	13	22
No answer	10	21	21

Although there was a significant percentage who preferred amelioration when the question was put in this way (the question implied a possibly serious decline in relations if the return of the Saar to Germany was insisted upon)—the majority still preferred the return to Germany. It is probable that the form of the question, suggesting an over-simple alternative, if anything served to increase the numbers of those who chose amelioration. The question would strongly suggest to the respondent that relations were bad, and that the return of the Saar to Germany would make things worse. Only a minority of Germans were prepared to treat Germany and France as a single interest unit as regards this sensitive issue.

Other figures reinforce this interpretation.[24] In April 1955, after the decision had been made to hold a plebiscite in the Saar to decide that region's future,[25] 80 per cent said it was up to the Saarland people alone to decide their future.[26] But 31 per cent maintained that Germany had not interfered enough in the settlement of the question—as if they feared the Saarlander would not take the right decision—25 per cent thought that the German government had intervened sufficiently and 6 per cent thought the government had intervened too much. At the same time 43 per cent said that the Saar should be returned to Germany (as the best solution to the problem), 27 per cent said the Saar should be independent, and only 13 per cent said it should be 'European'. In this case Europeanization, with its implication of some form of joint undertaking with France in the government of the Saar, was the least preferred solution.

[24] These are taken from Elisabeth Noelle and Erich Peter Neumann, *Jahrbuch der Offentlichen Meinung*, 1947–1955, (Allensbach am Bodensee: Institut für Demoskopie, Verlag für Demoscopie, 1956).

[25] See the account of the establishment of West European Union which was entrusted with the task of conducting the plebiscite in A. H. Robertson, 'Creation of W.E.U.', *European Handbook*, 11, 125–38.

[26] This view should be compared with the exaggeration of pro-German opinion in the Saar by Germans (reported in *Image*).

Further evidence about patterns of German attitudes towards France in the early 1950s concerned the proposal for a European Defence Community (EDC). The principle of an EDC had attracted considerable support in the winter of 1954–5. But a great deal depended upon the particular form of the proposal. Particular ways of putting the principle into practice could easily have led many to feel that disadvantage to Germany would result. Debates about EDC in the French Chamber at this time were reported in the German press, and the French request for some form of British guarantee attracted criticism. German views suggested that any modest favouring of French interests in the administration of the proposed community would have been sufficient to undermine West German support of the general principle. Support was encouraged by the conviction that Germany would have *at least* equality of control, and would *probably* acquire greater control in practice.

In reply to the question, 'Are you for or against a European Defence Community?' 49 per cent said they were in favour, 25 per cent said they were against, 19 per cent gave no answer, and 7 per cent said they did not know.[27] There was a clear majority in favour of the principle. Yet there was a general impression of doubts about French intentions over a wide range of issues, including the EDC.

A question was put in the following form: with which countries should we co-operate more closely (response as a percentage of those asked)?[28]

	March 1953	September 1954
USA	83	78
Britain	62	58
France	55	46
Italy	44	34

It will be noticed that, at both dates indicated, France occupied third place to the USA and Britain. Perhaps a more indicative aspect of the figures, however, was the relative decline in preference between the two dates. Preferences for cooperation with all four countries named had fallen between March 1953 and September 1954. (Perhaps a reflection of lessening interest in international cooperation in West Germany, an increasing self-reliance or intro-spection resulting from the defeat of EDC in the French Assembly in

[27] From *Image de la France*, winter 1953–4.
[28] From Noelle and Neumann, *Jahrbuch. Jahrbuch* figures are compiled from a compound question, and are in all cases out of 100%.

August 1954.) Yet the relative fall of 9 per cent in the preference for cooperation with France is greater than that for either Britain or the USA—4 per cent and 5 per cent respectively. Not only are these figures a reflection of German doubts about French intentions, but they are also an indication of the sensitivity of German public opinion to the apparent confirmation of these doubts.

Doubts about French intentions as regards the EDC are revealed by questions put in the winter of 1953–4; at this time it still seemed likely that the EDC Treaty would be ratified in the French Assembly. A representative cross-section of Germans was questioned by the authors of the *Image de la France* study about what they thought of French views of EDC.

Is France for or against a European Army?
For   12%   Against   33%
Is the attitude of the French people different from that of her government?
Different   8%   Identical   10%

Germans thought that the French were opposed to a European Army, and little distinction was made in the minds of Germans between the responsibility of the French government, and the responsibility of the French people for this attitude (44 per cent could not answer the second question). Of those who felt France was opposed to a European army, 38 per cent believed this was because of French fear of Germany, whilst only 7 per cent said this was not the case. However, 43 per cent either could not or would not answer the question. Interesting results were achieved, however, when the question was put in a rather different way. The Germans were asked:

Do the French fear that we will rapidly gain control of a European Army?

Yes   47%   No   4%

An accompanying question showed that 20 per cent of the Germans who answered felt this fear was justified, and 16 per cent felt the fear was groundless, a result which was significant both because of the large majority for those who stated that Germany would probably come to occupy a position of dominance in the European Army, and because of the 64 per cent who were unable to say that this was not the case.

Where defence was concerned the Germans were not prepared to trust the French fully. The German people in the early 1950s had misgivings about linking their fate too closely with that of the

French. A number of questions were put by the authors of *Image de la France* on the chances of cooperation in a European government. The answers to these questions provide indirect evidence of the preparedness of Germans to accept extra-national authority.

> Do you think it is possible to form a European Government of French, German, Belgium, Dutch, Italian and Luxembourger Ministers, which would govern European peoples?
> Yes   46%   No   12%

A majority felt that such a government would be possible. They were also prepared when questioned in this general way to concede a closer relationship with the French.

> Is it possible to achieve a happy Franco–German cooperation in such a Government?
> Yes   41%   No   8%

Yet it was, of course, always easier to agree to the possibility than the actuality. In qualification of the last question, 61 per cent said that France had not yet overcome her distrust of Germany.[29] And the question was put: who should have the last word, the German government or a European Parliament (response in per cent)?[30]

	February 1953	September 1955
European Parliament	37	32
German Government	14	42

In February 1953, more Germans were prepared to allow final responsibility to the supra-national institution. By September 1955, however, more felt that the German government should 'have the last word', than believed the European Parliament should have final control. On the other hand only 12 per cent said in March 1953 that Germany should not cooperate with France very closely.

Other evidence about German doubts appeared in questions about the EDC. Frequently approval of the general principle goes along with disapproval of some of the elements essential to it. More German people favoured that institution than were opposed to it. Despite this, there appeared some reluctance to accept the possibility of a French Commander-in-Chief in charge of the EDC, which would have been a formidable difficulty in its operation.

---

[29] Ibid.   [30] Figures from Noelle and Neumann, *Jahrbuch.*

Would you accept a European Army under a French Commander?[31]

No	26%
Yes—under conditions	11%
Yes	8%
Did not answer	40%

Only 8 per cent expressed unconditional support for such a move, whilst 26 per cent were definitely against. Forty per cent could not say that they would accept a French Commander. In this case the conclusion may reasonably be drawn that the Germans were not willing to accept directives from a non-German on defence questions. The *Image* study also contained evidence which suggested that the Germans continued to regard the French in some ways as an *out-group*.

The question was put: Who is responsible for the poor state of Franco–German relations (response in per cent)?[32]

	Less than 30 years	30–49	Over 50
France	56	65.5	66.5
Germany	3.5	2.5	6
Both	16	10.5	11
Groups and Personalities			
in France	3.5	3.5	3.5
in Germany	1.5	4	2.5

There was evidence here of the 'in-group–out-group' mentality. Germans had not yet come to encompass the French within a common framework of loyalties. Most Germans attributed blame to the French, and a very small percentage said the Germans were responsible.

There were also figures which suggested that Germans believed that the French were 'different' from them, and possessed of characteristics which were not entirely flattering from the German point of view.

Do you think the French way of life is different from ours?[33]
Yes 64%   No 10%   No answer 27%

When the reasons for this difference were enquired after, most suggested that the French took life easier, that they were more pleas-

---

[31] Ibid.
[32] Figures from *Image de la France*, winter 1953–4.
[33] *Image de la France*.

ant, that they were more cultured. Some of the implications of these differences deserve closer examination. When the virtues of the French in the eyes of German men and women were enquired after, the evidence was discouraging (percentage of those asked).[34]

	Men	Women
Charming	59	55
Cultured	53	29
Solid	4.5	2
Courageous	10	5.5

When questioned about the faults of the French, the most serious was felt to be that the French were 'complacent'.[35] Fifty-six per cent of the men and 48 per cent of the women felt this was the case. Amongst older men there was a tendency to talk about the differences and the faults of the French in racial terms. 'The French are a Latin people, the Germans Nordic.'

Most Germans subscribed to the view that the French made clear distinctions between work and life. In figures about German views of the French culture, there were suggestions of the belief that the French had good qualities. But these good qualities, it was felt, were offset by elements of unreliability, of 'rareness' and complacency, which might be essential offshoots of 'culture' and 'charm' but which were nevertheless better kept at a distance. These 'faults', if only because of the way in which they were named, suggested that certain characteristics of the French people were, in the view of many Germans, antagonistic to the German way of life.

Figures about the French character were reinforced by figures on German views of other aspects of French life. Questioned about the French economy, 37 per cent said the economy was not very good, and 11.5 per cent that it was bad. Twenty per cent thought that political disorders caused the troubles of the French economy and 14 per cent social conditions. The image of politics in France was unfavourable, and there was a suggestion of incompatibility with that of Germany. Although the majority thought Germany was a democracy,[36] only 34 per cent thought that France was too. Twenty-two per cent thought France was not a democracy, 33 per cent were evasive and 11 per cent did not know. As regards the international status of France, 72 per cent said 'No' to the question 'Do you think France is a world power?'

---

[34] Ibid.   [35] Ibid.   [36] Ibid., vol. 1, 156.

The figures quoted suggest that the German image of France in the period 1953–4 contained much that was detrimental to the French. More important than the belief that there were differences were the characteristics which explained the differences. The latter implied that the French were unreliable, complacent, Latin, in the minds of Germans. This impression about their character was borne out by the practice of their economy and political system. There were differences that were antagonistic to German values and the German way of life.

Deutsch's point was that when you had an amalgamated or a pluralistic security community, this would be revealed in the pattern of attitudes in one group towards the other. By the mid-1990s all the evidence was that the people of Germany and France had learned to be rather more discriminating in their judgements about each other and that by the early 1970s they had come to form a security–community. Donald Puchala's work, in which he applied the techniques of analysis developed by Karl Deutsch, is indicative of these changes.[37]

There were many illustrations of such changes. There had been a great outcry in France in the late 1950s when German troops were first allowed after the war into Northern France on training exercises. This was also the response when German troops were permitted to take part in training exercises in South Wales. The reaction was hostile. Yet a quarter of a century later a situation had been reached in which the member states of the European Community, as in the Maastricht Agreement, had accepted the possibility of a common defence policy. The Germans and the French had a high degree of cooperation about defence issues for a number of years and had got to the point of setting up a joint brigade, an integrated military unit of French and German forces, of which the British took rather a dim view. It would, of course, be ridiculous to claim that the territory of the whole of the European Union had come to form a pluralistic security community. But it was arguable that it had moved to a considerable extent in that direction, and probably involved the core states of France and Germany.

Evidence from *Eurobarometer* polls taken in summer of 1994[38] supported the view that Franco–German relations had moved in the direction of security–community. For Germans the French were

[37] Donald J. Puchala, 'Integration and Disintegration in Franco–German Relations 1954–65', *International Organization*, 24/2, spring 1970.

[38] *Eurobarometer*, 41, 1, summer 1994, as in Table X.

members of a small group of peoples regarded as being worthy of either a lot of trust or some trust. The others included the Danes, the Dutch, and the Belgians. The respective figures were for the French, around 70 per cent, for the Danes 85 per cent and for the Belgians around 65 per cent. The other member peoples were below this. Only about 52 per cent had a lot of trust or some trust in the British. The French by that date had come to trust the Germans more than any other European people, though there were a number of close seconds such as the Belgians. Around 74 per cent of the French had either a lot or some trust in the Germans. Only 46 per cent of the French trusted the British in this way. This evidence, though not substantial, was at least illustrative of major changes in the way the Germans and the French thought of each other compared with the early 1950s.

This is not the place for an examination of public attitudes relevant to security in all the member states, but one indication was that in the mid-1990s there was no evidence that any of the governments had in place plans for coping with military attack by partners. And there were no fortified boundaries between the member states. It was revealing that public attitudes across Europe strongly supported the setting up of common entry and visa arrangements which were to be agreed by the governments by 1996, which could not have been accepted in relations between the French and the Germans in the 1950s. The Shengen group of countries had gone a long way by the mid-1990s towards establishing what could be called a single social space: arrangements for a high degree of cooperation between police forces and national judiciaries, and what amounted to a passport union. In the core of the Community there had been between the 1950s and the mid-1990s major changes in the publics' attitudes towards other publics which justified the conclusion that a pluralistic security–community had emerged among the core-group—the original Six—and that there had been progress towards this in the area of the twelve as a whole.

A closer examination of poll materials in the 1950s compared with the 1990s illustrates these points.

5

CONCLUSIONS

I N Chapter 1 the points were made that institutional arrangements in the 1990s reflected the pattern of evolution of the European Community. At every stage adjustments took place which re-established the sovereignty of states in new circumstances. The approach concentrated upon adjusting the circumstances of the state so that it could coexist with the collectivity, and despite the increasing resilience of the collectivity it did not impose upon the different parts. There were appropriate compromises on policy, as well as in the institutional arrangements, and the states retained an extensive array of reserve powers, such as the right to withdraw from membership and to alter the terms on which they acceded. The need to find a new balance between autonomy and interdependence at various stages also explained the tendency for the Community to emerge in a series of successive phases. A phase of integration was followed by a phase of consolidation. But the bargains made at each juncture illustrated a giving and a taking, as new ways of defining sovereignty were sought.

It was in conformity with this pattern that concessions that could not be made at one stage, proved acceptable at a later stage. For instance majority voting was not acceptable in 1965, but was acceptable in the Single European Act and Maastricht Treaty twenty years later. Community budgetary arrangements were not acceptable in 1965 but were acceptable in 1970. Foreign policy arrangements were not acceptable in 1961 but were acceptable in the early 1970s, and any move towards the harmonization of defence policies was not acceptable until the 1990s. Direct elections to the European Parliament were not acceptable until 1974, not implemented until 1979, but then became a routine feature of the Community's working arrangements.

This list could be much extended. But the important underlying point is that such a pattern of evolution should not be interpreted as establishing the ascendancy of the Community and the concomitant undermining of the states. Rather new arrangements had to wait until ways could be found and understood by the governments which permitted a new reconciliation between state sovereignty and the emerging community. Integration in the European Community was not about submerging the states, but, as was stated in the introduction to this book, about understanding and adapting to new circumstances in the emerging interdependence of the sovereign states.

Students of the European Community in the mid-1990s could not but be struck by an apparent paradox: that, on the one hand, pressures towards an increasing centralization of arrangements under the heading of political and monetary union seemed to have increased, and were frequently linked in public discussion with the concept of federalism;[1] whilst, on the other hand, a number of members, most obviously Spain, Portugal, and Greece, even the new Germany, were obviously using the Community to develop their sense of their own identity as separate states, and, although the British had been most prominent in opposing federalism, no member government had shown any inclination in specific terms to abandon its sovereignty. This paradox is hard to understand and is perhaps too easily dismissed with the retort that the Community is *sui generis*, or that the supporters of further integration had simply not understood its constitutional implications, as the Bruges group argued.[2]

Running through the argument in this book are, therefore, two themes which might appear to be mutually exclusive: the survival and even entrenchment of the state on the one hand and the extension of the range of international organization in the European Union on the other. Does not any development in the latter inevitably lead to the weakening of the former by, for instance, challenging its sovereignty? The conclusion is that this was not necessarily the case: indeed there are now reasons for supposing that at the regional level, where the challenge might at first sight appear to have been at its strongest, the state and international organization were

---

[1] See the essays in *Contemporary European Affairs*, 1/1–2 (1989), edited by David Bell and John Gaffney, under the title '1992 and After'.

[2] See Alan Sked, *A Proposal for European Union* (London: The Bruges Group, Occasional Paper 9, 1990).

capable of being mutually reinforcing.[3] Thus the regionalization process need not get in the way of state building. Indeed, in the European Community, states such as Spain and Portugal sought membership in order to rediscover themselves as states, not to lose their identity.

Judgements about the implications for sovereignty of life in an interdependent world are too often naïve and sharply polarized. The slightest practical adjustment to the need for greater cooperation between states may be resisted as representing too great a compromise with the ideal of statehood, or stronger international organizations are hailed as a step towards a federalist millennium.

The pattern of evolution of the EU discussed in Chapter 1 was logically consistent with the main conclusions which could be drawn from the other three substantive chapters. The chapter which focused on the arrangements in the mid-1990s, Chapter 2, argued that consociation was then the most appropriate model of the Community, which acquired the title of *Union* in the Maastricht Treaty. It was argued that the current arrangements had to be understood in the context of their evolution, and that they could be interpreted in this context as aspects of consociation. Any view of the Union rested on prior assumptions about its essential character, usually summed up in a formula such as federalism, or hard intergovernmentalism, or, in this case, consociationalism. The conclusion here was that if history was taken into account it became clear that federalism and hard intergovernmentalism were not appropriate.

Consociationalism was the model which fitted the picture: the European Union was not a federation, in the sense that there was a centralization of powers, nor did it tend in that direction, because the appearance that powers were being steadily transferred to the centre was misleading in many ways. Many reserve powers had been retained by the states, and many Community competencies were shared by them in central mechanisms. According to the Treaty of Rome the Community had exclusive competence in a number of areas, such as the protection of the common market, but the implication of this for the powers of the centre varied considerably: as was indicated in Chapter 2, they ranged from strong to relatively weak. Terms such as pooling, or sharing, or transferring became very crit-

---

[3] This argument is developed in Paul Taylor, 'Regionalism and Functionalism Reconsidered', in A. J. R. Groom and Paul Taylor (eds.), *Frameworks for International Co-operation* (London: Pinter Publishers, 1990), 234–54.

ical: to say that sovereignty was shared or pooled was quite different from saying it had been lost or transferred.

The main features of the Union were revealed through the notions of *symbiosis* and *consociation*. There had evolved a level of Community activity which had a degree of self-containment, and which had its own values, and its own individual actors, who sought values defined at the European level. But this was linked with a set of discrete national polities. It was in accordance with this image that a number of institutions, despite doctrines about their leaning towards either the Community or the nations, usually reflected a subtle compromise between the two inclinations. The Presidency gave power to individual states, which remained anxious to retain and exercise it. In some ways the Presidency had helped more low profile states to emerge individually and separately onto the international stage. It had often been pointed out that it helped states such as Ireland, Holland, Belgium, and even Luxembourg to become major international players every few years. But at the same time the administrations of the states that had the Presidency were fully aware that they also needed to relate to the Community and they became a part of the transnational Community political system. They had been socialized within the system to the extent of seeking values within it which reflected the interests of the collectivity, and they promoted the idea that the interests of the collectivity and the states had to be compatible and symbiotic.

In terms of consociation the nations were the segments which remained concerned with their own autonomy, and which were headed by politicians who were concerned to maintain their own internal power. The politics of the community in which they engaged was about two questions which sometimes coincided and sometimes collided. It concerned the maintenance of the political élite's own power within the segments, and it concerned increasing the benefits from cooperation for their segments. But if the latter purpose conflicted with the former it was abandoned: never the other way round. But the trick was to avoid such contradictions by choosing goals which served both ends.

In the institutions of the Community, decision-making was dominated by the need to form a consensus among the élites which in effect constituted a cartel of national authorities. The history of the Community's development, and the theory of consociation, alerted the observer to the fact that the majority-voting arrangements were primarily an instrument for consensus-building. No governments could be regularly outvoted in them about matters which they believed to be important: cautious and more ambitious states equally recognized this. And there was great concern to maintain the principle of the proportionate representation of the states in the Community's institutions. The peoples and governments in the states were determined to retain their due representation in the bodies that formulated policy proposals and administered the resulting cooperative activities. And they insisted upon equality in their capacity to resist policies which they did not like.

As with the Presidency the doctrine on the role of the Commission was different from the practice. It was to speak for Europe but in practice states insisted upon maintaining the level of their representation within it, both in the executive committee and in the Secretariat. And despite the rule that no members of the Commission could be instructed by governments in practice there was compromise with this principle. There were coalitions of officials in the Commission and officials in the governments of the nations from which they came on questions they regarded as important. Governments firmly believed that by making the right appointments at senior levels they could ensure outcomes of which they approved. Lower down appointments were made on the basis of public examination, but even then existing heads had considerable discretion on whom they would appoint to vacancies from the list of candidates who had passed the examination. Every aspiring Eurocrat was well aware that a period on a *stage* in Brussels before passing the examination would stand them in good stead in that they would then be able to make friends and influence people.

In Chapter 3, in the account of relations between the European Union and non-members, a more future-orientated stance was adopted. The major problems of enlargement were considered: these were the costs of enlarging which were evaluated by reference to the present character of the Community. But a few further steps were taken: conceivable developments of the Union with regard to foreign policy and defence, and monetary integration were considered in their implications for relations with outsiders. Once again the reckoning of costs and benefits attempted here only made sense in the light of what the Union had become by the mid-1990s. The pattern of the arrangements for decision-making would be damaged by adding new members then, because those arrangements had gradually acquired a distinctive, very special character. The pattern of bargaining would become significantly more complicated, and with more damaging outcomes, because of what the Union *was* at the stage of its unique development in the mid-1990s. It would be easier for a smaller number of states to agree to further develop the Community in the light of a character which they had come to understand, than in the company of a group of states which had a limited understanding of the Union's special blend of converging and diverging interests.

The Community would also have difficulty in dealing with the economic problems associated with enlargement, not just because of the specific costs but because of a range of less tangible costs deriving from the effects of enlargement upon the Union as a community. What were the implications for the further development of the funds, and for governments' preparedness to accept redistribution, of turning it back into a looser form of international society? What were the implications of allowing more exceptions and departures from Community programmes for the coherence of the core, and for the *acquis communautaire*? In both cases there would be damage to the ways of working which had emerged and the understandings which lay behind them. The risk was that what had been achieved would be casually thrown away.

The dangers and likely costs of expansion were all too evident when it came to defence and security. Precisely when the existing members seemed capable of moving tentatively towards greater harmonization of foreign policy and defence policy, the step was contemplated of adding countries with different interests, traditions, and philosophies. From the point of view of the security of Europe, and of the future development of the UN, a shallower but wider Europe would be less effective. If NATO expansion was unwise, how could it be wise to enlarge the EU, and to accept states in the primary economic and social framework which could not be accepted in that for security and defence? What the UN needed was a more coherent position on the part of the Union states, and a greater preparedness to act together in paying bills and providing resources. Enlargement in this area too was inconsistent with the place which the Union had reached in its evolution, and with the role in the global organization which it was beginning to develop.

The chapter on public attitudes clearly identified patterns which reflected those encountered elsewhere. The distinction between attitudes relevant to sovereignty, competence, and security, developed by this writer, produced some useful results. It demonstrated that presenting such attitudes in dramatized dichotomous terms—either *with us* or *against us*—which might be called the Tebbit formula, after the Eurosceptical Conservative ex-Minister, was dangerously misleading. (Tebbit complained that many British nationals failed to support the English cricket team, and that such support was a proper test of nationality! It was curious that the British cricket team was still described as 'England'!) To imply such a dichotomy was to reveal a misunderstanding of how identity worked: that individuals either remained immovably attached to the values of some symbolic entity, usually, in British party politics, described as England, or identified wholly with an alternative, was a delusion. Those who asserted this in Britain often lacked the sensibility to acknowledge that a good part of the population of the British Isles was made up of other ethnic groups—Scots, Welsh, and Irish, and a fair range of immigrant communities.

The data contained in Chapter Four revealed a more complex, and normal, form of identity, in that individuals had multiple identities, with degrees of support for many different levels of organization, from family to nation to Europe. It was possible for the balance of support to shift from one level to the next, but it would be unusual for older loyalties and identities to be abandoned. Most importantly they revealed that West Europeans had become capable of distinguishing between questions concerning ultimate responsibility, which may be subsumed under the heading of attitudes to sovereignty, and questions about the location of competencies, that is, the question of who does what, and where. With regard to the latter, public opinion in the Union was complex and nuanced. It accepted the possibility of managing at the level of the Union a range of functions which Eurosceptics insisted were fundamental to national sovereignty. There was discrimination with regard to foreign policy and defence, which it was accepted—even in Britain—could involve the Union, and with regard to who could stand and vote in elections within the member states. People generally accepted that non-national EU citizens should have the right to vote in local elections, but objected to their standing as candidates. Individuals in Europe still identified primarily with their states' institutions and symbols, and thought of themselves as being mainly, but not exclusively, of their own country, but they were increasingly prepared to accept that important tasks—like defence and foreign policy—need not be dealt with exclusively by their own government.

In some ways the most important movement was the move towards security–community in the core area of the Union. The majority of individuals in France and Germany no longer saw each other as potential enemies with whom disputes could be settled by the use of violence. This crucial development suggested a movement towards cross-cutting cleavages, and overlapping interests across national frontiers, which was another illustration of the slow quickening of European identity. The overall picture, however, remained diversity in unity. It was a mirroring, at a different level, of the principles discovered in the evolution of the Union, and in its working arrangements and institutions.

Those who wished to preserve or restore older conditions of sovereignty had an interest in scaling down the unifying aspects of public attitudes, and had no hesitation about misrepresenting them. They wished to return to a more primitive version of the ideal of national self-determination, in which all important tasks were carried out directly by or within the state. They interpreted subsidiarity as a doctrine on the repatriation of functions which the Union had taken on, though in fact subsidiarity was an injunction about *effectiveness*—neither centralization in compliance with Federalist imperatives, nor renationalization to preserve the state: it could sanction transfers upwards if, for reasons of scale or effect, they could be done better there. Even in a cautious state like Britain public opinion was softer towards integration than was often implied, and was more nuanced, and more capable of being led by politicians. Of course it could be led back to a greater insistence upon exclusivity, and falling support after 1991 or thereabouts indicated this possibility. But it was not the absolute barrier to integration that was claimed, and the claim that public opinion definitely excluded this or that piece of integration was not supported by the evidence.

Two further questions need to be asked. What was the European Union for in the mid-1990s? (What was its purpose?) And, were there any limits to integration beyond which the portrait presented here would have to be discarded? (If integration continued would there come a point at which it made more sense to say that the sovereignty of states had been transferred, that it had become a federation, and was no longer a consociation?) The latter question is important because it relates to the claims of the Eurosceptics that further integration *must*, either now or later, endanger the state, and hence a stand should now be made. The argument of this book is that sovereignty has not been gradually eroded by integration, but could something happen which would bring this about?

The answer to the first question was that it brought greater benefits for the mass of the population than could be obtained if the economies and societies were more highly differentiated in the separate states. This is not an issue that needs to be dealt with at length here. There are many books on the economic benefits of integration. What might be added is that there were considerable social benefits in being able to move around within a larger space, and an inconvenience in being more confined in smaller ones. European workers and professionals now had the option of *exit* from their states within the Union as well as *voice*. In an age of developed and sophisticated arrangements for long distance travel it would certainly be psychologically disturbing to be faced with impedimenta, like currency restrictions, or visa requirements, that usually appeared to be mainly for the benefit of special private interests. Élites found it easier to evade such limitations. The business world was not entirely united on the need for greater openness between the member states. Some companies, especially those involved in the manufacturing sector, had come to believe by the mid-1990s that the large market brought benefits in great excess of costs. Other businesses, such as those with large involvement in the currency market, arbitrage, and some forms of insurance, were more likely to be ambiguous about proposals for integration like creating a single currency. There were a large number of businesses that actually benefited from the exchange rate system, and even from its performing badly. But for the majority of citizens in the mid-1990s the benefits of integration would probably exceed the costs in that operating in the larger market would bring greater efficiencies and fewer transaction charges.

One response to this was that liberalization should not be confined to the area of the European Union: rather it should be a global process of liberalization and deregulation. And whether liberalization or deregulation took place at the regional or global level there would inevitably be problems in areas which lost industry to new centres. But working through the region had several advantages even as an approach to global liberalization. It constituted a space which was big enough to bargain more effectively with global corporations, which were indeed concerned about any threat of regional exclusivity. That they were so concerned was a measure of the countervailing power of regions.

Working together in regions, governments would be more effective in their pursuit of internal social goals, to which, for all the difficulties in the way of their attainment in the late 1990s, they remained committed. They would find it easier to follow internally policies to maintain higher levels of employment, and persuade global corporations to accept the costs of doing this in return for access to the larger market. The large region would also be less dependent on maintaining a high level of exports to non-members—it would be economically more self-contained—and therefore able to accept a higher social charge on production. And regional authorities would have greater influence than individual member states on the formation of regimes which regulated international economic forces and the activities of the global corporations outside their frontiers. Regime creation at the global level was likely to be at the expense of the social purposes of medium-sized and small states. Indeed developing global regimes could have the disadvantage that it strengthened international order, but increased potential for *disorder* in the states. It would benefit élites in various states, who would find an increasing range of common interests, but this worldwide society of the rich would develop in opposition to the impoverished and contained populations within states. Regionalization was the only practical counter-strategy.

Were there limits to extensions of the scope of integration or management arrangements which were not compatible with the model of the European Union discussed in this essay? It was impossible in the mid-1990s to identify precisely such limits for the future since the conditions of sovereignty continuously altered in the light of the circumstances of the time, but there were indeed a number of guidelines which helped to avoid steering too close to the margin. It was necessary for states to retain the right to insist upon the principle of unanimity in areas of policy adjacent to those where the Community of necessity had a strong managerial role. If there were to be monetary integration, which required a strong role for common institutions, and centralized management of the areas of policy relevant to maintaining the monetary union, states needed to retain control of adjacent areas like taxation and spending.

It would be possible to extend strong community control to the point at which there was necessarily nothing left for states to control independently, but if that happened it could still be argued that states had retained sovereignty if certain conditions applied; this would be the case if all decisions of principle or policy were taken on the basis of unanimity, and the centralized powers concerned implementation and operation. But this would be an extreme situation, and, in the long term, such a balance of state and community powers would be hard to sustain. As suggested, the optimum distribution would be to have national control in areas that were adjacent to areas of community control. This might be called the *principle of balanced competencies*, which could be set alongside *subsidiarity* as a key principle for the governance of the European Union.

There were also good arguments for retaining the central principles of the present system with regard to foreign policy, and defence coordination. The consociation of states would be likely to acquire an increasing range of common interests. The view that economic integration had implications for the development of more aligned foreign policies was consistent with this argument. Time and experience would also strengthen the common bases of foreign policy. But because the states remained distinct, they rightly expected to retain their own arrangements for defining and seeking foreign policy goals. Accordingly the mechanisms of the CFSC should remain multicentric. And in external representation the argument favoured retaining separate but coordinated embassies and representations. If states were to be separate and individual alongside the collectivity they needed to have their own space in international society as well as a range of shared arrangements with partners, just like married individuals in domestic society.

Similarly, as regards defence forces, states needed to retain their own armies, though these would not be managed and located in the expectation of attack from partners. There would be a significant range of common interests embedded in the political and economic structures of the collectivity, as well as remaining distinctive ones; this indicates a need for a community armed force made up of integrated units, and joint command, control systems, and logistics, which could be used to defend the overarching interests abroad, and of course, could also act in cooperation with the United Nations as an element in peace-keeping forces. It should be noted, referring back to a point made in the Introduction, that such arrangements for dealing with relations with non-members would be different from those characteristic of arrangements between individual states, be they in the form of a new European federation, or the existing separate states: such a Europe would be unlikely to have proactive foreign policies, though it would be designed to allow appropriate collective military defence of the interests of the whole, and separate national defence of state interests. There could be varying coalitions of support among the partners for the latter. It followed also that the decision-making procedures should be consistent with the principles. Majority voting in the areas of foreign policy and defence should be strictly limited.

What about the powers of the European Parliament, which was likely to be an item on the agenda of the intergovernmental conference on institutional reform starting in late 1996? It is not proposed to spot the agenda here whether with regard to the powers of the Parliament, or the extension of qualified majority voting in the Council. In 1996 the European Parliament's powers were more striking for their limitations than their extent: it could not initiate or pass legislation, or raise taxes. It could veto a limited range of legislation, as was pointed out in Chapter 4, and it did have the power to veto the budget. But were there further accretions in its power that could challenge the theory of consociation? Only two changes could have that effect: they were simple but radical in that together they would be an important step towards federal arrangements. The first would be the extension of the independent right to raise revenue—to tax—to the European Parliament. The second would be the granting to the European Parliament of an exclusive right to legislate in specified areas, which would establish, beyond the doubts that now exist, that in those areas national legislatures were subservient. Neither was likely to be approved. It was doubtful whether the British Parliament could accept such a development, not because of political opposition, but because it would be a constitutional impossibility. It would fly in the face of the doctrine of the sovereignty of each and every British Parliament. If Parliament attempted to agree to this it would be acting in contradiction to the principles of the British constitution. A central principle was that there could not be contradiction between the European and national constitutions.

No particular expansion in the scope of integration, or making new policy areas subject to majority voting, *necessarily* meant a greater threat for sovereignty. In the mid-1990s it was simply untrue that any particular act of integration, such as monetary union, was a bridge too far. What mattered rather was that the principles of balanced competencies and of subsidiarity should be observed. A concession in one area should be seen in context, so that appropriate balancing restraints could be placed on further movement in adjacent areas. In any case developments in Europe in the 1990s suggested that traditional views about the hierarchy of policies had altered. Foreign policy and defence were not as sensitive as education and health, in that greater discretion for the Union was permitted in the former than the latter. Such sensitivities should be respected but not invented.

In every period through the history of the state—long before the European Community—there were views specific to that period about what could be permitted by way of extending competencies to common institutions without jeopardizing sovereignty. The history of the European Union illustrated this point well. As has been pointed out, it was striking in the mid-1990s that nationalist parties tended to be pro-European, and were prepared to accept extensive working within common arrangements in the Union. National autonomy could be reconciled with the perception that very little had to be done exclusively at the local level. In this case national autonomy became little more than a way of relating to other states and participating with them in larger systems. As long as the principle of the Luxembourg Accords was respected, that no states could be regularly outvoted on questions which their governments held to be vitally important, this system would be compatible with national sovereignty. Once again the important point was that the principle of the sovereignty and equality of states in the common system should be respected. This was perfectly compatible with the pooling or sharing of sovereignty. The proportionate representation of the segments in the common arrangements, with decisions taken on the basis of consensus, was of crucial importance.

Bibliography

Monographs and Collections

Birch, Anthony H., *Nationalism and National Integration* (London: Unwin Hyman, 1989).

Bulmer, Simon, and Scott, Andrew (eds.), *Economic and Political Integration in Europe: Internal Dynamics and the Global Context* (Oxford: Basil Blackwell, 1994).

Burrows, Bernard, and Edwards, Geoffrey, *The Defence of Western Europe* (London: Butterworth, 1982).

Butler, Sir Michael, *Europe: More than a Continent* (London: William Heinemann, 1986).

Cafruny, Alan, and Rosenthal, Glenda, *The State of the European Community: The Maastricht Debates and Beyond* (Boulder, Colo.: Lynne Reiner, 1993).

Calleo, David, *Beyond American Hegemony: The Future of the Western Alliance* (Brighton: Wheatsheaf, 1987).

Camps, Miriam, *Britain and the European Community* (Princeton: Princeton University Press, 1964).

Church, Clive H., and Philimore, David, *European Union and European Community: A Handbook and Commentary on the Post-Maastricht Treaties* (Hemel Hempstead: Harvester Wheatsheaf, 1994).

Coffey, J. I., and Solms, Friedhelm (eds.), *Germany, the EU, and the Future of Europe*, Center of International Studies Monograph Series, 7 (Princeton: Princeton University, 1995).

Dahrendorf, R., *Society and Democracy in Germany* (Garden City, NJ: Doubleday, 1967), 276.

Deutsch, K. et al., *Political Community and the North Atlantic Area* (Princeton: Princeton University Press, 1957).

Deutsch, Karl, and Foltz, William J. (eds.), *Nation Building* (New York: Atherton Press, 1963).

Dinan, Desmond, *Ever Closer Union? An Introduction to the European Community* (Basingstoke: Macmillan, 1994).

Etzioni, Amitai, *Political Unification: A Comparative Study of Leaders and Forces* (New York: Holt, Rinehart, and Winston, 1965).

George, Stephen, *The British Government and the European Community since 1984*, University Association for Contemporary European Studies, Occasional Papers 4 (London: Kings College, 1987).

George, Stephen, *An Awkward Partner: Britain in the European Community* (Oxford: Clarendon Press, 1990).

'Gessellschaft für Markt und Meinung Forschung m.b.h.' (unpublished), *Image de la France. Un Sondage d'opinion publique allemande*, winter 1953–4 (Frankfurt-am-Main, July 1954).

Gillingham, John, *Coal, Steel and the Rebirth of Europe, 1945–55: The Germans and French from Ruhr Conflict to Economic Community* (Cambridge: Cambridge University Press, 1991).

Groom, A. J. R., and Taylor, Paul (eds.), *Frameworks for International Cooperation* (London: Pinter Publishers, 1990).

Hallstein, Walter, *Europe in the Making* (London: George Allen and Unwin, 1972).

Hayes-Renshaw, Fiona, 'The Role of the Committee of Permanent Representatives in the Decision-Making of the European Community', Ph.D. thesis (London: London School of Economics, 1990).

Holland, Stuart, *Uncommon Market* (London: The Macmillan Press, 1980).

Jacobs, Francis B., *Western European Political Parties: A Comprehensive Guide* (Harlow: Longman, 1989).

Keohane, Robert O., and Nye, Joseph S., *Power and Interdependence* (Boston: Little, Brown, 1977).

Kitzinger, Uwe, *Diplomacy and Persuasion* (London: Thames and Hudson, 1973).

Lerner, Daniel, and Aron, Raymond (eds.), *France Defeats EDC* (London: Thames and Hudson, 1957).

Lindberg, Leon, *The Political Dynamics of European Economic Integration* (Stanford, Calif.: Stanford University Press, 1963).

Lodge, Juliet (ed.), *The European Community and the Challenge of the Future* (London: Pinter Publishers, 1989); 2nd edn., 1993.

McRae, K. (ed.), *Consociational Democracy: Political Accommodation in Segmented Societies* (Toronto: McLelland and Stewart, 1974).

Mathijsen, P. S. M. F., *A Guide to European Community Law*, 5th edn. (London: Sweet and Maxwell, 1990).

Mazey, S., and Richardson, J., *Lobbying in the European Community* (Oxford: Oxford University Press, 1993).

Michalski, Anna, 'Denmark and the European Union', Ph.D. thesis (London: London School of Economics, 1995).

Milward, A. S., *The European Rescue of the Nation State* (London: Routledge and Kegan Paul, 1992).

Morgan, Roger, *West European Politics since 1945: The Shaping of the European Community* (London: B. T. Batsford, 1972).

Newhouse, John, *Collision in Brussels: The Common Market Crisis of 30th June 1965* (New York: Norton, 1967).

Noelle, Elisabeth, and Neumann, Erich Peter, *Jahrbuch der Öffentlichen Meinung, 1947–1955* (Allensbach am Bodensee: Institut für Demoskopie, Verlag für Demoscopie, 1956).

Nugent, Neil, *The Government and Politics of the European Union*, 3rd edn. (Basingstoke: Macmillan, 1994).

Pickles, William, *How Much has Changed? Britain and Europe* (Oxford: Basil Blackwell, 1967).

Pierre, Andrew J. (ed.), *A Widening Atlantic? Domestic Change and Foreign Policy* (New York: Council on Foreign Relations, 1986).

Pryce, Roy, *The Politics of the European Community* (London: Butterworths, 1972).

—— (ed.), *The Dynamics of European Union* (London and New York: Croom Helm, 1987).

Shonfield, Andrew, *Europe: Journey to an Unknown Destination* (Harmondsworth: Penguin Books, 1972).

Sked, Alan, *A Proposal for European Union* (London: The Bruges Group, Occasional Paper 9, 1990).

Story, Jonathon (ed.), *The New Europe: Politics, Government and Economy since 1945* (Oxford: Basil Blackwell, 1994).

Taylor, Paul, *The Limits of European Integration* (London and New York: Croom Helm and Columbia University Press, 1983).

—— *International Organization in the Modern World* (London: Pinter, 1993).

Tsoukalis, Loukas, *The Politics and Economics of European Monetary Integration* (London: George Allen and Unwin, 1977).

—— *The European Community: Past, Present and Future* (Oxford: Basil Blackwell, 1983).

—— *The New European Economy: The Politics and Economics of European Integration*, 2nd edn. (Oxford: Oxford University Press, 1993).

Wallace, Helen, *Europe: The Challenge of Diversity* (London: Routledge and Kegan Paul for the Royal Institute of International Affairs, 1985).

Wallace, William, *Regional Integration: The West European Experience* (Washington: The Brookings Institution, 1994).

—— Wallace, Helen, and Webb, Carole (eds.), *Policy-Making in the European Community*, 2nd edn. (London: Wiley, 1983).

Wilke, Marc, and Wallace, Helen, *Subsidiarity: Approaches to Power-Sharing in the European Community*, RIIA Discussion Paper, 27 (London: Royal Institute of International Affairs, 1990).

Articles and Chapters in Edited Books

Almond, Gabriel A., 'Comparative Political Systems', *Journal of Politics*, 18 (Aug. 1956), 398–9.

Asmus, Ronald D., Kugler, Richard L., and Larrabee, F. Stephen, 'NATO Expansion: The Next Steps', *Survival*, 37/1 (spring 1995).

Bell, David, and Gaffney, John (eds.), *Contemporary European Affairs*, 1/1–2 (1989).

Brown, Michael E., 'The Flawed Logic of NATO Expansion', *Survival*, 37/1 (spring 1995).

Bull, Hedley, 'Civilian Power Europe: A Contradiction in Terms?' in Loukas Tsoukalis, *The European Community: Past, Present and Future* (Oxford: Basil Blackwell, 1983).

Burley, Anne-Marie, and Mattli, Walter, 'The Law and Politics of the European Court of Justice: Law as a Mask', *International Organization* (Oct. 1993).

Corbett, Richard, 'The Intergovernmental Conference and the Single European Act', in Roy Pryce (ed.), *The Dynamics of European Union* (London and New York: Croom Helm, 1987).

Denton, Geoffrey, 'European Monetary Cooperation: The Bremen Proposal', *The World Today*, 34/11, London: RIIA (Nov., 1978).

—— 'Restructuring the EC Budget: Implications of the Fontainebleau Agreement', *Journal of Common Market Studies*, 23/2 (Dec. 1984), 117–40.

Hoffman, Stanley, 'Discord in Community: The North Atlantic Area as a Partial International System', in Francis O. Wilcox and H. Field Haviland, Jr., *The Atlantic Community: Progress and Prospects* (New York: Praeger, 1963), 3–31.

Langeheine, Bernd, and Weinstock, Ulrich, 'Graduated Integration: A modest Path towards Progress', *Journal of Common Market Studies*, 23/3 (Mar. 1985).

Lijphart, Arend, 'Consociation and Federation: Conceptual and Empirical Links', *Canadian Journal of Political Science*, 22/3 (1979), 499–515.

Lindberg, Leon, 'Integration as a Source of Stress on the European Community System', *International Organization*, 2 (1966), 233–63.

Lodge, Juliet, 'The Single European Act: Towards a new Euro-Dynamism?' *Journal of Common Market Studies*, 24/3 (Mar. 1986), 203–23.

Moravcsik, Andrew, 'Preferences and Power in the European Community: A Liberal Intergovernmentalist Approach', *Journal of Common Market Studies*, 31/4, Dec. 1993.

Pinder, John, 'Positive Integration and Negative Integration: Some problems of Economic Union in the EEC', *The World Today*, 24, London: RIIA (Mar. 1968), 88–110.

Puchala, Donald J., 'Integration and Disintegration in Franco–German Relations 1954–65', *International Organization*, 24/2 (spring 1970).

Robertson, A. H., 'Creation of W.E.U.', *European Handbook*, 11, 125–38.

Schmuck, Otto, 'The European Parliament's Draft Treaty establishing the European Union (1979–84)', in Roy Pryce (ed.), *The Dynamics of European Union* (London and New York: Croom Helm, 1987), 188–216.

Sidjanski, Dusan, 'Pressure Groups and the European Economic Community', in Michael Hodges (ed.), *European Integration* (Harmondsworth: Penguin Books, 1972).

Smith, Anthony D., 'National Identity and "Europe" ', *International Affairs*, 68/1 (Jan. 1992).

Taylor, Paul, 'The New Dynamics of EC integration in the 1980s', in Juliet Lodge (ed.), *The European Community and the Challenge of the Future* (London: Pinter Publishers, 1989).

—— 'The European Union in the 1990s', in Ngaire Woods (ed.), *Explaining International Relations since 1945* (Oxford: Oxford University Press, 1996).

Thygesen, Niels, 'Towards Monetary Union in Europe—Reforms of the EMS in the Perspective of Monetary Union', *Journal of Common Market Studies*, 31/4 (Dec. 1993), 447–72.

Welfens, Paul J. J., 'The EU and Eastern–Central European Countries: Problems and Options of Integration', *Aussenpolitik*, 46/3 (1995).

References to Official Publications

Ad Hoc Committee for Institutional Affairs, *Report to the European Council* (Brussels, 29–30 March 1985), SN/1187/85.

Commission of the European Communities, 'Draft Treaty establishing the European Union', *Bulletin of the European Communities*, 17/2 (1984), 7–28.

—— *Bulletin of the European Communities*, Supplement 1/85, 'The Thrust of Commission Policy' (Luxembourg: 14 and 15 Jan. 1985a).

—— *Completing the Internal Market: White Paper from the Commission to the European Council* (Luxembourg: Office of Official Publications, June 1985b).

—— *The Inter-Governmental Conference: Background and Issues* (Luxembourg, 1985c).

—— *Bulletin of the European Communities*, Supplement 2/86, Single European Act (Luxembourg, 1986).

Commission of the European Communities, *The Principle of Subsidiarity*, SECK(92) 1990, Final (Brussels, 27 Oct. 1992).

—— *Eurobarometer*, 38, Dec. 1992, p. vii.

—— *Eurobarometer*, 40, Dec. 1993.

—— *Eurobarometer*, 41, July 1994.

European Council, *Texts of Agreement reached at European Council*, including documents SN517/88 and SN461/88 (11–12 Feb. 1988), 7.

European Parliament, *Debates* (July, 1973), 91.

—— *A New Phase in European Union* (Luxembourg: General Secretariat, 1985).

Evidence on the Implications of the Maastricht Treaty, House of Commons Foreign Affairs Select Committee (Feb. 1992), pub. Mar. 1992 as HC(1991–92 223–(ii)).

Index